NEW APPROACHES TO THE LITERARY ART OF ANNE BRONTË

New Approaches to the Literary Art of Anne Brontë

Edited by

JULIE NASH and BARBARA A. SUESS

Ashgate

Aldershot • Burlington USA • Singapore • Sydney

Published by
Ashgate Publishing Limited
Gower House
Croft Road
Aldershot
Hampshire GU11 3HR
England

Ashgate Publishing Company
131 Main Street
Burlington, VT 05401-5600 USA

Ashgate website: http://www.ashgate.com

British Library Cataloguing in Publication Data
New approaches to the literary art of Anne Brontë. -
    (Nineteenth century series)
    1. Brontë, Anne, 1820-1849 - Criticism and interpretation
    I. Nash, Julie II. Suess, Barbara A.
    823.8

Library of Congress Control Number: 2001091647

ISBN 0 7546 0199 4

Printed and bound by Athenaeum Press, Ltd.,
Gateshead, Tyne & Wear.

Contents

The Nineteenth Century
General Editors' Preface

The aim of the series is to reflect, develop and extend the great burgeoning of interest in the nineteenth century that has been an inevitable feature of recent years, as that former epoch has come more sharply into focus as a locus for our understanding not only of the past but of the contours of our modernity. It centres primarily upon major authors and subjects within Romantic and Victorian literature. It also includes studies of other British writers and issues, where these are matters of current debate: for example, biography and autobiography, journalism, periodical literature, travel writing, book production, gender, non-canonical writing. We are dedicated principally to publishing original monographs and symposia; our policy is to embrace a broad scope in chronology, approach and range of concern, and both to recognize and cut innovatively across such parameters as those suggested by the designations "Romantic" and "Victorian". We welcome new ideas and theories, while valuing traditional scholarship. It is hoped that the world which predates yet so forcibly predicts and engages our own will emerge in parts, in the wider sweep, and in the lively streams of disputation and change that are so manifest an aspect of its intellectual, artistic and social landscape.

Vincent Newey
Joanne Shattock
University of Leicester

Preface

Critics and biographers commonly cite an anecdote from Anne Brontë's childhood to explain her place within the famous literary Brontë family. In 1826, the Reverend Patrick Brontë returned from a trip with gifts for his four surviving children. To Branwell, the only boy, he gave a box of wooden soldiers. The next morning, each child chose a soldier and named him; over time they invented personalities and adventures for each soldier.[1] Anne named her soldier 'Waiting Boy', an apt alter ego for the youngest Brontë who would become known for her patience and passivity during her short life (Chitham 25).

Little is known about Anne Brontë's inner life, though the details of her isolated childhood in Yorkshire, her close relationship with her siblings (particularly Emily), her dissatisfying experiences as a governess, her venture into authorhood, and her tragic death at age 29 of tuberculosis have become part of the Brontë legend. What we do know about Anne Brontë is that she did much more than wait. She went to school, she traveled, she worked, and most of all, she wrote. Like her sisters, she began writing in childhood, escaping through her writing into the imaginary world of Gondal that she and Emily created together. Throughout her life, she wrote diary notes, poetry, insightful marginalia, and two very remarkable novels that are the primary focus of this collection.

In 1833, Branwell Brontë wrote that his youngest sister was 'nothing, absolutely nothing' (Chitham 25). Although literary critics have perhaps given her more credit than her brother did, there is no question that the complexity of Anne Brontë's work has just begun to be recognized in the last ten years or so. Her two published novels, *Agnes Grey* and *The Tenant of Wildfell Hall*, were widely read and discussed during her lifetime, but her works fell out of favor over time, criticized for being too religious and didactic – an ironic charge since Victorian critics cited 'coarseness' and 'vulgarity' as her biggest flaws. Although scholars have recently exhibited a renewed interest in her life and works, with a number of monographs, articles, and biographies published in the last decade, no-one has compiled a collection of scholarly essays examining her writings. This book, *New Approaches to the Literary Art of Anne Brontë*, brings together the ideas of some of the top Brontë scholars working today, as well as some bright, new critical voices, to examine the many layers of Anne Brontë's work.

The title of our collection refers to Brontë's writings as 'literary art' for a special reason. Ever since Charlotte Brontë's 'Biographical Notice of Ellis and Acton Bell', in which the surviving sister claimed that 'Acton' merely 'reproduce[d] every detail' from her experiences 'as a warning to others' (Chitham 136), many readers have assumed that Anne Brontë's talent lay in autobiography, in a strict representation of life as she knew it. This assumption has some truth to it. Anne, like her sisters, did use her experiences to help shape her works. Indeed,

James R. Simmons, Jr.'s essay in this collection, 'Class, Matriarchy, and Power: Contextualizing the Governess in *Agnes Grey*', demonstrates how accurate her portrayal of the Victorian governess is, making the novel 'a realistic examination of nineteenth-century class issues as well'. But Brontë's writings go one step further, in that they transform experience into art by coupling careful literary techniques with a boundless imagination.

That Brontë harbored ambitions for herself as a published author is evident in another anecdote recounted by Charlotte in her 'Biographical Notice' of her sisters:

> One day, in the autumn of 1845, I accidentally lighted on a MS volume of verse in my sister Emily's handwriting [and tried to] persuade her that such poems merited publication. . . .
>
> Meanwhile my younger sister quietly produced some of her own compositions, intimating that, since Emily's had given me pleasure, I might like to look at hers. (Chitham 129)

Far from waiting passively (and probably in vain) for Charlotte to 'accidentally' stumble on her own poetry, Anne 'quietly' but determinedly adds her work to the collection of poems, and begins to spend her evenings revising them for publication. Brontë saw herself as a writer, an artist, not merely a recorder of experience, as the essays collected here demonstrate in new ways.

There is no question that at least one purpose of Brontë's art was to instruct. As she writes in her 'Preface' to the second edition of *The Tenant of Wildfell Hall*, 'I will not limit my ambition to . . . producing "a perfect work of art": time and talents so spent I should consider wasted and misapplied' (30). Brontë believed strongly that literary art should instruct and improve the minds and lives of its readers. Her strong religious inclination has been well noted, if not always well understood, as Maria Frawley demonstrates in her essay, 'Contextualizing Anne Brontë's Bible'. As Frawley notes, '[a]lthough Brontë may have been devout compared to her sisters, she cannot be said to have had a straightforward, untroubled religious life'. Frawley's analysis of Brontë's Bible notes reinforces the complexity of the religious beliefs that also shape her novels. Marianne Thormählen adds to the discussion of Brontë's spiritual views in 'Aspects of Love in *The Tenant of Wildfell Hall*'. Readers may be surprised to realize that, besides the Bible and other religious readings, Brontë credits romantic love as one of the 'driving forces' of spiritual pilgrimage. In Brontë's novel, Thormählen writes, '[h]appiness in love is associated with determined resistance to forces that militate against the laws of God'. Lee A. Talley examines another of Brontë's religious influences, Evangelical Methodism, in 'Anne Brontë's Method of Social Protest in *The Tenant of Wildfell Hall*', arguing that 'Anne Brontë's Methodist heritage shapes her realistic approach to worldly and philosophical problems' in her second novel. Melody J. Kemp also cites the influence of Methodism on Brontë's work, specifically the Methodist emphasis on character formation and 'the belief that character could be self-determined' in 'Helen's Diary and the Method(ism) of Character Formation in *The Tenant of Wildfell Hall*'.

The belief that people could change and that no one was predestined either for damnation or glory is one way in which Anne Brontë distanced herself from her sisters, both of whose works contain at least the suggestion of inescapable fate. Agnes Grey, Helen Huntingdon, and Gilbert Markham are all fundamentally good characters that must overcome a number of personal flaws and delusions before they can be worthy of the happiness they eventually achieve. Perhaps the most controversial of these three characters is Gilbert Markham, *Wildfell Hall*'s peevish, violent, and self-important hero whose reformation continues to be debated by critics. This collection contributes a number of divergent views to this debate. In 'A Matter of Strong Prejudice: Gilbert Markham's Self Portrait', Andrea Westcott studies Gilbert's narrative as autobiography to demonstrate 'how little Markham is capable of change'. Westcott argues that Markham's melodramatic effusions in the novel's final section 'afford Brontë an opportunity to parody his clichéd romantic sentiments'. In contrast, Andrés G. López defends Markham, arguing that he has made a spiritual journey parallel to the ones made by Agnes Grey and Helen Huntingdon. In '*Wildfell Hall* as Satire: Brontë's Domestic *Vanity Fair*', Lopez describes Brontë as Victorian satirist and argues that her 'parallel narratives of growth . . . illustrate that men's and women's respective natures and experiences are similar', a radical belief given the common Victorian myth of separate spheres.

There is no question that one of Brontë's major themes was the double standard applied to the behavior of men and women. In her 'Preface' to *Wildfell Hall*, Brontë, under the pseudonym Acton Bell, answers the critics who are eager to discover the sex of the author:

> [I]n my own mind, I am satisfied that if a book is a good one, it is so whatever the sex of the author may be. All novels are or should be written for both men and women to read, and I am at a loss to conceive how a man should permit himself to write anything that would be really disgraceful to a woman, or why a woman would be censured for writing anything that would be proper and becoming for a man. (31)

Just as Brontë argues here for literary equality between the sexes, she uses her novels to make a case for equality in education, work opportunities, and marriage. Bettina L. Knapp's essay, 'Anne Brontë's *Agnes Grey*: The Feminist; "I must stand alone"', examines *Agnes Grey* as the medium through which 'Brontë's voice was raised against . . . offensive treatment accorded to governesses; against society's denigration of working women; against the legal status of married women who had to give over their dowries and fortunes to their husbands, thereby reducing them to slave status and keeping them virtual prisoners in their own homes'. The exploitation and second-class status of women is a theme that Brontë's second novel takes on even more directly, as the essays on *The Tenant of Wildfell Hall* demonstrate here.

Again, what enables Brontë to convey her moral and social outrage so powerfully is her ability to transform these issues into literary art. 'I love to give innocent pleasure' (30), Brontë writes in her 'Preface' to the second edition of *Wildfell Hall*, and the reader takes his or her pleasure from the way the story is told. Not surprisingly, Brontë's narrative choices have also been the subject of critical controversy, and the essays in this volume explore some of her narrative methods using different critical approaches. Garrett Stewart's essay, 'Narrative Economies in *The Tenant of Wildfell Hall*' addresses a common criticism leveled at Brontë's book, namely the 'openly odd' narrative structure of embedding one narrator's diary within the epistolary text of another narrator, thereby decentering the story. By exploring the text 'from the narrative ground up', Stewart attempts to answer the criticisms of the novel's narrative structure, pointing out that the novel has been 'blamed for failing to achieve at its center the directness it so markedly sets out to avoid'. In ' "I speak of those I do know": Witnessing as Radical Gesture in *The Tenant of Wildfell Hall*', Deborah Denenholz Morse approaches the issue of narrative structure in *Wildfell Hall* from a different angle, focusing on the ways in which Brontë's novel reads as testimony and, in its emphasis on reading as well as writing, almost forces the reader to become 'drawn into the role of witness'. The novel's readers thus become, according to Morse, judges of a society in which 'women and children suffer the domestic abuses chronicled in the novel'. Moreover, Brontë's 'pervasive use of the Bible as the undergirding structure of her novel points to the sacred Word as the legitimating source of her own words' which thus constitute 'a new vision of social and moral responsibility'. From a more specifically Christian perspective, the structure of *Agnes Grey* is more straightforward, but the essays in this collection demonstrate that even here, Brontë carefully chose her structure and symbolism to further her moral, social, and literary ends. Larry H. Peer's 'The First Chapter of *Agnes Grey*: An Analysis of the Sympathetic Narrator' presents the reader with Brontë's narrative challenge: How can she 'secure and maintain the sympathy of the audience for a hero with a character flaw?'. Peer's investigation of Chapter One examines Brontë's careful and effective use of symbolism. Marilyn Sheridan Gardner also works with symbolism in Brontë's first novel. In '"The food of my life": Agnes Grey at Wellwood House', Gardner examines the 'elaborate scenes of eating' in the novel's first ten chapters and concludes that '[w]hen Brontë places Agnes among the Bloomfields, she elevates dining into an educational exercise and raises eating into a metaphor for the way of life at Wellwood House'. This extended analogy reinforces Agnes' movement 'from the sacred confines of the parsonage to the profane venue of the worldly Bloomfields'.

The essays in this collection represent a diversity of theoretical and critical approaches, a factor that speaks to the richness of Anne Brontë's texts. *New Approaches to the Literary Art of Anne Brontë* offers new readings of Anne Brontë's novels and life and suggests new critical frameworks with which to approach them. While many of these essays place Brontë's writings in the context of her life and make comparisons to the more famous works of her sisters, they also recognize that her novels can and should stand alone. Brontë's narrative methods, her social criticism, and her religious convictions are individually worthy of study. Understood together, as we hope this collection will make possible, they reveal that the literary accomplishments of Anne Brontë make her an artist in her own right.

Note

[1] These elaborate stories and games were the beginning of the literary and artistic life of the Brontë children. They would evolve into the 'Great Glass Town' essays, stories, pictures, histories, and songs. Over the years, the Brontës would produce thousands of words of writing before they ever attempted publication.

Works Cited

Brontë, Anne. 'Preface'. *The Tenant of Wildfell Hall*. 1848. New York: Penguin, 1985.
Chitham, Edward. *A Life of Anne Brontë*. Oxford: Blackwell, 1991.

Julie Nash
Barbara A. Suess

Acknowledgements

We would like to thank Jean I. Marsden, whose Austen/Brontë graduate seminar at the University of Connecticut was the inspiration for this book. In addition, the advice and encouragement of our advisors, Regina Barreca and Lee Jacobus, have been invaluable. We received positive feedback and useful suggestions from numerous Victorian scholars during the course of assembling this collection, and we are grateful to all those who believed in this book – especially, of course, our contributors. Their dedication to and enthusiasm regarding Anne Brontë's works, and the level of professionalism with which they attend to their own, have made working on this project a pleasure. We also appreciate the guidance of the Ashgate staff members who diligently aided us with our project. Finally, we would like to thank our families, especially Quentin Miller and Ernest Adamo, for their enthusiastic support of this project from the beginning.

Chapter 1

Contextualizing Anne Brontë's Bible

Maria Frawley

'What, Where, and How Shall I Be When I Have Got Through?'[1] With this not-so-simple question before her, Anne Brontë embarked on a mission to read and study the Bible. Her notes indicate that her project was 'begun about December 1841'. Twenty years old, Brontë was likely at the time to have been working as a governess for the Robinson family of Thorp Green, although contemplating a permanent return home to establish a school with her sisters. Although she had begun to write poetry, both on her own and as part of the collaborative project known as the Gondal and Angrian Chronicles, it would be six more years before she published her first novel, *Agnes Grey*. All that we now know of this Bible-reading project is what can be deduced from the notes made on the Bible's flyleaves. She evidently worked her way through the entire text of the Old Testament, diligently noting the chapters and verses of particular interest to her. The first such entry notes passages from the Book of Deuteronomy, and the last from the Book of Malachi. The end page is dated 'April 30, 1843', and is followed by a passage from the Book of Proverbs (16.23), which reads, 'A man hath joy by the answer of his mouth and a word spoken in due season. [H]ow good is it'.

Biographers have long acknowledged that information about Anne Brontë's life is scant. As Juliet Barker writes in her introduction to *The Brontës*, a family biography, 'Though many have tried, it is impossible to write an authoritative biography of either of the two youngest Brontë sisters. The known facts of their lives could be written on a single sheet of paper; their letters, diary papers and drawings would not fill two dozen' (xviii). Even Edward Chitham, author of *A Life of Anne Brontë*, acknowledges that 'there are few documents directly relating to the life of Anne Brontë which could rank with the kind of primary sources usually studied by biographers', and concludes that 'we have to look elsewhere for ways to build up a picture of Anne Brontë and her life' (5-6).

Anne Brontë's Bible is evidently one such place, although commentators of her life and writing, including Chitham, have overlooked it. Given the sensitivity of Brontë's biographers to the importance of primary source evidence, it is especially perplexing that her Bible notes, which clearly constitute a sort of primary source evidence, have for so long gone unstudied. One explanation for this apparent lapse is that the Bible is housed not at Haworth Library, which holds most of the materials relevant to Brontë's life, but rather at the Pierpont Morgan Library in New York City. Perhaps more importantly, though, the notes on the flyleaves do not lend themselves to obvious interpretation. Brontë did not annotate the notes with commentary to clarify what the particular chapters and verses meant to her; rather, she simply listed chapters and verses, occasionally indicating special emphasis by underlining or writing 'esp.' for especially. Yet even this descriptive fact about her efforts and methods is potentially significant. This essay will suggest a few of the ways that the Bible notes might prove enlightening.

On the most basic level, Brontë's efforts to study the Bible reveal one of the ways that religious belief was *practiced* in Victorian England. As an apparently private pursuit, her project can give students of the period a glimpse into one of the ways that religious belief was expressed and practiced – that is, the everyday phenomenon of religiosity that tends to be overlooked by historical accounts, stressing as they do the public and institutional mechanisms for the expression of belief. As Robin Gilmour has written, 'religious experience in this period should not be confined to what happened or did not happen in churches and synagogues. William James' *Varieties of Religious Experience* (1902) is a much better title for a study of Victorian religion than that old music-hall turn, Faith and Doubt' (94). Even scholarly works sensitive to the need to address the variety of religious beliefs and practices of ordinary people tend to concentrate, Gail Malmgreen explains, 'not on the interior world of belief, but on the public expression of religion, and on religion as an engine of social action' (8). Brontë's study of the Bible exemplifies both a 'variety of religious experience' and the kind of private practice to which Malmgreen here refers, and suggests one of the ways that an individual's 'interior world of belief' was exercised and shaped.

The significance of Brontë's Bible is not just limited to what it reveals about variations of Victorian religious experience and history; it enables one to arrive at a more sophisticated understanding of her personal religiosity than that currently available in scholarship about her. For reasons I will examine in more detail in this essay, Brontë scholars have treated Anne Brontë's religion rather reductively. Only recently have they begun to critique the received versions of Brontë's religion, which depicts her as quietly pious and distinctly orthodox in her beliefs. Brontë's Bible study has implications both for our understanding of Victorian social history and for Brontë's personal history. Although seemingly separate, these threads in fact converge through a shared emphasis on the boundaries between obedience and initiative and the role of the individual in achieving a kind of self-reformation.

Contextualizing Brontë's Bible Study

No social or intellectual history of the Victorian period is without an extensive section on religion, and although an adequate summary of the vast literature on the topic is beyond the purview of this essay, it is clear that Anne Brontë's Bible study belongs to a particular historical moment in the religious experience of her nation. 'The religious life of this period was intense and disputatious', Gilmour writes, 'and its problematic presence can be felt wherever we look in nineteenth-century literature' (63). Brontë lived and wrote precisely at the time that many of the most public manifestations of religious crisis emerged, with attempts at the reformation of the structure of the Church of England, conflicts with Dissenting or Nonconformist churches, and reaction to German historical criticism of the Bible being three of the most often-cited examples of the alleged crisis. More pervasive, if less difficult to pin down, is the evangelical temper associated with this period, one linked as inextricably, Richard Altick shows, to a middle-class ethos and the rise of industrialism as to distinctions between 'high church', 'low church', and 'broad church'.[2]

Adding another dimension of complexity to this moment in Britain's religious history is, of course, the concomitant and relatively rapid development of many areas of science. Many literary historians have seen in these developments, particularly in advances in geological findings during the first half of the century, a source for the expressions of religious doubt that seem to accrue throughout the literature of the period and that provide a backdrop to expressions of faith. Advances in scientific understanding complicate considerably the version of religious life that would exist were one to examine only early Victorian conflicts within sects associated with definitions of low, broad, and high church. Nevertheless, as Gilmour persuasively argues of 'first-generation Victorians', which would include Anne Brontë:

> It has become increasingly clear that their objections to Christianity were overwhelmingly *moral*, objections to certain key doctrines of evangelical religion in which some had been reared but all had experienced in the religious culture of the time. The Atonement, chiefly, hell, everlasting punishment, original sin – a God who required the obedience of his creatures on those terms was a God who did not deserve worshipping. . .' (87)

Although Brontë cannot be said to belong to a group of early- to mid-Victorians 'object[ing]' to Christianity, she clearly did concern herself with the very concepts and doctrines that Gilmour lists here, perhaps most significantly, as her Bible notes suggest, with the nature of obedience. And, while her Bible study does not reveal a movement from faith to doubt or vice-versa, it does suggest an urge to learn about and think through for herself the doctrines that occupied public debate.

Despite the insights that social historians have made about religious belief in Victorian England, it is difficult to further contextualize Brontë's project because relatively little is known about institutionalized or private Bible study in nineteenth-century England. Popular works of Biblical commentary by Richard Mant and George D'Oyly were published and updated well into the Victorian period, as was Thomas Hartwell Horne's 1818 *Introduction to the Critical Study and Knowledge of the Holy Scriptures*. These are the types of works to which, for example, major public figures such as William Gladstone turned when they embarked on a systematic study of the Bible.[3] Little information exists within Brontë family history, however, to help us place Anne's Bible study relative to that which other family members may have conducted, or to understand what motivated her to undertake her reading at this particular moment in her life. Beginning at roughly the same time she commenced her position as a governess at Thorp Green, she may have anticipated reading and studying the Bible with the children under her care. One might similarly speculate that she sought in Biblical passages solace while in a difficult and isolating situation. Nevertheless, nothing about her Bible study is mentioned in her 1841 diary paper nor in anything else I have discovered by or about Anne Brontë. It was apparently undertaken in private and, like so much about Brontë's work, has gone unrecognized by biographers and critics as well.

One can safely assume that Brontë's study of the Bible reflects a desire to achieve a more thorough understanding of the scriptures than she presumably got through listening to Sunday sermons or through discussions with her family members. Her pursuit implies as well that she assumed personal responsibility for her relationship with God, an idea that was at the heart of Anglican Evangelicalism.[4] Both Anglican Evangelicals and Methodists argued for the individual right – even duty – to read and study the Bible for one's self. As Christine Krueger writes,

> Attacking the mystification of scripture that demanded of 'legitimate' readers expertise available to a select few, they maintained that God would reveal to babes what he concealed from the wise. Indeed, scripture itself imposed on the individual a duty to attend to that Word, the authority to interpret it, and the duty to spread it – to speak for God. (8)

Many Victorians embarked at various points in their lives on relatively systematic studies of the Bible in the spirit that Krueger here summarizes. Suggesting the centrality of Bible study to the evangelical mood that characterized the first half of the century, Altick notes that the 'Bible, interpreted with utmost literalism, was the supreme guide to conduct' (165-66). 'In addition to a common literary and argumentative vocabulary', he writes, 'the Bible provided the accepted cosmogony, a considerable part of ancient history as it was then known, and above all the foundations of his morality' (203). It is in the end fruitless to try to ascertain with more precision Brontë's motivations in undertaking this project or to determine with any precision the gradations of influence that Methodism and Anglican Evangelicalism had on her own beliefs – or, for that matter, attitudinal differences toward Bible study within these groups. Nevertheless, it is apparent that Brontë, like most of the general educated public, was steeped in this dimension of her cultural heritage. The extensive notes jotted down on her Bible's flyleaves should be understood as a manifestation of this cultural heritage.

Anne Brontë's Religion

The notes help one to appreciate the complexities of Brontë's personal history as well. Anne has long been considered the most pious of the sisters; as her sister Charlotte herself put it, 'She was a very sincere and practical Christian, but the tinge of religious melancholy communicated a sad shade to her brief, blameless life' (qtd. in Chitham 136).[5] Although Brontë may have been devout compared to her sisters, she cannot be said to have had a straightforward, untroubled religious life. One of the most obvious examples of her need to think through her religious understanding occurred late in 1837 or early in 1838 when she was living at the Roe Head school. Collapsing physically, Brontë experienced what today would be thought of as a psychosomatic crisis, one with distinctly 'religious overtones' (Chitham 52). During this episode, she consulted, evidently on several occasions, the Moravian minister James la Trobe. Existing records of their encounters indicate that Brontë and la Trobe conversed about the Bible. As summarized in Chitham's biography, la Trobe

> found her 'very well acquainted with the main truths of the Bible respecting our salvation', but evidently Anne saw Bible precept as a series of requirements rather than 'God's gift in His Son'. Her heart, however, 'opened to the sweet views of salvation, pardon and peace . . . and welcome to the weary and heavy laden sinner, conscious more of her noting loving the Lord her God than acts of Enmity to Him'. (54-55)

Chitham concludes that 'for the evangelical Anne, this encounter may have provided a conversion experience, after which she could discard her theological worry' (55). Yet, given the intensity with which she later approached the Bible as an object of study, it seems more sensible to view the la Trobe episode as one stage in the intellectual development of her religious belief. One might also reason that when Brontë embarked on a study of the Bible in 1841, it was not to acquaint herself with supposed Biblical truths. Already well-schooled in basics, as the la Trobe episode indicates, she would instead be studying at a more rigorous level of thinking.

A second point in Brontë's personal history that illustrates the complexity of her religious experience and adds credence to the notion that her beliefs evolved throughout her life occurred in 1848, shortly before she died. A Liverpool minister, Dr. David Thom, had written to her (as Acton Bell) to respond to some of the religious ideas expressed in her writing. 'A Word to the Elect', an anti-Calvinist poem of Brontë's, had appeared in *Poems by Currer, Acton, and Ellis Bell* (1846), for example, and her second novel, *The Tenant of Wildfell Hall* (1848), revealed some of Brontë's thoughts on the issues of sin, eternal damnation, and universal salvation.

Thom's original letter is not extant, but her response, dated 30 December 1848, is enlightening. In it, Brontë wrote of the doctrine of universal salvation, writing that she embraced it 'with a trembling hope at first, and afterwards with a firm and glad conviction of its truth'. Continuing, she explains, 'I drew it secretly from my own heart and from the word of God before I knew that any others held it' (qtd. in Barker 580). Her letter suggests, then, the importance of the *process* through which her beliefs developed over time as they were shaped and validated by her reading. They were the result of both feeling and thought – specifically, apparently, study of what she believed to be God's word as expressed through the Bible.

Despite the complexities suggested by these and other aspects of Brontë's experience and writing, scholarship on her religious beliefs has focused reductively on ascertaining Calvinist or Wesleyan leanings within her Methodist heritage. In an article on Brontë's feminism, for instance, Marion Shaw contrasts Brontë's religious beliefs to those espoused by the fictional character of Mr Brocklehurst, the horrifically mean Calvinist Methodist who appears in *Jane Eyre*. Describing Brontë as 'an Arminian Methodist', Shaw contends that in 'this milder form of evangelicalism, she stands as a mediator between Calvinist determinism and Romantic naïveté' (127). Much of the effort exerted to pinpoint Brontë's beliefs has depended, in turn, on imprecise understandings of the extent to which she may have been influenced by three central figures in her life: 1) her Aunt Branwell, who has been unfairly associated with a hellfire-and-brimstone type of Calvinism; 2) her mother, Maria Branwell, who died when Brontë was an infant but whom Brontë would nevertheless have come to associate not with her mother's Methodist upbringing but with the more moderate beliefs of the Church of England which she had joined; and 3) her father, the Reverend Patrick Brontë, for whom 'belief in conversion, the mainspring of Evangelical teaching' was a 'cornerstone' of life (Barker 44), but who was formally affiliated with an Anglican church and is known to have preached his belief in the essential goodness and infinite mercy of God.

When Brontë biographers and critics have moved beyond assertions of these influences, they have typically sought to locate within her poetry and fiction evidence of particular religious concerns, with poems such as 'Self-Communion' and 'A Word to the Calvinists' providing the primary source for evidence. Timothy Whittome, for example, sees Agnes Grey's reference to '"the glorious heaven beyond, where both may meet again and sin and sorrow are unknown"', lines that conclude Brontë's novel, as 'an affirmation of Anne's own beliefs' (40). Brontë's reaction to the notion of a spiritual elect and, alternately, her consideration of the possibility of universal salvation, particularly as represented in *The Tenant of Wildfell Hall*, have been the major subjects of such inquiry. Although insightful, this approach to Brontë's religion implies that its primary interest lies in the extent to which it appeared in and possibly influenced her literary efforts.

In sum, there are several critical limitations to these approaches, one being that they exclude consideration of religiosity associated with the everyday. As

Chitham writes, 'Anne's understanding of religion included the duty of morning and evening prayer, church attendance and a moral way of life, which had to be learnt' (27). An equally significant shortcoming is that such approaches unduly assume that Brontë's religious convictions were almost entirely molded by those around her. Yet she revealed in many ways an independence much like that traditionally associated with her more famous sisters, especially her attitude toward unfamiliar ideas and experiences (such as living and working away from home).[6] In the end, much of the existing scholarship on Anne Brontë assumes an overly simplistic notion of authorship. While it would be foolish to argue that Brontë was not impacted by her familial surroundings, the notes that she made on the flyleaves of her Bible suggest that she took a great deal of personal responsibility for her own beliefs and that these beliefs simultaneously shaped and were shaped by other aspects of her life, including her professional writing. That she made the effort to study the Bible, that she apparently wanted to do so on her own, and that the task was undertaken with enough rigour to have lasted nearly a year and a half combine to reveal considerably more independence and initiative than scholars usually credit to Brontë.

Anne Brontë's Bible

It would be convenient for a discussion of Brontë's Bible project if the notes she took revealed several distinct themes, but such is not the case. Instead, the chapters and verses noted illustrate wide-ranging interests and concerns impossible to summarize in an essay. A few examples will illustrate the breadth of response implied by Brontë's simple listing of chapters and verses. She begins with the Book of Deuteronomy, a collection of laws that express the principle that God rewards those who follow his laws. The first chapter cited in her notes is the eighth, which counsels its readers to 'keep the commandments of the LORD thy God, to walk in his ways, and to fear him' (8:6) and which reminds its readers in a variety of ways of the value of humbling experiences. Curiously, Brontë also singled out of the Book of Deuteronomy chapters 23 and 24 both of which begin by itemizing a series of rules to be followed. The first verse of chapter 23 reads, 'He that is wounded in the stones, or hath his privy member cut off shall not enter into the congregation of the LORD', and chapter 24 begins, 'When a man hath taken a wife, and married her, and it come to pass that she find no favour in his eyes, because he hath found some uncleanness in her: then let him write her a bill of divorcement, and give it in her hand, and send her out of his house'. The third verse of chapter 25 similarly instructs readers that judges, upon finding a wicked man guilty, may give him '[f]orty stripes'.

     It is tempting to speculate on the relationship of these and other verses within the five chapters of Deuteronomy that Brontë noted to interests that we know her later to have developed: divorce, for instance, is central to the social and historical contexts of *The Tenant of Wildfell Hall*. Similarly, verse nineteen of chapter eight warns that those who 'walk after other gods, and serve them, and worship them . . . shall surely perish', another theme that surfaces in Brontë's second novel, as when Helen Huntingdon agonizes over the destiny her sinful husband would meet were there not an all-forgiving God. But what do we make of chapter 23, verse 25, which reads, 'When thou comest into the standing corn of thy neighbour, then thou mayest pluck the ears with thine hand; but thou shall not move a sickle unto thy neighbour's standing corn'? Rather than despair that no such interest in fields of corn and attendant neighborly relationships later appears in Brontë's fiction or poetry, we might look instead for less transparent ways that such verses may have had meaning for her. One might reasonably conclude, for example, that many of the verses of all five Deuteronomy chapters that Brontë selected for emphasis implicitly concern the challenges and complexities of obedience. Obedience – to one's self, one's family, and to God – was an issue with which Brontë struggled both in her writing and in many of her personal experiences.

Brontë seems to have been especially taken with the Book of Psalms, the Book of Proverbs, and the Book of Ecclesiastes; the latter two are prefaced in her notes with the phrase 'the whole of'. Within the Psalms, a book that 'speaks to God in prayer and of God in praise and in professions of faith and trust'[7] Brontë singled out several chapters and verses that center around God's treatment of the sinner, obviously an idea that would later occupy her attention as a poet and novelist. Psalm eleven, for instance, includes the following: 'The Lord examines the righteous, but the wicked and those who love violence his soul hates. On the wicked he will rain fiery coals and burning sulfur, a scorching wind will be their lot' (11:5-6). An even more prominent theme emerging in the particular Psalms she selected has to do with one's fear of God's anger and concomitant desire for God's mercy. Psalm four, the first within the Book noted by Brontë, begins, 'Answer me when I call to you, O my righteous God. Give me relief from my distress; be merciful to me and hear my prayer' (4:1). Psalm six, the second to be noted by Brontë, begins, 'O Lord, do not rebuke me in your anger or discipline me in your wrath' (6:1), and continues to express the bodily and psychic anguish of the speaker before ending more confidently, 'The Lord has heard my cry for mercy; the Lord accepts my prayer. All my enemies will be ashamed and dismayed; they will turn back in sudden disgrace' (6:9-10). In a relatively rare gesture, Brontë indicates ambivalence in her notes on the Psalms, writing '*perhaps* the 38th' (emphasis mine). Curiously, this passage begins the same as Psalm six (i.e., 'O Lord, do not rebuke me in your anger'), details the speaker's bodily and psychic affliction, but ends on a decidedly more plaintive note: 'O Lord, do not forsake me; be not far from me, O my God. Come quickly to help me, O Lord my Savior' (38:21-22). Finally, many of the last Psalms selected by Brontë seem to emphasize not an angry God's treatment of the miserable sinner, but rather a benevolent and awe-inspiring God who is 'good to all' and 'has compassion on all he has made', as in Psalm 145, verse eight,[8] and who 'remains faithful forever', as in Psalm 146, the last of 42 Psalms noted on the flyleaves.

Brontë scrutinized closely other books of the Bible as well. On the flyleaves she pencilled in 'The whole book of Job', noting, 'especially the 14th chapter', which she underlined for additional emphasis, before registering the '11th to 15th' verses. Within Job she also noted the 23rd to 29th verses of the 19th chapter and the 28th chapter in its entirety. She approached the Book of Proverbs in much the same way, writing 'The whole book' in her flyleaves but singling out 'especially the 11th chapter 7th and 8th verses & the 14th ch. 32nd verse'. Similarly, she noted 'The whole of Ecclesiastes, but especially the 3rd chapter, 21st verse'. Through their use of direction and emphasis, these comments provide greater insight into Brontë's interests and concerns. The fourteenth chapter of Job conveys, predictably, the despondent mood of its speaker, but verses eleven through fifteen are noteworthy in their evocation of a sense of promise and hope. They read:

> As the waters fail from the sea, and the flood decayeth and drieth up: So man lieth down, and riseth not: till the heavens be not more, they shall not awake, nor be raided out of their sleep. O that thou wouldest hide me in the grave, that thou wouldest keep me secret, until thy wrath be past, that thou wouldest appoint me a set time, and remember me! If a man die, shall he live again? all the days of my appointed time will I wait, till my change come. Thou shalt call, and I will answer thee: thou wilt have a desire to the work of thine hands.

The question that Job asks stands out not only because it is the only one raised in this chapter, but also because of its starkly honest grappling with the possibility of an afterlife. Job expresses his desire to be remembered in much the same way as Anne Brontë once did, writing in the poem 'The Shadow of Christ', 'Remember me! Oh! My God for good – ' (42). The passage is remarkable as well for its movement between various degrees of certainty, statements of which frame the central question of an afterlife. Although the opening lines suggest a disheartening certainty that there is no hope of life after death, the central question, 'If a man die, shall he live again?', undercuts the proposition with which he began. Either the answer Job assumes here is 'No!', or he is contemplating an alternative that would counter commonly held assumptions of his time. The way the passage ends seems especially worthy of comment, for after raising the unanswerable question, Job makes two promises: the first to wait through his 'appointed time', a phrase that echoes the more overtly apocalyptic 'till the heavens be no more', and the second to answer the call from the Lord. 'Thou shalt call, and I will answer thee' in this sense echoes the Proverb Brontë chose to end her notations: 'A man hath joy by the answer of his mouth and a word spoken in due season' which, like Job's dual references to an 'appointed time', suggests that Brontë was intrigued by ontological propositions that relate temporality to being.

Two additional aspects of the passage from Job deserve commentary in light of Brontë's other writing. Job issues a multi-faceted plea to God and ends with his request to be remembered. His plea begins with an expression of his desire to be hidden as in 'the grave'; 'keep me secret', he writes. These are desires that many of Brontë's fictional and poetic characters express and that Brontë herself was said to embody. In an often-quoted passage, Charlotte Brontë wrote that Anne 'covered her mind, and especially her feelings, with a sort of nun-like veil'; memorializing her sister in another biographical notice, she wrote that her youngest sister 'ever waited at a Secret Sinai, listening in her heart to the voice of a trumpet sounding long and waxing louder' (qtd. in Frawley 1, 20).[9] What is especially intriguing about these remarks is the way Charlotte implicitly associates her sister's secrecy with religiosity.

As I have argued in *Anne Brontë*, secrecy is problematized in critical ways in Brontë's literary work, most often by being represented as a condition that characters struggle against even as they accommodate it. Job's wording implies that it is not something about himself, but rather he himself, who wants to be hidden, made secret. My emphasis on personhood here is intentional, for it is also implied by the phrase 'till my change come', which Job uses to demarcate a shift in his relationship with God and in the duration of his 'appointed time' on earth. Fulfillment of desire, and of self, is something over which Job has only limited control, and his use of a vocabulary of waiting both in this passage and in others helps to underscore the passivity of his posture.

It is just this passivity that underwrites Brontë's question, 'What, Where, and How Will I Be When I Have Got Through?' – a question that positions Brontë, like Job, as waiting anxiously for a 'change', what might be thought of as a personal reformation, to come. The question with which Brontë opened her Biblical reading project is especially revealing because very similar questions occur to Brontë's fictional heroines and poetic personae at key narrative moments, just as they had to Brontë herself in her diary papers. Such questions reveal, I believe, the connection between her reading of the Bible and her lifelong concern with self-examination and the ways in which the self could be transformed by experience. A November 1834 diary paper co-written by Emily and Anne, for example, includes the line, 'Anne and I say I wonder what we shall be like and what we shall be and where we shall be, if all goes on well, in the year 1874' (Wise and Symington I 124-25). In her own diary paper of 1841 Brontë wrote, 'I wonder what will be our condition and how or where we will all be on this day four years hence' (Wise and Symington I 239). Turning the lens on herself later in the diary paper, she speculates, 'What will the next four years bring fourth? Providence only knows' (Wise and Symington I 239).

Brontë's 1845 diary paper includes questions posed in an almost identical format, but ends with a slight twist on the theme. 'What changes all we have seen and known; and shall we be much changed ourselves?', she asks before concluding, 'I hope not, for the worse at least. I for my part cannot well be flatter or older in mind than I am now' (Wise and Symington II 53). The interest that Brontë showed in her own self-development translated to her fictional heroines as well, both of whom struggled with questions of God's will and His justice. In language akin to Job's request to God for a hearing, Agnes Grey, for example, asks herself, 'Is it likely that my life all through will be so clouded? Is it not possible that God may hear my prayers, disperse these gloomy shadows, and grant me some beams of heaven's sunshine yet' (137). In *The Tenant of Wildfell Hall*, Helen Huntingdon agonizes that the degradation of living with her husband has so changed her as to make her almost unrecognizable to herself, and perhaps to God, at one introspective moment thinking, 'how immeasurably changed' she was (275).

Such moments remind us that for Anne Brontë the idea that one's personhood is mutable – that identity itself is not necessarily a stable given – was both promising and, yet, simultaneously threatening. The question with which Brontë prefaced her study of the Bible, 'What, Where, and How Shall I Be When I Have Got Through?', was one that she posed and re-posed to herself at key moments in her life and within her writing and suggests that she thought of it as potentially life-transforming. I have focused in this essay on a very select sample of the chapters and verses that Brontë noted. She lists in total seventeen books from the Old Testament and itemizes along the way almost 120 specific chapters and even more verses, so there is far more to be said on the subject of Brontë's Bible. What these limited examples reveal, however, is that for Brontë the Bible was much more than a book to own and carry with her to the services conducted by her father in Haworth or to take from home as a source of consolation and comfort during the isolation of governessing. It was a text valued both as an instrument of self-education and, correlatively, as a device to foster self-transformation. Analyzing Brontë's Biblical reading project in these terms suggests that the emphasis on an individual responsibility for developing a relationship to God through studying the Bible, so often associated with Victorian versions of Evangelicalism, contributed to and even cultivated a particular kind of subjectivity, one linked in Anne Brontë's case at least to a belief in the potentialities of self-reformation.

In *Agnes Grey* Brontë signals her respect for the cottager Nancy Brown and for Agnes Grey herself via a reference to the 'well-used Bible' that Agnes takes from the shelf. Locating with ease a particular passage that Nancy has requested to hear, Agnes tells Nancy, ' The wisest person . . . might think over each of these verses for an hour, and be all the better for it' (73). Clearly Anne Brontë's own Bible was equally 'well-used', providing her not only with a wealth of material to contemplate as she worked her way through thorny theological issues but also, and perhaps more importantly, with the language to map her way beyond personal contemplation to broader questions of being.

Notes

[1] All quotations from Anne Brontë's Bible are transcribed from pencilled notes on the Bible's flyleaves. The Bible is an Authorized Version, published in London by Longman, Hurst, Rees, Orne and Browne in 1821. Permission to reprint this material from MS PML 17769 has been granted by the Pierpont Morgan Library.

[2] Richard Altick, *People and Ideas: A Companion for the Modern Reader of Victorian Literature*, devoted, respectively, to 'The Evangelical Temper' and to 'Religious Movements and Crises'.

[3] I am indebted to Bill McKelvy, then of the University of Virginia, for this information. McKelvy responded to my request for information to VICTORIA, the internet discussion group.

[4] For an excellent discussion of evangelical doctrine and the literature of the nineteenth century, see Elisabeth Jay's *The Religion of the Heart: Anglican Evangelicalism and the Nineteenth-Century Novel*.

[5] This passage originally appeared in Charlotte Brontë's 'Biographical notice of Ellis and Acton Bell' (19 September 1850) in the preface to the 1850 edition of *Wuthering Heights* and *Agnes Grey*.

[6] For a more thorough discussion of the ways Brontë revealed her initiative and independence, see my study *Anne Brontë*, particularly chapter two.

[7] I take this descriptive phrase from the Introduction to the Book of Psalms found in *The Holy Bible: The New International Version* (610).

[8] 'The Shadow of Christ' is a 'manuscript that was purchased at the sale of Ellen Nussey's effects as the work of Anne Brontë'. Although The Brontë Society finds the attribution 'doubtful', I believe it to be accurate (letter to Maria Frawley 6 December 1996).

[9] The first remark originally appeared in Brontë's 'Biographical notice of Ellis and Acton Bell' (19 September 1850) in the preface to the 1850 edition of *Wuthering Heights* and *Agnes Grey*. The second is from Charlotte Brontë's 'Introduction' to 'Selections from Poems by Acton Bell', first published in the 1850 edition as well.

Works Cited

Altick, Richard. *Victorian People and Ideas: A Companion for the Modern Reader of Victorian Literature*. New York: Norton, 1973.

Barker, Juliet. *The Brontës*. New York: St. Martin's, 1995.

Brontë, Anne. *Agnes Grey*. 1847. Intro. Anne Smith. London: J. M. Dent and Sons, 1985.

-----. Notes on flyleaves of King James Bible. Ms. PML 17769. Pierpont

Morgan Library, New York.

-----. *Poems by Currer, Ellis, and Acton Bell*. London: Aylott and Jones, 1846.

-----. 'The Shadow of Christ'. Poem with commentary, attributed to Anne
Brontë. Ms. BS 1. The Brontë Society, Haworth.

-----. *The Tenant of Wildfell Hall*. 1846. Intro. Winifred Gérin. Ed. G. D.
Hargreaves. Harmondsworth: Penguin, 1979.

-----. 'Introduction'. *Wuthering Heights* and *Agnes Grey*. London: Smith, Elder,
1850. Rpt. *Complete Poems of Anne Brontë*. Ed. Clement Shorter. London:
Hodder and Stoughton, 1920.

The Brontë Society. Letter to Maria Frawley. 6 December 1996.

Chitham, Edward. *A Life of Anne Brontë*. Oxford: Blackwell, 1991.

Frawley, Maria. *Anne Brontë*. New York: Twayne, 1996.

Gilmour, Robin. *The Victorian Period: The Intellectual and Cultural Context of English
Literature, 1830-1890*. New York: Longman, 1993.

The Holy Bible: The New International Version. Grand Rapids: Zondervan, 1988.

Jay, Elisabeth. *The Religion of the Heart: Anglican Evangelicalism and the Nineteenth-
Century Novel*. Oxford: Clarendon Press, 1979.

Krueger, Christine L. *The Reader's Repentance: Women Preachers, Women Writers, and
Nineteenth-Century Social Discourse*. Chicago: University of Chicago Press,
1992.

Malmgreen, Gail, ed. *Religion in the Lives of English Women, 1760-1930*.
Bloomington: Indiana University Press, 1986.

Shaw, Marion. 'Anne Brontë: A Quiet Feminist'. *Brontë Society Transactions* 21.4
(1994): 125-35.

Whittome, Timothy. 'The Impressive Lessons of *Agnes Grey*'. *Brontë Society
Transactions* 21.1-2 (1993): 33-41.

Wise, T. J. and J. A. Symington, eds. *The Brontës: Their Lives, Friendships and
Correspondence*. 4 vols. Oxford: Shakespeare Head Press, 1932.
Philadelphia: Porcupine Press, 1980.

Chapter 2

The First Chapter of *Agnes Grey*: An Analysis of the Sympathetic Narrator

Larry H. Peer

The standard judgment of Anne Brontë as a novelist is reflected in George Saintsbury's *The English Novel* (1913). There he writes that the 'third Brontë sister is but a pale reflection of her elders' (243), missing the point that her talent and achievement are of a different order than her sisters'. Her method is not the same, but it is not less sophisticated. A clue to Brontë's literary refinement is given by Derek Stanford, who asserts that

> Any [writer] . . . who is truly able to remember his childhood [can] write an incomparable book. What Anne remembers to perfection are the incidents and state of late adolescence and early womanhood under certain forms of stress. In the story of the governess in *Agnes Grey*, we meet with all those moments of hope and fear, those happenings, productive of keen joy and pain, which a young susceptibility and lack of experience inevitably guarantee to their possessor. But the two things mainly remarkable about the record of early impressions is the accurate, sober, unmisted fashion with which each detail is presented; and the stoic and un-self-pitying manner in which these griefs and hardships are described. (230)

Actually, at the beginning of *Agnes Grey*, the young heroine has every requirement for deserved happiness but one. She has intelligence, youthful vigor, beauty, even a kind of wit, and certainly good-naturedness. Everywhere it is clear that she has the love of those around her. Indeed, one of the central points of the first chapter is that she thinks of herself as happy. Her goal in life is to develop and grow emotionally until she is ready for marriage with a man she can love, thus finding the beginnings of self-fulfillment she deserves. The only threat to her well-being, a threat of which she is not totally aware, is herself: good as she is, she is deficient in the kind of mental toughness gained through hard experience that she will need to survive gracefully her impending ordeal.

It is clear that, with general plot and characterization of this kind, Anne Brontë gives herself difficulties of a high order.[1] Although Agnes' weakness is submerged, it constantly threatens to result in serious harm. Yet she must remain sympathetic or the reader will not wish for or delight sufficiently in her success. To put this another way: Brontë portrays Agnes in the act of growth (the opposite, for example, of Proust, who shows characters in the act of decay). The English novel up to her time typically portrayed growth by showing a character with a flaw (such as Agnes' lack of mental toughness) which, during the course of the narrative, is corrected. The greatest example of master of this fabulative technique is found in Jane Austen's novels.

But character flaws, however submerged, tend to alienate the reader. The rhetorical problem, then, is how the author can secure and maintain the sympathy of the audience for a hero with a character flaw. One solution to this problem is to find some way for the reader to laugh at the mistakes committed by the central character. In *Tom Jones*, this is achieved partly through the invention of episodes producing sympathy and relieving any serious anxiety we might have and partly through direct and sympathetic commentary. In *Emma*, since most of the episodes must illustrate the heroine's faults and thus increase our emotional distance or our anxiety, Austen uses sympathetic laughter to keep us 'in tune' with the heroine. In *Don Quixote*, every crazy gesture the hero makes gives further reason for sympathizing with the strange but well-meaning character, and we can thus laugh at him in somewhat the same way we might laugh at our own faults, in a loving spirit.

Another solution to the problem of maintaining sympathy despite faults is to use the heroine herself as the narrator of her own experience. This is not the 'central intelligence' Henry James uses to view the world of the book primarily through the central character's own eyes, but a general method of showing the story through Agnes' eyes in order to ensure that we travel with the heroine rather than stand against her. But Brontë does not provide, in the unimpeachable evidence of Agnes' own conscience, proof that the heroine's many redeeming qualities are genuine; such evidence could be given through authorial commentary. What we see in *Agnes Grey* is the employment of a sustained inside view of the heroine, which leads the reader to hope for the good fortune of the character with whom he or she travels. An analysis of the first chapter of *Agnes Grey* shows the three ways this sustained view operates.

First of all, it must be remembered that the story is not an autobiography, but a novel. The narrative 'I' is Agnes, not Brontë. However, Brontë's basic strategy is to link the narrative 'I' to facts about the author herself. This creates the kind of credibility that exists when the characteristics of a sympathetic author rub off on a fictional character. The strategy is not new with Brontë, nor is it uncommon in literature of the time, especially Romanticism. What *is* remarkable is its aptness, its perfection. Consider, for example, the following passage, the fourth paragraph of the novel:

Of six children, my sister Mary and myself were the only

> two that survived the perils of infancy and early childhood. I,
> being the younger by five or six years, was always regarded as the
> *child*, and the pet of the family: father, mother, and sister, all
> combined to spoil me – not by foolish indulgence, to render me
> fractious and ungovernable, but by ceaseless kindness, to make
> me too helpless and dependent – too unfit for buffeting with the
> cares and turmoils of life. (4)

Here are stated facts true enough about the lives of both Anne Brontë and Agnes Grey: six children, of which the narrator is the youngest, this child being the family 'pet' and, significantly, the child lacking in the toughness required to survive the turmoils of life. The differences are also obvious: altered children's names, the possibility of the mother's role spoiling the child (stronger for Agnes than for Brontë, whose mother passes away early on), and the number of children who survived the perils of infancy and early childhood.

In *Agnes Grey*, linking the narrative 'I' to facts about the author establishes the novelist's self-dramatization, and the reader is invited to investigate the tension between her 'book-self' and her literal, physical self. This is, above all, a Romantic strategy, where egoistic imperatives are both a formal and a thematic issue in the novel. Brontë's own Haworth childhood reflects the 'perils of infancy' motif found in the book, giving us the notion of the world as a condition of painful and trying experience. From the opening sequence to the end of the narrative, the principle of absolute self-possession is what enables the heroine (and, of course, Brontë herself) to survive and to deserve happiness. The ultimate reason for Agnes'/Brontë's journey through hard experience is to find refinement through trial. When Agnes/Brontë says just before the end of chapter one, 'But some weeks more were yet to be devoted to preparation. How long, how tedious those weeks appeared to me! Yet they were happy ones in the main – full of bright hopes and ardent expectations', we realize that we have a journey-symbol which, coupled with the narrator's insistent use of words and phrases such as 'anguish', 'different feelings', 'circumstances might be changed', 'feeling of sadness', 'looked so sad', and so on defines the tension between the narrator and the heroine and brings us along with them.

A moment in the first chapter signals the ultimate meaning of the journey. When Agnes' father loses his fortune in a shipwreck, the heroine responds in this way:

> Disappointed he was; and bitterly, too. It came like a thunderclap
> to us all, that the vessel which contained our fortune had been
> wrecked, and gone to the bottom with all its stores, together with
> several of the crew, and the unfortunate merchant himself. I was
> grieved for him; I was grieved for the overthrow of all our air-

> built castles: but, with the elasticity of youth, I soon recovered
> from the shock. (6-7)

[The 'elasticity of youth' is the theme of the journey; Agnes' developing elasticity will allow her to absorb the punishment of hard experience and make something of it without being broken by it.] And the elasticity stretching between the narrative 'I' and the author allows the reader to be brought along with the story.

The second way the sustained inside view operates relates more closely to the typical reader's experience. Agnes gains another kind of credibility, not from her link to Brontë but from her link to the novel's reader. In *Tristram Shandy*, Sterne calls our attention to the differences between the hero's relationship to his life experience and the reader's own, creating a gulf between us and the fictional speaker. But in *Agnes Grey*, the common attitudes of the heroine are those with which the typical reader is familiar and comfortable. There is, in other words, a kind of respectable, easily understood, and almost clichéd set of notions that strike an empathetic chord. The reader is likely to say to himself or herself, 'Yes, I understand what Agnes means' or 'I have felt just that way myself'. For example:

> Mary and I were brought up in the strictest seclusion. My mother, being once highly accomplished, well-informed, and fond of employment, took the whole charge of our education on herself, with the exception of Latin – which my father undertook to teach us – so that we never even went to school; and, as there was no society in the neighborhood, our only intercourse with the world consisted in a stately tea-party, now and then, with the principle farmers and tradespeople of the vicinity (just to avoid being stigmatized as too proud to consort with our neighbors), and an annual visit to our paternal grandfather's; where himself, our kind grandmamma, a maiden aunt, and two or three elderly ladies and gentlemen, were the only persons we ever saw. Sometimes our mother would amuse us with stories and anecdotes of her younger days which, while they entertained us amazingly, frequently awoke – in me, at least – a secret wish to see a little more of the world. (4-5)

Anyone brought up on seclusion, in a close-knit family environment, educated formally and informally by parents, immediately recognizes this description as perfectly apt, right down to the 'kind grandmamma', and the wish to grow in stature and confidence until it is appropriate to go into the world and 'test the waters'. Agnes uses the words of a child from a respectable and loving family, the kind of family that has, in modern times, been at the center of civilization. Of course, Agnes (and, by implication, her family) will stand in stark

contrast to the spoiled brats and supercilious parents she will meet as the novel
develops from the first chapter. The terrible families at Wellwood and Horton are
quite familiar to the average reader: they represent the other pole of family
relations right down to our own day. In other words, there are still parents who
want everything good for their children as long as it does not require their own
interest, devotion, time, and effort. The resulting lack of self-discipline on the
children's part can always be predicted, just as we know what is going to happen
to Agnes as she enters the uncivilized 'outer' world. The expectations are so clear,
the results so predictable, that the plot and all that goes with it would be an
unbroken cliché were it not for the suspense we feel at moving along with Agnes
to see how she will survive it. Agnes' 'secret wish to see a little more of the world'
is fraught with danger as well as with opportunity.

[All this recalls the anecdote about Mr Brontë and the mask experiment.
Each of his children was invited to wear a mask and answer his questions from
behind it, the idea being that disguise would allow the children to speak more
freely than speaking face-to-face allows. Anne, then no more than four, was
asked what a child like her most wanted from life, and her answer was 'age and
experience' (Gérin 19-20). This, of course, is what Agnes wants, but further, what
we all want and gain from life, even from those aspects of life that are so obvious,
commonplace, and predictable as to be almost clichés, and which, by extension,
we are going to gain by reading the novel. The anecdote illuminates Brontë's
novel if we see the work as another mask through which we are told what is to be
gained from life.]

It seems to me that the most easily understood and perfectly done but,
surprisingly, most often criticized aspect of the novel pinpoints the second way
the sustained inside view of the heroine works. What Agnes actually learns to do
is cope, not conquer in a blaze of glory. She is spiritually mature enough to know
that, after all, to do those things well that are the common lot of all mankind is
the truest greatness; to quietly make something dignified out of the human idiocy
around us is the ultimate civilizing act. Agnes has a quality that allows her to do
this: she has a self-possession born of a moral education in a loving home. The
style of the novel reflects this; there is an effortless virtuosity in catching the
tiniest implications and nuances of character and situation unmatched in the
nineteenth-century novel, except, perhaps, in Jane Austen and, in a certain way, in
Stendhal. Brontë/Agnes is a center of differentiation, but of just the sort of
character and situation differentiation we all understand basically out of typical,
mundane human experience. In other words, this kind of style is not to be
criticized, but rather to be highly praised.

Beyond stylistic characteristics, however, are the symbols that are at the
core of the third way we access Agnes. There are two kinds of symbolism
popular in the nineteenth-century novel: the 'immediate' kind, in which symbols
are woven into the plot, and a 'secondary' kind, in which symbols stand out from

the plot, 'interpretable' like an allegory. Brontë's use of the first kind is crucial for an understanding of the novel's meaning, and it represents a metaphysical structure that always aptly fits Agnes and her circumstances.

Like so many of her fictional contemporaries (Robinson Crusoe, Tom Jones, Pamela, Jane Austen's heroines, and so on), Agnes begins her history in a state of innocence, even exaggerated innocence, represented by a closed and simple physical setting, in Agnes' case the parsonage. As the novel develops, Agnes will be tested in other physical locations, each place representing a kind of experience and a measure of her character. But her beginnings in the parsonage give the reader the inside view with which he or she empathizes. One might say she is the parsonage, and vice versa, with all related positive and negative characteristics. For example, Agnes, like a country parsonage, is more-or-less self-contained and respected, but also limited in view, provincial. To entitle the first chapter 'The Parsonage' is to reveal to the reader the closed and simple personality of Agnes, along with her ability to flower under crisis.

Another way of looking at this idea is to read carefully the first few sentences of the novel, which include the lines,

> All true histories contain instruction; though, in some, the treasure may be hard to find, and when found, so trivial in quantity, that the dry, shrivelled kernel scarcely compensates for the trouble of cracking the nut. (3)

The reader may be tempted at first to see Agnes' story as only a 'shrivelled kernel', but he or she must still crack the nut to find out if that is indeed all it is. To regard the story as a nut to be cracked open is not only interesting but perfectly apt, inasmuch as the careful removal of an inner treasure or nourishment from an outer shell is how Agnes learns throughout the novel as well as how she teaches, as in chapter eleven when she 'pries open' the Bible to extract its meaning:

> Whether this be the case with my history or not, I am hardly competent to judge. I sometimes think it might prove useful to some, and entertaining to others; but the world may judge for itself. Shielded by my own obscurity, and by the lapse of years, and a few fictitious names, I do not fear to venture; and will candidly lay before the public what I would not disclose to the most intimate friend. (1)

Shielded as a four-year-old by her mask or later by a 'kernel' (one may use any of the many metaphors Brontë suggests), she is able to speak her mind freely. Speaking shyly from behind any mask, whether a mask of obscurity or something else, has the charm of a child revealing a 'great truth' to a parent, and it helps us go along with Agnes indulgently, rather than criticize her for hiding.

One of the most interesting symbolic linkages occurs at the end of chapter one:

> But the morning brought a renewal of hope and spirits. I was to depart early; that the conveyance which took me (a gig, hired from Mr Smith, the draper, grocer, and tea-dealer of the village) might return the same day. I rose, washed, dressed, swallowed a hasty breakfast, received the fond embraces of my father, mother, and sister, kissed the cat – to the great scandal of Sally, the maid – shook hands with her, mounted the gig, drew my veil over my face, and then, but not till then, burst into a flood of tears. The gig rolled on; I looked back; my dear mother and sister were still standing at the door, looking after me, and waving their adieux. I returned their salute, and prayed to God to bless them from my heart: we descended the hill, and I could see them no more. (14-15)

Here we find three sets of four actions that play out the drama (in three acts, as it were) of her entrance into the experience that begins in chapter two. In the first act, Agnes rises, washes, dresses, and eats. In act two, she embraces her father, then mother, then sister, then cat. Finally, she says farewell to the maid, gets into the gig, draws the veil over her face, then bursts into tears. The syntax is perfectly balanced and perfectly expected as a typical set of farewell actions. The first set of actions is related strictly to her own person, the second to those closest to her, and the third draws her away into a new world. This encapsulated drama is the microcosm of the whole novel, both structurally and thematically. The compactness of this little drama is like the balance, symmetry, and compactness of the entire narrative, and the very domesticity of the actions figures forth the novel's meaning about doing common things well and coping in a civilized way with the real world.

> 'It's a coldish mornin' for you, Miss Agnes', observed Smith; 'and a darksome un too; but we's happen to get to yon' spot afore there come much rain to signify'.
> 'Yes, I hope so', replied I, as calmly as I could.
> 'It's comed a good sup last night, too'.
> 'Yes'.
> 'But this cold will happen keep it off'.
> 'Perhaps it will'.

Here ended our colloquy. We crossed the valley, and
began to ascend the opposite hill. As we were toiling up, I
looked back again: there was the village spire, and the old grey
parsonage beyond it, basking in a slanting beam of sunshine – it
was but a sickly ray, but the village and surrounding hills were all
in sombre shade, and I hailed the wandering beam as a propitious
omen to my home. With clasped hands, I fervently implored a
blessing on its inhabitants, and hastily turned away; for the
sunshine was departing; and I carefully avoided another glance,
lest I should see it in gloomy shadow, like the rest of the
landscape. (15)

One of Brontë's favorite images, the veil, plays a prominent part in this
passage. It seems to represent a covering of Agnes' innermost feelings, a kernel, a
mask allowing her to speak out her true self, for behind the veil she is able to
burst into tears. As she crosses the landscape in the gig, moving further and
further away from ignorant innocence toward 'age and experience', she notices
that the sunshine is departing her little child's world. Agnes is both the grey
parsonage (the 'grey' is the link, of course) and the parsonage's sunlight, or rather
the parsonage lit by a 'slanting beam of sunshine'. She is thus, at the conclusion
of chapter one, seen as the colorless village child and the bright beam who will
light the lives of those with whom she comes in contact as she gains experience.
This symbol creates suspense, for who knows how one's attempt to cope with life
will turn out? The reader is brought to wish for more on Agnes' landscape than
'gloomy shadow', even hoping that the light of her integrity and humanity will
illuminate the darkened landscape of mortal existence.

Agnes Grey is a surprisingly good novel, given Brontë's neglected station.
Her rhetorical problem is to secure sympathy for the heroine, which she does by
employing a sustained view of Agnes. Her strategy is threefold: link the narrative
'I' to facts about the author, link the narrative 'I' to the reader's familiar and
comfortable world, and spin a web of symbolic reference that ties the reader to
Agnes' fortunes. Thus we empathize with a character in the act of growth, learn
to love her, and perhaps in some measure even learn to be like her.

It is important to recognize that this is the first novel in English literature
that employs this strategy in the creation of a true *Bildungsroman*. *Agnes Grey* is the
archetypal representation of the interaction between the self and the world, where
the process of the education of the self by common human experience is the
point. It may be that Brontë's novel is neglected because modern readers are not
interested in *Bildung* (which might also explain why we no longer read true classics
such as Goethe's *Willhelm Meister*, Stendhal's *Vie de Henri Brulard*, and other works
contemporary with Brontë). Also, it may be that Charlotte's and Emily's ways of
writing have such surface appeal that the quiet and powerful stillness of Anne's

style is obscured by comparison. In any case, the strategy of *Agnes Grey* is clearly employed, carefully woven to reader response, and linked to the great works of the Continental tradition.

Note

1 Wayne C. Booth's *The Rhetoric of Fiction* (1961) is one of the clearest pieces of scholarship on the problem of rhetoric, characterization, and plot. I am indebted to the strategy of his book's excellent discussion of Jane Austen in the formulation of my argument here. All references to *Agnes Grey* are from the Sheakespeare Head edition, edited by J. J. Wise and J. A. Symington.

Works Cited

Booth, Wayne. *The Rhetoric of Fiction.* Chicago: University of Chicago Press, 1961.
Brontë, Anne. *Agnes Grey.* Eds. Hilda Masden and Robert Inglesfield. Oxford: Clarendon, 1988.
-----. *Agnes Grey. The Shakespeare Head Brontë.* Eds. J. J. Wise and J. A. Symington. Oxford: Basil Blackwell, 1931.
Gérin, Winifred. *Anne Brontë: A Biography.* London: Allen Lane, 1976.
Harrison, Ada and Derek Stanford. *Anne Brontë: Her Life and Work.* New York: Methuen, 1959.
Saintsbury, George. *The English Novel.* London: J. M. Dent and Sons, 1913.

Chapter 3

Class, Matriarchy, and Power: Contextualizing the Governess in *Agnes Grey*

James R. Simmons, Jr.

'The figure of the governess', notes Katherine Hughes in *The Victorian Governess*, 'must be one of the most familiar and abiding images in nineteenth-century literature' (xi), and certainly even the casual reader of the Victorian novel would have to agree. In works as diverse as Charlotte Brontë's *Jane Eyre*, William Makepeace Thackeray's *Vanity Fair*, Harriet Martineau's *Deerbrook*, and Mrs Henry Wood's *East Lynne*, the plight of the governess is intrinsic to the development of the novel as a whole. Though there may be a tendency to attribute the ubiquity of the governess in nineteenth-century fiction to the belief that this is merely a result of the parallel found in the vast numbers of them employed in England during the Victorian period – some 21,000 in 1850 (Pool 250) – it is interesting to note that during that same year there were roughly two *million* men, women, and children employed in factory work in England (Cobden 104). Yet in very few novels were the heroes or heroines factory workers. Hughes accounts for some of the appeal of the fictional governess by noting that the 'transformation of the governess into a major literary character was inseparable from the wider process of feminization which the novel had been undergoing since the middle of the eighteenth century' (ix), and though this is certainly true, there must be more to the popularity of the fictive governess, for otherwise the struggle of the female factory worker might have sufficed to carry the torch of feminism in literature just as well. So what accounts for the Victorian fascination with the governess?

As the most recognizable Victorian novel about the life of a governess, Charlotte Brontë's *Jane Eyre* may provide an answer. Class consciousness, it has been pointed out, is a central issue in the narrative. As Mary Poovey has shown in *Uneven Developments: The Ideological Work of Gender in Mid-Victorian England*, as a governess Jane is middle class by birth, yet working-class in that she works for wages (131). Similarly, Susan Fraiman notes that a conflict in the novel is the question of 'where does Jane belong', and part of Jane's quest for self is to discover if she is a 'middle- or working-class girl' (617). No doubt class consciousness, a subject on the minds of many Victorian readers, is of paramount importance in *Jane Eyre* and other novels about governesses. However, it is in a novel by another Brontë that we find the most realistic portrayal of the life of a governess. In terms of class representations and historical accuracy, nowhere is the governess more realistically depicted than in Anne Brontë's *Agnes Grey*.

In *Agnes Grey*, Agnes confronts obstacles similar to those that many governesses working in England at mid-century faced, primarily the tribulations of attempting to serve as a surrogate mother while in fact having little of the authority or power of the natural mother. While this lack of authority seems, at least superficially, to be the result of the fact that the children whom Agnes teaches realize that she is simply a mother figure, and thus they feel less inclined to obey her than they might their natural parent, the problem is in fact more complex. Consequently, it would be reductive to assume that Anne Brontë is merely making a statement about motherhood in *Agnes Grey*, especially since the disrespect shown by the children is not the most problematic aspect of Agnes' tenure as a governess: on the contrary, her strongest commentaries – veiled though they may be at times – are about class considerations. In this novel Agnes exists as neither strictly a servant nor one of the family, and like many governesses, the fluid parameters of Agnes' world find her treated as a pariah by the children she teaches and the other staff and servants alike. Ultimately though, it is Agnes' ill treatment by the parents of her charges in the Murray and Bloomfield households who undermine her authority, and in no small part because they see her as being of a lower class than themselves. Agnes' power is therefore circumscribed by class considerations, and like many actual upper-class Victorian children, the Bloomfield and Murray offspring cannot forget that their governess is merely a paid subordinate. To this extent, class undermines Agnes' power perhaps more than the fact that she is not the natural mother of the children, because although she attempts to establish a maternal family relationship, there is no disputing that her relationship with the children is primarily economic, and that she works as a governess because she is of a less-affluent class.

In this sense, one may see Agnes' struggle as emblematic of the conflicts facing the emerging English middle class as well. In *Agnes Grey* Anne Brontë has presented a depiction of the life of a governess that differs greatly from the more sensational, romanticized portraits found in most of the other novels of the period. Because *Agnes Grey* is likely lesser known than Brontë's more popular novel *The Tenant of Wildfell Hall*, and perhaps the least frequently read of any work by the Brontë sisters other than Charlotte's *The Professor*, it is probable that many of the readers who come to this novel are already aware that Anne Brontë was herself a governess.[1] Dickens, Thackeray, Wilkie Collins and many others employed governesses; Elizabeth Gaskell and George Eliot were instructed by governesses; Harriet Martineau's sisters were governesses; and even Anne's sister Charlotte briefly worked as a governess. However, Anne Brontë alone among the most prominent literati of the nineteenth century worked for an extended period as a governess, and perhaps had her experiences been more pleasant she might never have been a novelist at all. Yet it is her personal experience that allows Brontë to write authoritatively about the inner struggles concerning class issues that the governess faced daily, and it seems safe to assume that Agnes' life is probably more realistic than the lifestyle of many fictional governesses whose stories were penned by authors who were not themselves governesses.

The question is, however, were Anne Brontë's experiences, and by extension Agnes', typical of the experiences of governesses during the nineteenth century? Readers today presume to know about governesses' lives primarily because they know about fictional governesses such as Jane Eyre and Becky Sharp. But is it wise to take at their word the Brontës, Thackeray, Martineau, Trollope, or any of the other literati who wrote about governesses? Factual and fictional accounts often differed greatly, and as with so many other working-class occupations, twentieth-century perceptions of governesses are largely based on accounts by middle-class fiction writers, not upon accounts by the people who actually worked in these occupations. But to truly understand the Victorian cultural constructions of what governesses were expected to be like, and therefore by extension attempt to understand if Agnes' situation is indeed emblematic of Victorian class prejudices, it is important to examine the lives of actual Victorian governesses, and determine to what extent conflicts based on class existed between employee and employer, and how they limited the power of the governess. The answer to the question of what a governess' life was really like can be found by exploring some of the working-class lifewriting by governesses during the period. By doing so, it becomes clear that *Agnes Grey* makes one of the Victorian period's strongest statements about class, matriarchy, and power, statements that have long been overlooked as merely the stylistic explorations of a young novelist struggling to write her first work.

The Governess in Fact and Fiction

Governesses, it seems, were everywhere in Victorian fiction, and literary accounts of their unhappiness and mistreatment were prevalent as well – although often these accounts were disputed. 'Insolence to a governess is an old stock complaint' wrote the novelist Charlotte Yonge in 1878. 'In real life, I never heard of it from anyone by birth and breeding a lady'. Yonge admitted that she had heard of *one* instance, 'from a thoroughly vulgar employer', but that otherwise mistreatment by employers was more fiction than fact: the stuff novels are made of (34).

Certainly in fiction the governess as victim had been an idea for decades, and even in Jane Austen's Regency-period comedy *Emma* the plight of the governess is alluded to – one of the few darkly negative references in an Austen novel. In that novel, Jane Fairfax, elegant and accomplished but poor and an orphan, faces the prospect of a life as a governess, and she is none too happy that the meddling Mrs Elton seems determined to find her a situation before she is ready. Jane makes her thoughts on her prospects as a governess clear as she refers to the employment agencies that place governesses as 'offices for the sale – not quite of human flesh – but of human intellect' (Austen 193). When Mrs Elton misunderstands her and thinks Jane alludes to slave trading, Jane replies that she meant not the slave trade but the 'governess trade . . . but as to greater misery of its victims I do not know where it lies' (193).

Like Jane Fairfax, the poor but accomplished woman had few alternatives in terms of a career, and when supporting oneself became inevitable, governessing was indeed the most viable option. One such factual counterpart of Jane Fairfax was Nelly Weeton, whose *Journal of a Governess, 1807-1825* presents a fascinating look at the life of a governess during the early nineteenth century, as it was written long before mid-century novels such as *Jane Eyre* and *Agnes Grey* made the life of a governess fashionable reading material. Reading Weeton's life account, it seems that despite Yonge's disclaimer, governessing may have been every bit as wretched as some middle-class novelists led us to believe.

Ellen 'Nelly' Weeton was born on Christmas Day, 1776, the second child of a sea captain in her majesty's navy and his schoolmistress wife. Although her father originally told Weeton's mother that he 'wish[ed] his children to be all boys', because 'unless a father can provide independent fortunes for his daughters, they must either be made mop squeezers, or mantua makers' (Vol. I 6), she was a great favorite of her father's nevertheless. After the death of her two older siblings, Nelly was the only child until her brother Thomas was born when she was four.

In relation to Weeton's future, and especially as it applied to her brother Thomas, her father's words were to be prophetic. Her father was killed in a sea battle with an American warship in 1782, and thus her mother found herself at an early age as a widow with two children to care for. While the family's economic resources were limited, they possessed enough for Nelly's brother to acquire a good education, often at the expense of Nelly and her mother doing without. Weeton was fortunate in that her mother was able to help educate her at home, but she was denied the advanced education available to her brother and other men of the period. 'Oh!', she wrote, 'how I have burned to learn Latin, French, the Arts, the Sciences, anything rather than the dog trot of sewing, teaching, writing copies, and washing dishes every day' (Vol. I 14). Still, Weeton was able to read and write, although she was allowed to read very little popular literature, because her mother thought that she 'should be entirely ruined for any useful purpose in life if [her] inclinations for literature were indulged', and therefore her mother 'treated all [her] efforts in this way with decided discouragement; so much so as to damp [her] spirit for ever' (Vol. I 14).

Weeton's mother died in 1797, and thus she says 'I was left before I was twenty one, an unprotected orphan' (Vol. I 24). Her brother was but sixteen, and an articled clerk, and she was the sole support for the two of them. By way of the laws of primogeniture at the time, her brother derived enough income to provide for his needs, but Weeton had only the family's home to live in and little else. Consequently, she continued to run her mother's school, although the small income she derived from it (about seven shillings a week) provided barely enough to cover the family's accrued debts, much less for her to feed and support herself. Her mother had expected that Thomas would provide for Nelly when he found gainful employment, but on this count she was sadly mistaken. Upon the completion of his articles, Weeton's brother almost immediately married a girl with no dowry, and they eventually moved into the family home, which, of course, belonged by law to Thomas. Shortly thereafter, the brother whom she had worked so hard to help support, informed her that if she wished to remain in the house she must pay thirty guineas a year for board, 'nearly the whole of [her] income' (Vol. I 36). Eventually, however, Thomas' mother-in-law convinced him and his wife that Nelly 'should not live with them at all; that such a kind of family was very unpleasant' (Vol. I 37). Nelly found herself homeless, unwanted, alone, and with few prospects.

As a woman with some education but little else in the way of resources, Weeton took perhaps the only step available to her, in that she decided to embark upon a career as a governess. Through a friend, she heard about an advertisement that had appeared in *Gore's General Advertiser* on 9 November 1809 that read, 'WANTED, in the neighborhood of Kendal, a GOVERNESS, to superintend the Education of a Young Lady. None need apply but such as can give good references as to ability and character' (Vol. I 201). Weeton applied for the job and was interviewed by the retainer for the Pedder family who told her that she 'would be treated as an equal by them, more as a companion to Mrs Pedder than as a governess to Miss P, to assist her in regulating the management of the family such as Mr P. wished his to be' (Vol. I 202). After the retainer asked what salary she would expect – she told him thirty guineas[2] – he engaged her, and thus, she was soon to embark on a career that she would remain in for the majority of her adult life.

Weeton found herself situated at 'Dove's Nest', a home built in the late eighteenth century by a Mr Benson, who was the Wordsworths' landlord while they were residents of Dove Cottage.[3] There she was to instruct the Pedder's ten-year-old daughter Mary, and to serve also as a companion to Pedder's young wife. Initially, the situation seemed pleasant enough, causing Weeton to write in her journal that 'at present, I am treated with a degree of respect and deference, which my conduct shall, if possible, continue to deservedly extract' (Vol. I 212).

This idyllic life, however, was not to last. In February, the Pedder child was warming herself near the fire, and Weeton and Mrs Pedder left the room for not more than 'one whole minute' when 'I heard a scream' (Vol. I 232). The child's apron caught fire, and in an instant 'her thighs, legs, and arms were shockingly burnt indeed. The skin hung from her poor trembling limbs like shreds of paper' (Vol. I 233). Despite the best efforts of the local surgeon, by the next morning Mary Pedder was dead.

The situation at Dove's Nest would take a decided turn for the worse after this, but not, as might be expected, because of the death of the child. Weeton's services were retained as a companion for Mrs Pedder, primarily because her husband wanted Weeton to try to instill some knowledge into his beautiful but uneducated wife. Weeton noted that in fact Mr Pedder was little grieved by the loss of the child, and cared about nothing other than drinking. 'He is scarcely ever sober, and often out of temper, except when drinking and singing with the workmen and servants', Weeton wrote. 'Whilst the dead body of his only child lay in the house, he was drinking, morning or evening, with any person who called in the kitchen. He could even attempt to excite laughter in the room of death itself, and make that room the scene of several quarrels with his wife, without the slightest reason' (Vol. I 237). Although Mr Pedder frequently argued with and even beat his wife, he initially remained civil to Weeton. Soon, however, even this was to change.[4]

Eventually Pedder was not merely content to abuse his wife, and he soon turned his attentions to Weeton. She noted that his manner started to change, especially when he was drinking. The first time that this occurred he berated her for no obvious reason, saying that if she did not watch what she said, 'he and [she] should part very soon' (Vol. I 279). Weeton apparently stood her ground, and told him: 'Sir, I am ready to go at any time. I will never stay anywhere, an unwelcome inmate; for, of this I am certain, no person could possibly take fewer liberties than I do' (Vol. I 279). Though Pedder backed down on this occasion, he became increasingly hostile. As a result, Weeton found herself going out of her way to avoid Pedder, and as a consequence she led a 'sad, idle life, for I am not required to do much. I scarcely stir from my seat from morning to night, employing my time in sewing for the family or myself, writing and reading when I have nothing else to do; for were I to be walking often in the garden or elsewhere, I might occasionally meet with Mr P., who might discover something or other to excite his displeasure' (Vol. I 280). Indeed, from this time forth, Mr Pedder's attitude toward her was 'grossly insulting', and 'he [made] use of tones, gestures, and language approximating much more to the blackguard than the gentleman' (Vol. I 281).

With no money nor prospects, Weeton had no alternative but to remain in Pedder's employment until she could take it no longer. His behavior degenerated even further, both toward Weeton and his own wife:

> I am scarcely permitted to either speak or stir in his presence; nor ever to maintain any opinion different to his own. When in a violent passion (which is but too frequent), on the most trifling

occasions he will sometimes beat and turn his wife out of doors. Twice she has run away to her father's – oh! . . . and then such a house! Mr P Roaring drunk and swearing horridly, and making all of the men about the house drunk. I have thought at such times, I really could not stay any longer, particularly when he has been in violent passions with me, which has occurred six or seven times. As he at one time found fault with everything that I did, I have ceased to do anything I am not asked to do. (Vol. I 301)

As might be expected, ultimately Weeton could bear the strain no longer, and she left the Pedder's in 1811. After traveling on her modest savings for a few months, Weeton took another position as governess, this time with the Armitage family at High Royd. Mr Armitage was in textiles, and both he and his wife were young and not yet 30. Nevertheless, they already had six children, and would have a seventh while Weeton worked for them: they would eventually have fifteen children in all.

Although in this situation Weeton would not suffer the abuse that she had at the hands of Pedder, at the Armitage home she would be overcome by loneliness. Like many governesses, she was regarded as no better than a typical servant. 'There has been a great deal of company since I came' she would write, 'but, though I dine or drink tea with them, I am obliged to leave the room with them so immediately after I have swallowed it, that I may truly be said to see little of them' (Vol. II 58). Thus, just as Becky Sharp would find in *Vanity Fair* – 'I am to be treated as one of the family, except on company days, when . . . I dine . . . upstairs' (Thackeray 79) – the position of the governess was a lonely one, and this seems to have been what distressed Weeton the most. 'It is well that I have so little time for reflection, or otherwise I should almost weep myself into the grave; for my present situation is a most painful one! Forgotten, it seems . . . and totally excluded from all rational society here, I must sink into melancholy if my days were not so occupied as almost to preclude thought' (Vol. II 87). 'Sometimes', she noted, 'I sit with my face resting on my hands, indulging in melancholy, weeping bitterly; for no one interrupts me, no voice soothes, advises, or pities. . . .Why am I thus treated? What have I done, Oh Father, to deserve to be thus deserted and neglected?' (Vol. II 87).

One cannot help but pity Weeton, alone and offered only the alternative of caring for often unmanageable children: 'The children, though well ordered by their parents, when out of their sight are as unruly, noisy, insolent, quarrelsome, and ill-tempered a set as I have ever met with' (Vol. II 59). To further make the situation abhorrent was the fact that the Armitages seemed to care little as to what progress their children made in their studies, merely that they were cared for by someone: as Weeton explains, 'I have never, since I came here, received the slightest acknowledgment of the improvement of my pupils. It appears like a tacit degree of dissatisfaction with me: and when I do labour hard indeed' (Vol. II 74). And although she appreciated the fact that her employers were kind to her – 'I have no cause of just complaint; but I know of some who are treated in a most mortifying manner' (Vol. II 62) – more than at any other time of her life the relative working-class status of the governess was apparent to her: 'A *governess* is almost shut out of society; not choosing to associate with servants, and not being treated as an equal by the head of the house or their visitors, she must possess some fortitude and strength of mind to render herself tranquil and happy; but indeed, the master or mistress of the house, if they have any goodness of heart, would take pains to prevent her feeling her inferiority' (Vol. II 62).

Here, well into her journal, the reader discovers what Weeton felt was most injurious about the life of a governess. Weeton felt that she was middle-class, but that all around her regarded her as being working-class. Although she found this situation preferable to many she knew of, the fact that she was equated with the other servants in the esteem of her employers was unacceptable to her. For Weeton, the working-class status afforded her made the situation untenable, and rather than endure this indignity, she decided to leave her place. Upon the death of her aunt, she was left a small inheritance that allowed her to leave the Armitage home in 1814, and despite the fact that she was afterwards offered several other governessing positions, she chose to pursue this line of work no longer. She eventually married – unhappily, it is unfortunate to note – and she never again worked as a governess, although she did open a school and finished her career as an educator in that capacity. Yet her insights and experiences, which provide us with one of the earliest and best records of life as a governess, bear some retrospection, particularly in regard to the place of the governess in society, and to how the real-life governess compares to her literary counterparts.

The Governess as a Working-class Woman

Both of the situations in which Nelly Weeton found herself were deplorable, but for different reasons. In the first, although she was verbally abused and harassed, she realized that she was treated no differently from anyone else in the house, including the master's wife. Thus, even in her displeasure, she was not alone, and ironically she seemed to find some comfort in this. She was not treated poorly because she was not on a social level with the Pedders, and as she noted Pedder himself often drank and cavorted with his servants. Ultimately, it was only when she almost literally feared to what depths Pedder's behavior would take him next that she left. Overall though, it seems apparent that had Pedder refrained from his debauchery, she probably would have remained in her position for as long as it was available.

It is just as obvious that although the Armitages treated her with respect and attended to her needs, she was clearly no more than a servant in their eyes, and thus class consciousness was the root of her unhappiness. She was never abused, verbally or physically, she was allowed every necessity, the home was comfortable and nice, and even the children, though boisterous as children will be, did, as her accounts attest, progress under her tutelage and eventually become good students.[5] What seems to have accounted for her manifest unhappiness was her recognition that she was quite clearly viewed as little more than a servant in the house, and this obviously bothered her. After all, her father had been a respected naval officer, and her brother would become a well-known attorney. Poverty alone had reduced her to dependant circumstances, and she quite justifiably thought that she should have been viewed as more of a social peer than she was. She was not, however, and thus she was wretched. That this was a common occurrence for many governesses would seem apparent, and as I will illustrate later with *Agnes Grey* it was corroborated in literature as well. To be viewed as a member of the working classes, to be seen as being no better than the stable hand or postboy, was a hard fact with which many a governess had to contend.[6]

Perhaps this would explain why many governesses like Weeton eventually returned to the schoolroom. Although the pay was better as a governess, and the living conditions (in terms of physical comfort) were preferable as well, the pressures of social ostracism for many with middle-class sensibilities were too great to bear. Many governesses found themselves employed by families with even less social pedigree and education than they had. However, because of the industrial revolution and the money made by the rising middle classes, educated women from good families often found themselves in a position of inferiority when clearly they felt that in some respects they were equal, or even superior to their employers. At least in the schoolroom, they were afforded the respect that was denied them in many governessing positions, and the respect that they often received from the people in their communities seems to have been immense. Even the Brontë sisters eventually gave up governessing and attempted to open their own school. Although they were unsuccessful, it seems obvious that they preferred teaching in the schoolroom as opposed to the drawing room.

Yet though it may seem to be anticipating too much to claim that Weeton's situation was typical, as Mary Smith's account will show, Weeton's experiences were, it seems, not atypical at all. First published in 1892, *The Autobiography of Mary Smith, Schoolmistress and Nonconformist* offers an inside look at the life of a governess in the middle and latter part of the nineteenth century, a period when the fictive governess was a popular stock figure in Victorian literature. Smith was born in 1822 to working-class parents: her father was a boot and shoemaker, and her mother was a cook at the Gloucestershire vicarage. Her mother died when she was two, and her father began sending Mary to a dame school when she was four. When her father remarried, her stepmother wanted

Mary to be educated only with an eye toward employment in a trade and thus she viewed 'reading as a . . . species of idleness' (26). Mary, however, found that she loved to read, and her father encouraged her in her literary pursuits, and saw to it that not only was she educated in the social graces – 'Correct and lady-like manners were considered to be almost the be all and end all of a girl's education' (29) – but that her love of reading was encouraged as well. Thus, she was allowed to read 'the best English authors', and she found herself reading and enjoying 'Addison, Steele, Dryden, Young, Pope, [and] the Taylors' (33). She soon came to be seen as a child prodigy; yet as a working-class child she was destined for a life of labor, not leisure.

Smith's first experience as an educator was running a school for an elderly couple, but because the owners of the school were financially unstable, this position soon became untenable. She advertised for a position as governess and was hired by the Sutton family at Scotby. She seems to have liked the Suttons, and was particularly impressed by the rigid discipline in the house. 'The children were spoken to rather than scolded, and prompt obedience was expected at all times', she wrote. 'In their behavior toward servants, and anyone under them, very rigid rules were enforced. Nothing was to be taken or done for them by a servant without the ready "thank thee", or "obliged to thee", as soon as they were able to articulate the words' (137-38). But just as had been the case with Weeton, although she found herself in a good position, she was little more than a servant, and as such, she had the 'feeling that, do what [she] could, [she] was living a sad, monotonous, profitless life, so far as anything [she] desired or wished for was concerned' (140).

Smith's manifest unhappiness as a governess was caused by a sense of class consciousness. Like Weeton, Smith would attempt to rectify this by seeking a position in a classroom, which, although still seen as working-class, at least meant that she was not living in home where she was so demonstrably regarded as working-class by employers and servants alike. She found this opportunity when her former employers contacted her with the opportunity to run their school anew, with the promise that they were at last financially secure: she left Scotby to take the position because it seemed to afford more gratification than the position of governess. Unfortunately, the Osborns were financially no better off than before, and yet again, Smith was forced to seek employment as a governess.

Smith recognized that the duties of a governess were rapidly changing, at least in terms of what was now expected. 'I was brimful of knowledge, which had been gathered from my vast and multifarious reading in history, science, and literature', she wrote, 'but I was dismayed. Every advertisement I read, even for farmer's families in the country, required music and French, and the various components of what was called a "genteel education"' (169). While the families of the children had no such knowledge themselves in many cases, 'it gratified the vanity of ignorant parents, who were able to boast of their daughters having learned French' (169). Thus, she found herself unemployable for many positions, despite her knowledge and qualifications. She lived at home with her father, whilst she looked for a position as a governess.

When she did finally find a position, she discovered that she had entered a middle-class nightmare. Here again finances were a problem, and she noted that although she 'was to have fifteen pounds for the year', she was paid nothing, and 'instead of this [she] was reminded of the privileges [she] enjoyed' (165). One of those 'privileges' was access to the family's library, but, she notes, 'it was unkindly said that I had soiled two of these volumes, and in consequence I agreed to take them as part of my salary' (165). It appears that in many ways this family went out of their way to mistreat and offend Smith, as she noted that

> I found that in the school and in the house, whatever I did failed
> to please. My patience, hard work, and endurance of unjust
> criticism were all in vain. I was needlessly made to feel affronts
> for which there was no excuse, and slighted day after day without
> any possible reason. Any new or interesting book, I found was
> put into a drawer and locked up, contrary to custom, and much
> to my mortification: I was piqued constantly with petty
> annoyances. (63-64)

Once again, her position became untenable: 'I grew sadder and poorer every day, refusing to say anything about my wants, but feeling them intensely' (179). As a result, she once again left her situation, this time without ever receiving her pay.

Her next job was one that found her in Bristol, although she noted, 'strange to say, from the first I had a miserable presentment that in some way – I could not tell how – I should not succeed' (179). The lady of the house had three children, the youngest of whom was five weeks old, and 'what I was wanted to do or teach, seemed somewhat a mystery' (180). Soon Smith had a feeling that the family – who was clearly trying to ascend the social scale – wanted her 'evidently, as it appeared to [her], for *show*' (180). She was needed merely so that the family could have a governess, not because it needed one, or was able to afford one. Smith noted that in fact the meals were irregular and scant, and that she often noticed tradespeople, like the washerwoman they employed, were often turned away without being paid. 'I was sore vexed that I had come into such a house', she noted, 'and I knew I could not stay – sham being an abomination in my sight' (181). After just a week, Smith asked to be released from the situation, and her mistress refused, probably only because of the social indignity that the family would suffer after having a governess for such a brief period of time. Still, Smith was persistent, and in another week she left their employment, despite their objections.

Eventually Smith would open her own school, and only then did she find happiness. Although her earnings were meager, she was happy at last, and she was also able to read at the end of the day, as her time was her own. In this capacity she was to remain for the rest of her life, but by her own recollections this was a time of intense happiness. Finally, as an independent woman, she found the fulfillment she had so long desired.

As Weeton, Smith, and other women evince, Victorian governesses seemed to lead isolated, lonely lives. They were often well-bred and well-educated, yet because they had little money and few prospects, they found themselves employed by people who could be seen as intellectually and sometimes even socially inferior if not for monetary accruement. Because of their education, and often too because they were born of middle-class families, governesses believed that they were decidedly middle-, and not working-class. That they were justified in believing so is certainly reasonable, but they found that they could not escape the fact that to society in general, they were regarded as working-class. Governesses employed by the middle and upper classes generally found that their employers saw them as little better than the washerwoman or stable hands with whom they worked, because they were, after all, still servants, and service was a decidedly working-class occupation. These concerns with class stratification are manifested in many of the extant journals and autobiographies written by nineteenth-century governesses, and class concerns are often the central issues pervading these accounts. Because governesses were women with education and breeding, they felt oppressed and discriminated against as they labored for employers who clearly regarded them as servants. To add to this indignity, domestic servants saw them as working-class as well, and furthermore, servants often resented the fact that governesses saw themselves as more than servants, and they tempered their behavior toward governesses accordingly. In this sense, no matter how we today regard governesses – and it is generally that they were middle-class women in service positions – overwhelmingly they were regarded as working-class by society during the nineteenth century.

Class Consciousness and *Agnes Grey*

Having only briefly examined two autobiographical accounts by governesses – neither of which were in print during Anne Brontë's lifetime – it is clear that *Agnes Grey*'s Agnes leads a day-to-day life that greatly resembles those of her factual counterparts. Agnes Grey, the daughter of an impoverished clergyman and his wife, is forced to work to help support her family. Well-read, and a lady in the sense that she is a model of propriety and decorum, Agnes finds life among the families of the middle and upper classes quite different from what she imagined. 'How delightful it would be to be a governess! . . . how charming to be entrusted with the care and education of children!' Agnes says early in the novel (Brontë 69). Yet, as she is soon to discover, she is looked upon as less than a servant: with an ostensibly middle-class background, yet forced to work in a service capacity among the rich, she is often beneath the contempt of even the household servants.

Although only nineteen, Agnes decides to take a job that characteristically calls for the employee to spend more time educating and disciplining the employer's children than their own mothers do. Although Agnes takes her first position in the Bloomfield household despite the fact that she has no formal education, she is confident that she can perform well: 'whatever others said, I felt I was fully competent to the task; the clear remembrance of my own thoughts and feelings in early childhood would be a surer guide than the instructions of the most mature adviser' (69). Clearly, the only training that Agnes feels is necessary for the position is that she emulate her own mother, or enact a transference of her mother's relationship with her and her sister onto the relationship that she will have as a governess to the Bloomfield children. 'I had but to turn from my little pupils to myself at their age', Agnes states, 'and I should know, at once, how to win their confidence and affections' (69).

Unfortunately, Agnes' assumption that she can wear the mantle of mother with the ungovernable Bloomfield children is a mistaken one, especially in the sense that she is determining her behavior toward them based on the assumption that they will regard her as a surrogate mother. The children, however, recognize that as a paid employee and economic dependent Agnes is essentially a working-class servant, even if better dressed and better educated than most. Thus, because she cannot span the invisible barrier of class consciousness, she is without the power of discipline based on respect, a real mother's most essential power, and so, as a mother-figure in the Bloomfield household, she is an abject failure. This causes her to abandon her intentions of treating the children lovingly, because as the children have little or no respect for her they spurn her gentler attempts at discipline. Thus, as Agnes slowly comes to realize that her own theories of how to properly raise children will not work in this situation, she begins a degenerative spiral in both her theories and practice toward raising the Bloomfield children. Rather than the love and care that she received from her mother, she resorts to the almost purely physical modes of force that she deems necessary to control the children. 'Sometimes, exasperated to the utmost pitch, I would shake [Mary Ann] violently by the shoulders, or pull her long hair, or put her in the corner' (88), Agnes says, and one might note that this type of action is not discipline on her part, but retribution. Agnes is simply physically reacting to Mary Ann's actions, and not attempting to teach the child anything.

Like Weeton and Smith, Agnes finds herself regarded as a nobody, and a nobody has no power and little self-esteem. While some members of the Bloomfield family treat her with total indifference, such as Uncle Robson, who 'seldom deigned to notice [her]; and when he did, it was with a certain superciliousness of tone and insolence of manner' (102), to the majority of the family Agnes is not invisible; however, she is clearly a servant in every sense of the word. Agnes seems to expect that as a governess she will be treated differently from the other 'invisible' servants, but indeed 'every visitor disturbed [her], more or less', and though she downplays the reason, at the heart of the matter it seems that it is 'because they neglected [her]' (106). She is, in fact, even expected to pay obeisance to the children, and 'even calling the little Bloomfields by their simple names [was] regarded as an offensive liberty, as their parents had taken care to show [her], by carefully designating them *Master* and *Miss* Bloomfield in speaking to [her]' (118). No doubt this is a measure designed to make sure that Agnes knows her place, although she notes that she was 'slow to take the hint, because the whole affair struck [her] as so very absurd' (118).

It is precisely this deliberate obstinance on Agnes' part, the refusal to act completely subservient, which angers her employers. They want, and expect, a servant (be she a governess) to act like a servant. Whereas Weeton and Smith had played their parts in a more malleable fashion until they could take it no more, and only then did they leave their employers, Agnes seems determined to resist the efforts to put her in her place. [Although Agnes hates her position at the Bloomfield house, it is the Bloomfields who sever the ties by firing her, claiming that she has failed to improve the children significantly.] While certainly the children did not improve substantially under Agnes' care, it is likely that Agnes' inability to 'know her place' greatly contributed to her dismissal. So, in an effort to 'redeem [her] lost honour' (108), Agnes searches for another position.

Agnes next takes a position as a governess in the Murray household. Here she almost immediately feels relegated to a position of little consequence in the household, as even the servants who unloaded her luggage were 'neither of them very respectful in their demeanour to [her]' (117). Yet [Agnes seems to already have learned from her past experiences, and her failure as a governess for the Bloomfields has perhaps taught her what is expected from her in her occupation. She therefore 'determined to be wiser, and began at once with as much form and ceremony as any member of the family would be likely to require'.] Agnes thus calls the children Miss and Master, despite the fact that she regards it as 'a chilling and unnatural piece of punctilio between the children of a family and their instructor and daily companion' (118). Trying at last to act the part expected of her, 'it was with a strange feeling of desolation' that she begins her new job.

Attempting to fit into a working-class role no doubt leads to Agnes' intense dissatisfaction, just as it did with Weeton and Smith. It is worth noting that Agnes qualifies her role as the children's 'instructor *and* daily *companion*' (my italics), not content to see herself as just an instructor, but also in the more equitable position of 'companion' as well. A technical definition of a governess is 'a woman who is employed to take charge of a child's upbringing and education', the operative terms here being 'employed' and 'education'. It is doubtful that her employers consider her their children's companion, and indeed probable that Agnes is considered a teacher only (if called upon to introduce Agnes, it is likely that the Murrays would refer to her as their children's governess or teacher – but not as their companion). Although Agnes professes to be willing to change and therefore seems to indicate at last her willingness to accept her subservient role, clearly she still feels that she serves as a 'companion' to the children and, despite her efforts, she is still resistant to being subsumed in a position regarded as working-class.

Attempting to act less as an equal and instead in a more subservient role is much more difficult than Agnes had anticipated, especially when she learns that although she is regarded as a servant by the family, the servants themselves ostracize her. Agnes soon comes to recognize that she will have the respect of no-one in the house, and that even 'the servants, seeing in what little estimation the governess was held by both parents and children, regulated their behavior by the same standard' (128). Clearly the children are used to treating all domestics with insolence, and Agnes notes that though she attempted to defend the servants and instruct the children to treat them better, the servants 'neglected [her] comfort, despised [her] requests, and slighted [her] directions' (128). What Agnes fails to realize is that her attempts to teach the children to respect the servants likely fail because they view their governess as a servant too, and thus they are disinclined to learn moral lessons from one whom represents the object of the lessons. On the servants' part, as Agnes indicates on many occasions, she holds herself above them, and thus their behavior reflects their own disdain for her air of superiority. Ultimately, these factors combine to contribute to Agnes' mental anguish, and her claim that 'I sometimes felt degraded by the life I led, and ashamed of submitting to so many indignities' (128).

Like Weeton and Smith, being equated with a servant at best, or a nobody at worst, is the obstacle that Agnes is never able to overcome, and of course it undermines her ability to discipline the children. She seems to fare better once the male children are removed, yet she still seems to lack any pretense of respect from the girls, something, again, that a mother usually has and that is an intrinsic part of successful motherhood, especially in terms of administering moral discipline. As she once again tries to assume the role of mother, Agnes tries 'unsuccessfully to replace her charges' materialistic values with values she had been taught at home, those of truthfulness, piety, and compassion' (Costello 116-17), all of which the girls completely disregard. Moreover, her influence with Rosalie and Matilda Murray is even less than with the Bloomfield children. The Murray girls, who are older and certainly more class conscious than the Bloomfield children, see little reason to listen to or respect an individual whom they clearly see as a social inferior. Matilda's greatest fault is her proclivity toward foul language, yet Agnes is unable to effect any sort of change in Matilda's use of expletives. The social polish that a mother might be able to give Matilda is apparently beyond Agnes' powers, and thus in the one area where Matilda clearly needs improvement, Agnes is completely ineffective. Certainly, Mrs Murray herself has never been able to improve her daughter's deportment, but simply by the act of hiring a governess it is implied that she does not intend to: she wants someone else, a hireling, to do it. As that hireling, Agnes applies her powers of motherhood as taught and exemplified to her, and once again, she fails: the restrictions of her working-class position simply do not empower her to succeed.

Even the girls' mother admits that a governess' power is restricted, almost by design, by dint of the governess' working-class status. As Mrs Murray tells Agnes, a good governess 'lives in obscurity herself', and indeed, Agnes is told that governessing 'is just the same as any other trade or profession' (207), words no doubt offensive to a woman of education and breeding. And even as she administers her warning, Mrs Murray reminds Agnes that she is lucky even to be told this, as many employers 'would not trouble themselves to speak [to her] at all' (207) and would merely replace her without notice. In effect, Mrs Murray indicates that a governess is a servant, and that a servant is of a class far beneath his or her employers, a class of no consequence. It is obvious that it is impossible for a governess to function as a second mother when the governess is of no consequence or importance.

As with her first position, Agnes' employment in the Murray household is defined by unhappiness and ineffectiveness. She is stunted by her inability to influence the Murray girls and depressed by her ostracism by the servants and the family. By all appearances she seems destined for a life of unhappiness as a governess, forever forced to submit to the will of people with whom she actually has much more in common than they would care to admit. The death of her father, however, enables Agnes to return to her own home, where she co-manages the family school with her mother. Like Weeton and Smith, Agnes therefore ends up in the schoolroom, happy to be free from the wretchedness of governessing. It is at home where Agnes also finds once again a position of equality, and indeed Edward Weston proposes to her by claiming that Agnes is the 'only . . . person in the world' who will 'suit [him] for a companion' (249). Thus, it is only at the end of the novel that Agnes finally finds equality as a companion; at last she is happy and freed from the restriction of class. Consequently, once Agnes has children of her own, she is a happy and ideal mother, and her children lack 'no good thing that a mother's care can give' (251). At the end of the novel Agnes is at last empowered as an effective matriarchal figure, and one unfettered by the restrictions and limitations of class constraints.

It seems obvious that Agnes' own middle-class sensibilities exacerbate her unhappiness as a governess, a situation that many real-life governesses faced themselves. Today *Agnes Grey* is arguably the second-least-respected novel in the Brontë canon, and Priscilla Costello notes that '*Agnes Grey* is ordinarily either ignored by literary critics or treated summarily as a charming though not too serious endeavor' (113). However, in the context in which it has been examined here, it is clear that this novel is something more than a quotidian account that centers around and relates a woman's experiences. Perhaps because she herself was a governess, Anne Brontë knew how a feeling of subservience could work on a proud and intelligent mind, and accounts by governesses such as Weeton and Smith indicate that Anne Brontë's novel realistically represents the life of a governess during the nineteenth century. Consequently, by contextualizing *Agnes Grey* in a cultural framework, as well as by examining it in a comparative format in regard to working-class autobiographies written by governesses during the nineteenth century, it is obvious that Anne Brontë's little-known novel should not only be recognized as an accurate depiction of the life of a governess during the nineteenth century, but as realistic examination of nineteenth century class issues as well.

Notes

[1] Anne Brontë briefly served as a governess for the Ingham family at Blake Hall in 1839, and in 1840 she took a position as governess for the Robinson family of Thorp Green, near York. She remained in this position until she resigned in 1845, just before the dismissal of her brother Branwell, who was serving as a tutor to the Robinsons' son – and may have been having an affair with Mrs Robinson as well.

[2] The editor of Weeton's memoirs, Edward Hall, noted that 'The boldness of Miss Weeton in demanding more than 10*s.* a week for her services can be gauged by comparison with the proposed salary of schoolmasters in the Report of Brougham's Education Committee, ten years later, recommending that it 'ought certainly not to exceed twenty-four pounds a year' with permission to augment it as best he could. And Charlotte Brontë had to be satisfied with much less many years later' (202).

[3] Long after Weeton had left the area, Dove's Nest was also to be the home of Felicia Hemans in the 1830s. Near Wansfell and overlooking Windermere, the area has long since become known for the literati who made their residences there during the late-eighteenth and early-nineteenth centuries. Weeton mentions only one of these individuals, Samuel Taylor Coleridge, and this when he was staying with the Wordsworths, who had by then moved to Allan Bank. 'There are many characters here worth observation', Weeton wrote in 1810. 'S. Coleridge, the conductor of a new and valued publication entitled *The Friend* resides only a few miles hence' (223). To make Weeton's single mention of the famous people living around her even more anomalous, by then Thomas DeQuincey was in the area as well, having taken up residence at Allan Bank. Yet

on no occasion does Weeton mention any of the famed literati in the area other than this single reference to Coleridge.

[4] It is not inappropriate here to comment on Pedder's desire to retain Nelly's services, especially given that it would not be unusual for readers to expect that his motives may have been sexual, especially given his libertine behavior on other occasions. Nelly herself never considered this possibility, and in fact, her descriptions of herself make the reader feel that she was not viewed by Pedder, or anyone else, as an object of desire. At this time Nelly was 35, and as she claimed not just plain but ugly. One reference seems to vividly confirm this as well. 'I have had a sad broken out face since I came here. I have had another boil on my face very near the former, only a little nearer the ear. I neither lanced, nor poulticed it, but when ripe, let out the matter with a needle, and then washed it with a little cold water. I think the mark will disappear soon. The one that Dr. Marwood lanced will leave a small mark like a seam' (240).

[5] In yet another instance where art would imitate life, just as in *Agnes Grey* where Agnes becomes a friend and correspondent with one of her former charges, Nelly, too, became a friend to Sarah-Anne Armitage. Although it is not clear to what extent the relationship flourished, they did correspond quite affectionately on occasion.

[6] The complexity of this situation may be illustrated by Mrs Blenkinsop's comments in *Vanity Fair,* as she notes that the servants hated governesses because 'they give themselves hairs and hupstarts of ladies, and their wages is no better than you or me'.

Works Cited

Austen, Jane. *Emma.* 1816. Ed. Stephen M. Parrish. New York: Norton, 1993.

Brontë, Anne. *Agnes Grey.* 1847. London: Penguin, 1998.

Cobden, John. *The White Slaves of England.* 1853. Shannon, Ireland: Irish University Press, 1971.

Costello, Priscilla H. 'A New Reading of Anne Brontë's *Agnes Grey*'. *Brontë Society Transactions* 19.3 (1987): 113-18.

Fraiman, Susan. 'Jane Eyre's Fall from Grace'. *Jane Eyre* by Charlotte Brontë. Ed. Beth Newman. Boston: Bedford, 1996. 614-31.

Hughes, Katherine. *The Victorian Governess.* London: Rio Grande, 1993.

Martineau, Harriet. 'The Old Governess'. *Sketches from Life.* London: Whittaker, 1856.

Pool, Daniel. *What Jane Austen Ate and Charles Dickens Knew.* New York: Simon and Schuster, 1993.

Poovey, Mary. *Uneven Developments: The Ideological Work of Gender in Mid-Victorian England.* Chicago: University of Chicago Press, 1988.

Smith, Mary. *The Autobiography of Mary Smith, Schoolmistress and Nonconformist, A Fragment of a Life*. London: Bemrose & Sons; Carlisle: Wordsworth Press, 1892.

Thackeray, William Makepeace. *Vanity Fair*. 1847. Ed. Peter Shillinsburg. New York: Norton, 1994.

Weeton, Ellen. *Miss Weeton's Journal of a Governess, 1807-1825*. Ed. Edward Hall. 2 vols. New York: Augustus M. Kelly, 1969.

Yonge, Charlotte. *Womankind*. Leipzig: Bernhard Tauchnitz, 1878.

Chapter 4

'The food of my life':
Agnes Grey at Wellwood House

Marilyn Sheridan Gardner

Anne Brontë uses references to food throughout *Agnes Grey* to measure degrees of civilized behavior in the different households in which she situates her heroine. Brontë incorporates a widening variety of fare to mark Agnes' ongoing acculturation into the Victorian society she hungers to experience and constructs scenes of eating where table manners correspond to the values of the houses Agnes inhabits. The correlation between food and house, however, appears most often in the novel's first five chapters, which cover Agnes' departure from home and her tenure with the Bloomfields of Wellwood House. Agnes' attitudes toward food, as well as the preparation of food and the manner of its consumption, evolve as she moves from the parsonage to Wellwood. As Brontë elaborates her scenes of eating, food becomes more than just a necessary component for Agnes' survival. When Brontë places Agnes among the Bloomfields, she elevates dining into an educational exercise and raises eating into a metaphor for the way of life at Wellwood House.

Claude Lévi-Strauss in *The Raw and the Cooked: Introduction to a Science of Mythology* offers an insight into the process of civilizing through the agency of food. Using raw, cooked, and decayed foods, Lévi-Strauss mediates among primitive, cultured, and sophisticated societies to theorize how natural beings are synthesized into civilized citizens (142). In a similar manner, Brontë's discourse on Victorian society in *Agnes Grey* uses food as a metaphorical register of culture and demonstrates, through scenes of eating, an aversion to what she apparently perceives as the dehumanizing effects of over-civilization.

Brontë designs Agnes' movement in life as a progression into society, expanding the analogy of natural to cooked food to accompany Agnes' transition from the sacred confines of the parsonage to the profane venue of the worldly Bloomfields. Brontë appears to privilege an intermediate position in the civilizing process, a mid-point she seems to endorse as the ideal. As Brontë adjudicates between the sacred and the profane, Lévi-Strauss mediates between savagery (raw) and decadence (rotten). Lévi-Strauss' mid-point, which he represents by cooked foods, is depicted by Brontë as a moderate state in the civilizing process that I have termed the 'decent', or the 'respectable'.[1] Decency, as I use it in my discussion of *Agnes Grey*, expresses Brontë's theoretical model of perfected human relations – the community. Agnes, Alice, and Mary provide Brontë's paradigm for community. The Grey women, once abroad in the world, strive always to maintain respectable, modest, and moral circumstances, and to embrace neither solitude nor society. Agnes, her mother, and her sister share in a close-knit community that begins with just the three of them. The men they marry and incorporate into their community all meet their requirements of decency.[2]

The Grey parsonage symbolizes a sacred location, a representation Brontë accentuates both by its connection to the nearby village church and by Richard Grey's profession as a man of God. To increase the parsonage's air of purity, Brontë elides scenes of eating from parsonage life, and instead depicts nourishment at the parsonage as primarily of the spiritual kind. Although Brontë illustrates a variety of pleasant family activities at the parsonage – the Greys at work by the fire, walking the nearby hills, or chatting with one another (4) – dining together, a primary communal activity, appears conspicuous by its absence. Brontë does employ meal-times in Chapter One, such as Agnes' 'hasty breakfast' before her departure to Wellwood House (13), or the occasional 'stately tea-party' held for the village locals (3) to mark the passage of daily life at the parsonage; but she particularizes no foods in Chapter One, even Richard Grey's 'favorite dishes' (7), by description or name. Brontë, by avoiding details of food at the parsonage, suggests a vegetative environment, a pastoral atmosphere she underscores by depicting Agnes and Mary at work in the family garden. Brontë stresses the Greys' seclusion and comfort in what she paints as a near-perfect natural environment.

In 'Eat – or Be Eaten: An Interdisciplinary Metaphor', Mervyn Nicholson comments: 'Traditionally, paradisal visions depict the origin of human society in a setting of *human* harmony expressed as *natural* harmony – as abundant food, typically vegetarian' (199). Brontë omits any references to meat at the parsonage, but instead depicts animals in symbiotic relationships with the Greys. Family pets, anthropomorphically represented, lend their tactile presence to the pleasures of the parsonage; Agnes' kitten is her 'dear little friend', and Agnes romps with the cat, strokes her 'soft bright fur', and holds her in her lap while she sleeps (12). Agnes' and Mary's pigeons, too, are pets, and Agnes feeds them, strokes them, even kisses them (12), as she kisses her cat (13). The well-fed pony is also esteemed by the Greys; the family had determined their favorite 'should end its days in peace, and never pass from our hands' (6). But the Greys' economically-driven necessity to sell their pony forebodes the coming disruption of their family, as the pony's conversion from protected pet to marketable product presages Agnes' own transformation from family 'pet' to Bloomfield commodity (2).

Through conventional depictions of peaceful domestic activities, Brontë paints the Grey parsonage as a tranquil Eden. Brontë disrupts her orthodox rural paradise, however, through the actions of her male character. Despite the nurturing labors of Alice, Mary, and Agnes, the idyllic conditions of their home are subverted by Richard's weakness in the face of worldly temptation. Richard's engagement in 'mercantile pursuits' (4) represents an abandonment of his home, where, as Nancy Armstrong defines domestic desire, Alice's virtues alone should have sufficed to tame his ambition and transform his appetite for wealth (6). Brontë first links food with desire when Richard Grey's destructive action brings hunger for the first time to the Greys' dining table. After Richard loses his fortune, Brontë correlates the Greys' diminished prospects with a decreased amount of foods at their table. Agnes tells us the meals produced by their humble hearth were 'always plain', but rations were further reduced as their income declined until meals were 'simplified to an unprecedented degree' (7).

The Greys' cutback in groceries results from their necessity to repay outstanding bills at 'Mr Jackson's, another at Smith's, and a third at Hobson's', local purveyors to whom the Greys incur obligations during their period of 'brightening prospects' (4), and Brontë unites the liquidation of their food-debt with their forfeiture of other anticipated pleasures. As Nicholson observes, desire upsets the harmonic balance of paradise, but it is economic necessity that drives forth the occupants and engenders the animal hunt: 'The Fall is signaled by the start of a struggle for food; the sentence laid on Adam to toil by the sweat of his brow marks the constitution of food as *coercion*, not just the coercion *of* humans but coercion *by* humans – of earth, its creatures and subtextually of other humans' (199).

When the Greys' visions of prosperity evaporate, life at the parsonage appears as uninspired and dreary as their limited rations. Although the Grey women rally to support Richard, his grief appears inconsolable. Brontë implies that Richard's remorse is a spiritual illness in which his physical symptoms manifest only after his refusal of the sustenance and comfort provided by the women of his house. Richard Grey's inability to accept food or solace from his family signals the failure of the Greys as an integral unit, for Richard's risk of his family's security profanes the parsonage with commercialism and breaches the Greys' self-containment with the corruption of outside interests. Ultimately, Richard's misplaced desire for more than his allotted portion destroys the safe haven all the Greys once enjoyed. Brontë depicts Richard's sin as a financial gluttony that results in his moral bankruptcy.

Even though Brontë supplies few details of the Greys' diet at the cottage, we do learn that meal-preparation takes up a considerable portion of Alice's and Mary's time. Although we are not shown the Greys communing through the sharing of meals, both Alice and Mary Grey are reported to be proficient cooks; Agnes says, 'all the cooking and household work that could not easily be managed by one servant girl was done by my mother and sister, with a little occasional help from me' (7). As Lévi-Strauss reasons a cook to be a 'cultural agent' in the civilizing process, observing that the cook converts raw ingredients from their natural state into a 'cooked' or cultured form (275), the Grey women's culinary skills imply their abilities to cope with the outside world. Alice, Mary, and to a lesser extent, Agnes, are willing and able to provide the necessary forms of culture for their family through their production of cooked foods.

Although Agnes always vaguely wishes to see more of the world, her exit from home occurs only in the aftermath of Richard Grey's transgression against the sanctity of his home. Brontë again correlates food and other desires when Agnes' hunger for experience augments her aspirations to exonerate her financially-strapped family from further provision of her 'food and clothing' (10). Even though Richard has irrevocably compromised the green world of her youth, Agnes leaves the parsonage having internalized from her mother and sister a communal way of life that she will seek to restructure in other places.

When Brontë removes Agnes from the reserved atmosphere of the Grey cottage, she chooses to depict a lively environment more able to represent Agnes' hunger for worldly experience. When Agnes enters her first employment with the Bloomfields, a young family with a new fortune derived from trade, Brontë constructs the nouveau riche domestic conditions of Wellwood House to accord with Agnes' inexperience. Agnes, hopeful of her own 'unused faculties' and 'unknown powers' (10), approaches Wellwood to discover a 'new, but stately mansion' (15) with a lofty iron gateway, green lawns, and a plantation of newly-planted 'upstart' trees (75). Agnes finds everything at Wellwood to be functional and modern, arranged in the best taste the considerable fortune of Mr Bloomfield can afford. The Bloomfields' veneer of civilized polish proves to be as thin and as easily disturbed, however, as Agnes' facade of confidence.

Brontë designs the Grey parsonage as a place of tacit restraint, while she depicts Wellwood as an environment that encourages explosive and unpredictable behavior. For instance, as Agnes enters Wellwood, Brontë modifies Agnes' formerly calm demeanor to reflect the anxiety Agnes imbibes from the atmosphere of her new surroundings. At the time of her arrival at Wellwood House, Agnes is, she writes, 'near nineteen, but, thanks to my retired life and the protecting care of my mother and sister, I well knew that many a girl of fifteen, or under, was gifted with a more womanly address, and greater ease and self-possession' (15). Brontë uses Agnes' injunction to herself, 'Be calm, be calm, whatever happens', to betray Agnes' immediate agitation upon entering the strange house (16). To emphasize Agnes' intimidation, Brontë has her speak 'in the tone of one half-dead or half-asleep' (16).

Brontë illustrates Agnes' induction into the adult behavior expected of her at Wellwood by repeated references to Agnes' heightened color. Agnes' complexion appears to glow beneath her skin's surface in tints of red and purple, the blood pumped by the 'rebellious flutter' of her heart (16). Brontë matches Agnes' inner confusion with her disheveled appearance:

> the cold wind had swelled and reddened my hands, uncurled and
> entangled my hair, and dyed my face of a pale purple; add to this

my collar was horribly crumpled, my frock splashed with mud,
my feet clad in stout new boots, and as the trunks were not
brought up, there was no remedy, so having smoothed my hair
as well as I could, and repeatedly twitched my obdurate collar, I
proceeded to clomp down the two flights of stairs . . . (16)

Brontë accentuates that Agnes' face is 'dyed' by her flush, using the resulting stain
image to reflect Agnes' movement toward the Wellwood dining room as a
progression from the sacred to the secular realm. Agnes descends to the dining
room of Wellwood House to experience what Nina Auerbach refers to as an
'initiation into physicality' (44). Auerbach explores the maturation of Jane
Austen's heroine, Elizabeth Bennet, and centers her discussion on Elizabeth's
participation in the Pemberley dining episode in *Pride and Prejudice*. In Auerbach's
interpretation, Austen uses the Pemberley scene of eating to anticipate Elizabeth's
elevation to mistress of the house, but Brontë's use of the Wellwood dining scene
differs significantly: Brontë depicts Agnes' passage down the Wellwood staircase
to the scene of eating as a descent, not a rise, into the secular world.

Both Brontë and Austen accompany the emerging maturity of their
heroines with an exchange of their original houses for new dwellings; Brontë's
parsonage with its shadowy boundaries and intangible sustenance is, like Austen's
Longbourn, supplanted by a place of solid architectural design and substantial
food. At Pemberley Elizabeth Bennet becomes fully aware of the opulence and
abundance of Darcy's world, as Pemberley's staff showers her with a wide variety
of foods, especially choice fruits (268). But Brontë's view of the material world is
considerably darker than Austen's, as their different uses of the scene of eating
makes plain. Brontë concentrates on the consuming nature of society, connecting
physical appetites with social ambitions that feed off one another. As Nicholson
observes: 'Eating represents life-energy enslaved by its own impulses, by the
contingencies of the physical world' (196). While Austen uses the dining scene at
Pemberley to connote the favorable outcome of Elizabeth's and Darcy's
differences, Brontë uses the dining scene at Wellwood to establish what will be
Agnes' negative experience among the Bloomfields.

Agnes' ingestion of the Bloomfields' food marks her induction into
Wellwood's economy, a process Elizabeth C. Hirschman terms 'commoditization'
(4). Commoditization, as Hirschman sees the process, occurs when 'one person
views another individual as an entity to be used for his/her own purposes from
the outset of their relationship' (4). According to Hirschman, commoditization
'requires no guise of emotional commitment or personal involvement':

Persons who commoditize others want no responsibility for
them and seek no emotional involvement, they view the other as
something to be used, discarded, and then forgotten. In essence,

they view the other as a commodity, a generic good or service
that can be used as desired and abandoned without feelings of
remorse or regret. (4)

Brontë chooses the dining room as the seat of power at Wellwood, and
the dining table as the instrument of subjugation. A Victorian dining room links
multiple powers, as Helena Michie observes, noting the dining table itself is the
traditional location not only of the scene of eating but the scene of socialization:

> The dinner table is an important locus of interaction in Victorian
> culture. In the novel, it is the place where characters, plots, and
> subplots come together to enjoy and to produce the rich
> complexities of Victorian fiction. In etiquette and conduct
> books, it is the central social space where the rules that govern
> Victorian society are made manifest. (12)

Agnes had hoped Mrs Bloomfield would be a motherly sort of woman who
would welcome her as a member of the family, but Mrs Bloomfield, Agnes finds,
appears more interested in control than comfort. Brontë's meal of leftovers for
Agnes predicts Mrs Bloomfield's disregard for both Agnes' feelings and her
physical well-being.

The Bloomfield dining room over which the mistress of Wellwood
presides offers Agnes little in the way of genuine hospitality. Ostensibly, Mrs
Bloomfield's manners appear as impeccable as the appointments of her new
mansion; she greets Agnes with apparent civility and quite properly invites her to
partake of a 'little refreshment' upon her arrival (16). Mrs Bloomfield's kindness,
however, proves to be as superficially assumed as Wellwood's civilized exterior.
Brontë establishes tensions between Agnes and the 'awful lady' in Agnes' first
meal at Wellwood House, a repast Agnes is forced to endure under Mrs
Bloomfield's steady gaze. Mrs Bloomfield, 'somewhat chilly in her manner', is 'a
tall, spare, stately woman, with thick black hair, cold grey eyes, and extremely
sallow complexion' who greets an apprehensive Agnes with 'due politeness'
tempered by a 'cool, immutable gravity' (16-17). Brontë serves up Agnes' youth,
warmth, and unease to Mrs Bloomfield's devouring eye, emphasizing from the
beginning Agnes' role as a disposable commodity in the Wellwood household.[3]

Brontë appears to connect the physical with the secular, rather than the
natural, and conveys the idea that civilization is a de-humanizing force. She
combines the occasion of Agnes' first meal in Wellwood's dining room with not
only Agnes' initiation into physicality but also her introduction to the civilizing
process. Brontë's depiction of Agnes' dining experience delineates what will be
Mrs Bloomfield's continuing participation in Agnes' general discomfort. Mrs
Bloomfield establishes her ascendancy over Agnes by forcing Agnes into the

unladylike position of eating in front of her, for, as Michie points out, the conventional heroine eschews the coarseness of eating in public and always 'laughs, flirts, and presides over presumably empty plates' (12). As Michie observes, 'in novels and conduct books that deal so closely with dinners, tea, and other social gatherings', there is never 'any mention of the heroine eating' (12). Dining is a social occasion, and real hunger – if ever experienced by the heroine – must be satisfied in solitary, even secretive, locations.

While Mrs Bloomfield occupies herself with observing Agnes eat, Brontë allows Agnes to observe shortcomings in the arrogant lady's own manners. For instance, because Agnes arrives after one in the afternoon (15), Mrs Bloomfield's offer of refreshment apparently consists of the remains from the family luncheon, leftovers not even sent to the kitchen for re-heating. Further, the foods Mrs Bloomfield offers her new employee appear both inappropriate and unappetizing, while at the same time, the provision of abundant meat for Agnes' meal represents an extravagant and unnecessary expenditure. Mrs Bloomfield's choice of nearly inedible but certainly expensive meat for Agnes' repast typifies what Agnes will find at Wellwood – an environment where largess grants little satisfaction. Mrs Bloomfield, in her role as a proper Victorian hostess, should have understood that a young lady like Agnes would have a delicate appetite reflecting her femininity and social class. The hearty meal of potatoes and meat Mrs Bloomfield offers would be, according to Michie's evaluation of menu choices, more suitable to male appetites and to servants doing physical labor than the dainty palate of a virginal parson's daughter (15). Agnes first experiences the dichotomies of money and manners at Wellwood House in her forced ingestion of Mrs Bloomfield's politely offered but inappropriate repast – a costly meal that is at the same time economical, for no special food need be prepared for a person of Agnes' status.

Despite Agnes' immaturity, she comprehends – but is unable to oppose – the insult implied by Mrs Bloomfield's offensive choice of food for her luncheon.[4] Agnes describes the difficulties of her dining experience and the doubtful quality of the food:

> I would gladly have eaten the potatoes and let the meat alone, but having got a large piece of the latter on my plate, I could not be so impolite as to leave it; so, after many awkward and unsuccessful attempts to cut it with the knife, or tear it with the fork, or pull it asunder between them, sensible that the awful lady was a spectator to the whole transaction, I at last desperately grasped the knife and fork in my fists, like a child of two years old, and fell to work with all the little strength I possessed. (17)

Because the Bloomfields have more money than the Greys, Agnes has supposed they will also be more well-bred in their manners and conduct. Brontë's use of Mrs Bloomfield to correct Agnes' erroneous assumption introduces Agnes to the ways of the civilized world.

From the occurrence of Agnes' first meal at Wellwood, Brontë proliferates food references to underscore the Bloomfields' parvenu aspirations in ways that register the ambitions of both the Bloomfields and Agnes as unrequited appetites. Eating at Wellwood House continues to have little to do with the satisfaction of physical hunger; indeed Brontë depicts no scenes of repletion among its residents. Instead, Brontë develops the appetites of the Bloomfields to accompany their economic success. Brontë oversupplies their table with foodstuffs and emphasizes the frequency of their meal-times to imply the Bloomfields' material greed.

Lévi-Strauss offers an observation that as people become more civilized, they invent dining rituals to note their cultural refinement; simple cooking and the activity of eating elaborates in increasingly complicated patterns until food and culture are served up and absorbed in combination at the table (164). Mervyn Nicholson, too, perceives what he terms the 'immense socio-political significance' that can be read in fictional dining scenes and surmises that the particular inclusion of meat is a convention used to connote the power of the provider (205). Reasoning that meat is expensive and can only be procured through the pain and death of an animal, Nicholson terms meat 'a metonym for status at the exclusion – and at the expense – of others' (205). Relating the Bloomfields' meat-laden menus to the behaviors of Agnes, Mrs Bloomfield, and Mr Bloomfield, Brontë deepens her connection between gluttony and socio-economic ambition. Brontë develops the association by repeated references to meat, suggestions she uses to demonstrate the order of authority regulating Wellwood House.

While the mistress of Wellwood has proved a force to be reckoned with, Agnes' nemesis is the master of the house. The patriarch of Wellwood House is, according to Agnes, unprepossessing in appearance. A man of 'ordinary' stature, Mr Bloomfield has a 'pale, dingy complexion, milky blue eyes, and hair the colour of a hempen cord' (25-26). Brontë characterizes Mr Bloomfield as a man who insists on the constant appearance of respectability for his family, and satires his frequent stipulation of 'decency' in matters of food and dress. Significantly, Brontë depicts Mr Bloomfield as having a 'large mouth', a feature she uses as an engulfing image representing both his dictatorial interference in the domestic affairs of Wellwood, and his unappeasable appetite for food, especially meat (26). Nicholson observes the authority implicit in eating meat: 'Total control is what the scene of eating enacts, especially when the food consumed is flesh. Eating meat is an assertion of power, because another living being has to be put to death to provide it. To eat it is to assert life/death control' (205).

Mr Bloomfield is the primary meat eater at Wellwood House, and the dispenser of meat at the table. As Mr Bloomfield serves up slices of mutton, he establishes Agnes' position at the table as the least important of his dependents. She is the last to be offered meat. Agnes says:

> There was a roast leg of mutton before him: he helped Mrs Bloomfield, the children, and me, desiring me to cut up the children's meat; then, after twisting about the mutton in various directions, and eyeing it from different points, he pronounced it not fit to be eaten, and called for the cold beef. (26)

When Mrs Bloomfield inquires: 'What is the matter with the mutton, my dear?', a querulous Mr Bloomfield replies: 'It is quite overdone. Don't you taste, Mrs Bloomfield, that all the goodness is roasted out of it? And can't you see that all that nice, red gravy is completely dried away?' (26).[5] Brontë uses the dining room of Wellwood to exhibit Mr Bloomfield's 'large mouth' busy at once with the tasks of eating and governing, as Mr Bloomfield continues to be unhappy with both the food placed before him and his wife's management of it. While Mrs Bloomfield attempts to placate her husband, he continues to be displeased, and when the unacceptable mutton is replaced by an equally unacceptable joint of beef, Mr Bloomfield disseminates his aggravation from Mrs Bloomfield all the way down to the kitchen staff. Mr Bloomfield declares the beef to have been cut incorrectly by servants – incompetent 'savages' – who should not be allowed to '*touch*', let alone eat, the 'decent' meats of the civilized Wellwood table (26).

Brontë continues Mr Bloomfield's table conversation as an interrogation of his wife that not only questions her household management, but also broadcasts his authority to all present. For instance, unsatisfied by his luncheon even while eating it, Mr Bloomfield inquires 'what there was for dinner':

> 'Turkey and grouse,' was the concise reply.
> 'And what besides?'
> 'Fish.'
> 'What kind of fish?'
> 'I don't know.'
> '*You don't know?*' cried he, looking solemnly up from his
> plate, and suspending his knife and fork in astonishment.
> 'No, I told the cook to get some fish – I did not
> particularize what.'
> 'Well, that beats everything! A lady professes to keep
> house, and doesn't even know what fish is for dinner! professes
> to order fish, and doesn't specify what!' (26-27).

Mr Bloomfield's preoccupation with his meals is superseded only by his obsession with the timeliness of their consumption. Brontë uses mealtimes at the Bloomfields to regulate the chronological course of Agnes' days, and relates the consumption of food to the passage of time. Thus Brontë signifies Wellwood's temporality and sets it apart from the timelessness of the Grey parsonage. While Agnes has remained a child for her entire parsonage lifespan, she matures quickly at Wellwood, and Brontë emphasizes Agnes' advancement into adulthood by an acceleration of her food intake. For instance, although Agnes does not arrive at the Bloomfields until afternoon, she is compelled to dine with Mrs Bloomfield no less than three times during the course of her first day. After Agnes' first luncheon, she is allowed to acquaint herself only briefly with the Bloomfield children before it is time to eat again, for after a preliminary visit to the school-room and a brief walk in the garden, Agnes and the children are expected in the dining room: 'When we re-entered the house it was nearly tea-time. Master Tom told me that, as papa was from home, he and I and Mary Ann were to have tea with mamma for a treat; for, on such occasions, she always dined at luncheon time with them, instead of at six o'clock' (22). Brontë again underscores the importance of the Wellwood dining room and its debilitating influence when at half past nine the same evening, Agnes says, 'Mrs. Bloomfield invited me to partake a frugal supper of cold meat and bread. I was glad when that was over' (23).

As Agnes discovers on her first day at Wellwood, nothing is permitted to disrupt or rearrange the inflexible meal times of the Bloomfields. Bells ring out the eating times, and the meals are served up in apparently inexhaustible progression.[6] Agnes describes the routine of dining as a tyrannical imposition dictating the progression of her days and abbreviating the mental and physical development of her pupils. Agnes says: 'by dint of great labour and patience, I managed to get something done in the course of the morning, and then accompanied my young charge out into the garden and adjacent grounds, for a little recreation before dinner' (24).

Mornings offer Agnes no reprieve. As she struggles to arrange Mary Ann's hair and dress the recalcitrant child in suitable clothing, Agnes is always aware of the approaching breakfast time. Agnes describes a relatively good morning as a revolution between two locations where the education of Wellwood takes place – the school-room and the dining room: 'When all was done (with Mary Ann), we went into the school-room, where I met my other pupil, and chatted with the two till it was time to go down to breakfast. That meal being concluded, and a few civil words having been exchanged with Mrs Bloomfield, we repaired to the school-room again. . .' (24). Brontë brings together Mr Bloomfield's parvenu aspirations in his insistence that Agnes address his off-spring as 'Master and Miss Bloomfield', that she keep their apparel spotless, and that they are presented at the table on time (25). When Mr Bloomfield happens upon the children playing in soiled clothing, he tells Agnes: 'Let me *request* that in future, you will keep them *decent* at least!' (25). Mr Bloomfield insists on a condition of decency for his household, a state of being which constantly eludes him because he does not follow through with the responsibilities of his authority. When Mr Bloomfield again chastises Agnes for her care of his children, his complaint about her lack of concern appears to echo his own governing ineptitude, for while Mr Bloomfield reserves all punishment to himself, he delegates to Agnes his obligations and culpabilities. When Mr Bloomfield, enraged once more over his children's less than perfect appearance as they play out in the snow, engages in a heated exchange with Agnes in which he exercises control over both governess and children through physical domination:

> 'But I INSIST upon their being got in!' cried he, approaching nearer, and looking perfectly ferocious.
> 'Then, sir, *you* must call them yourself if you please, for they won't listen to me,' I replied stepping back.
> 'Come in with you, you filthy brats; or I'll horsewhip you every one!' roared he; and the children instantly obeyed. 'There, you see! they come at the first word!'
> 'Yes, when *you* speak.'
> 'And it's very strange, that, when you've the care of 'em, you've no better control over 'em than that!' (40).

While retaining total authority of the 'horsewhip' to himself, Mr Bloomfield says to the powerless Agnes: 'Do go after 'em and see them made decent, for Heaven's sake!' (40).

Brontë uses Mr Bloomfield's insistence on mealtime punctuality to indicate the newness of his social position and his unease with his prosperous circumstances. Often, however, the mandatory intricacies of Mary Ann's toilette prevent Agnes' timely arrival with the children for breakfast. Of these mornings Agnes writes:

> frequently, when after much trouble and toil, I had, at length, succeeded in bringing [Mary Ann] down, the breakfast was nearly half over; and black looks from 'mamma', and testy observations from 'papa', spoken at me, if not to me, were sure to be my meed, for few things irritated the latter so much as want of punctuality at meal-times. (34)

Breakfast seems hardly over at Wellwood House before the lunch hour approaches, and Agnes is not spared the company of the Bloomfield elders even during the midday meal. As Agnes scrambles to answer the summons of the bell, she says: 'I dined with the children at one, while he and his lady took their luncheon at the same table' (25). Brontë details the monotonous regularity of all Agnes' days by references to the fixity and frequency of Wellwood's meal times, interruptions that occlude spiritual reflection or true communication. Brontë emphasizes Agnes' isolation as she depicts Agnes' difficulty in writing to the Greys. Agnes says:

> In the afternoon we applied to lessons again; then went out again; then had tea in the school-room; then I dressed Mary Ann for dessert; and when she and her brother were gone down to the dining-room, I took the opportunity of beginning a letter to my dear friends at home; but the children came up before I had half completed it. (27)

Agnes' attempts to write home are always interrupted. For instance, Tom Bloomfield commands his sister to dispose of Agnes' personal property, especially her writing materials. Agnes reports the incident between Tom and his sisters: '"Mary Ann, throw her desk out of the window!" cried he, and my precious desk, containing my letters and papers, my small amount of cash, and all my valuables, was about to be precipitated from the three-story window' (39). On a further occasion, as Agnes in a moment of 'unusual repose', plans a letter to her mother, Mr Bloomfield bursts into the school-room to upbraid her for negligence of his children and the room, designating both properties by references to meat: 'Just look at that carpet, and see – was there ever anything like it in a Christian house before? No wonder your room is not fit for a pigsty – no wonder your pupils are worse than a litter of pigs!' (45). Mr Bloomfield's remarks are apparently meant to establish him as atop the hierarchy of his home, but instead they appear to imply his own gluttonous propensities to the condition of his house and children.

Absenting herself or the children from the dining room does not appear an option at Wellwood; Agnes is not allowed to punish the unmanageable youngsters by curtailing their food or banishing them from the table. Agnes describes her attempt to control the naughty children by keeping them from meals. Tom Bloomfield reacts to Agnes' interference with his time for dining with a fury that imitates his father's tyrannical control of the scene of eating. Agnes says:

> Once, I told them that they should not taste their supper till they had picked up everything from the carpet; Fanny might have hers when she had taken up a certain quantity, Mary Anne when she had gathered twice as much, and Tom was to clear away the rest.
>
> Wonderful to state, the girls did their part; but Tom was in such a fury that he flew upon the table, scattered the bread

and milk about the floor, struck his sisters, kicked the coals out
of the coal-pan, attempted to overthrow the table and chairs,
and seemed inclined to make a Douglas-larder of the whole
contents of the room . . . (45)

Mrs Bloomfield, well-trained by her husband in the absolute necessity for
promptness in the serving of meals, does not correct Tom's outburst in any way,
but only orders the nursery-maid to 'bring Master Bloomfield his supper' (46).
Again Tom's behavior parodies his father's: "'There now", cried Tom,
triumphantly, looking up from his viands with his mouth almost too full for
speech. "There now, Miss Grey! you see I have got my supper in spite of you:
and I haven't picked up a single thing!'" (46).

While the girls do not express their disdain for Agnes with the ferocity of
their brother, their passive resistance is almost as difficult for Agnes to endure.
When Mary Ann misbehaves and Agnes attempts to chastise her, Agnes says the
child lies prostrate like a log till dinner or tea time, when, 'as I could not deprive
her of her meals, she must be liberated, and would come crawling out with a grin
of triumph on her round, red face' (31).

On the occasions when Agnes is permitted to eat in just the company of
the children, she is never certain of being completely out of sight of the
Bloomfields. Mr Bloomfield in particular makes a point of spying on Agnes.
Agnes describes Mr Bloomfield's interruptions as calculated to catch her and the
children at a disadvantage; Mr Bloomfield would, Agnes says, 'unexpectedly pop
his head into the school-room while the young people were at meals, and find
them spilling their milk over the table and themselves, plunging their fingers into
their own, or each other's mugs' (43).

Although Agnes attempts to remain aloof from the corruption she
perceives at work among the Bloomfields, Brontë gradually draws her closer into
the violence that permeates Wellwood. Brontë exhibits the Bloomfields'
influence at work in Agnes' desire to inflict corporal punishment on the children.
'A few sound boxes on the ear', Agnes thinks, or 'a good birch rod might have
been serviceable' in controlling the children (28). Although Agnes does not go so
far as to actually strike them, Brontë shows Agnes increasingly relying on bodily
force to restrain them. Of young Tom, Agnes says: 'I determined to refrain from
striking him even in self-defense; and, in his most violent moods, my only
resource was to throw him on his back, and hold his hands and feet till the frenzy
was somewhat abated' (28). Mary Ann in particular annoys Agnes to the point of
rage; Agnes says: 'Sometimes, exasperated to the utmost pitch, I would shake her
violently by the shoulders, or pull her long hair, or put her in the corner' (32).

Agnes tries valiantly to curb her impulse toward violence by deflecting her
anger. When Mr Bloomfield accuses her of neglecting her duties, Agnes responds
by attacking the school-room hearth. Agnes expresses her exasperation with the

uncontrollable situation: "'It puts *me* quite past my patience too!'" muttered I, getting up; and, seizing the poker, I dashed it repeatedly into the cinders, and stirred them up with unwonted energy; thus easing my irritation, under pretense of mending the fire' (45).

Although Mr Bloomfield reserves as his own the right to inflict punishment, the propensity for violence appears infectious. For instance, Tom Bloomfield expresses his burgeoning taste for authority when Agnes scolds him for threatening his sister with his raised fist. When Agnes says: "'Surely, Tom, you would not strike your sister! I hope I shall *never* see you do that'", Tom retorts, "'You will sometimes; I am obliged to do it now and then to keep her in order'" (20).

The violence of Wellwood goes from top to bottom, penetrating to the lowest household positions. Brontë conveys its contagion by Agnes' conversation with Betty, the children's nurse:

> 'Oh, Miss Grey!' [Betty] would say, 'you have some trouble with them childer!'
> 'I have indeed, Betty; and I dare say you know what it is.'
> 'Ay, I do so! But I don't vex myself o'er 'em as you do. And then, you see, I hit 'em a slap sometimes; and them little uns – I gives 'em a good whipping now and then – there's nothing else ull do for 'em, as what they say. Howsever, I've lost my place for it.'
> 'Have you, Betty? I heard you were going to leave.'
> 'Eh, bless you, yes! Misses gave me warning a three-wik sin. She told be afore Christmas how it mud be, if I hit 'em again; but I couldn't hold my hand off 'em at nothing – I know not how *you* do.' (46)

Despite Betty's admiration for Agnes' self-restraint, Brontë shows Agnes as gradually acquiescing to the predatory atmosphere of Wellwood. Brontë reflects the change in Agnes through the adjustment of Agnes' view of the Bloomfield offspring, young children Agnes had once envisioned as 'buds unfolding' (11). Brontë depicts Agnes transferring her images of children from vegetable to animal, as her pupils evolve in her mind from 'tender plants' (11) to 'tiger's cubs' (43).

Brontë constructs Wellwood's garden as the antithesis of the Grey parsonage bower through her continuing contrast of vegetable and animal images. Mr Bloomfield's carnivorous appetites are particularly reflected by the children's quarrelsome behavior in the garden. Unlike Agnes and Mary Grey, the Bloomfield children do not work together in their garden; each child has its own separate and jealously guarded plot (20). Brontë marks the dangerous nature of the Wellwood garden by her inclusion of a 'forbidden' but open well in its precincts (43). The uncovered well, a yawning orifice into the earth, appears as a symbolic representation of the Bloomfields' unquenchable appetites, and Brontë employs its presence in the garden as an echo of Mr Bloomfield's all-consuming large mouth.

The Bloomfields grow fine, splendid, but inedible flowers in Wellwood's 'tastefully' laid out garden (20), but beneath the lovely blossoms of roses, dahlias, and polyanthus the real productivity of the garden goes on; a variety of cruel traps for innocents of the lower creation – mice, moles, weasels, birds – are stretched about the green lawn in tangles of sticks and cord (21). Young Tom Bloomfield wants to catch himself some birds in his traps, he informs Agnes, so he can 'cut them in pieces', then 'roast' them alive to see how long they will live, and what such a dish will 'taste like' (21). When Tom finally procures an entire brood of nestlings, he tells Agnes he plans to 'fettle 'em off. My word, but I *will* wallop 'em! See if I don't now. By gum! but there's rare sport for me in that nest' (49).

Brontë uses Tom's remarks to break Agnes' stoic resolve to refrain from physical force, for this time Agnes succumbs to Wellwood's coercion to violence, as 'urged by a sense of duty', she dispatches the baby birds herself. Brontë depicts Agnes' involvement in the bloodletting as an inevitable consequence of Agnes' association with Wellwood; even the stone Agnes chooses to crush the birds has already been designated as an instrument of death. Agnes says:

> at the risk of both making myself sick, and incurring the wrath
> of my employers – I got a large flat stone that had been reared
> up for a mouse-trap by the gardener, then, having once more
> vainly endeavored to persuade the little tyrant to let the birds be
> carried back, I asked what he intended to do with them. With
> fiendish glee he commenced a list of torments, and while he was
> busied in the relation, I dropped the stone upon his intended
> victims and crushed them flat beneath it. (50)

When Brontë has Agnes kill the nestlings before Tom can torture them, the blood Agnes spills marks her inclusion into the eat-or-be-eaten secular world. Significantly, Brontë incorporates her heroine directly into the profane scene of killing that, though out of sight of the dining room, nonetheless supports the Bloomfields' 'decent' scene of eating (83).

By involving Agnes in the death of the birds, Brontë brings to the forefront the unavoidable but unmentionable association between death and meat on the table. Meat on the table 'epitomizes pleasure which elides a horrifying process of death', Nicholson observes: 'The process by which the flesh becomes food is elided: the killing and dismembering of an animal becomes an abstract act of commercial exchange, clean, neat, orderly. . .' (205). Nicholson believes meat to be the 'ultimate in commodity fetishism', for animal flesh appears in kitchens and at tables as a mere unrecognizable object; thus 'a ham sandwich seems to have nothing to do with the slaughter of a pig' (205). Brontë determinedly upsets the niceties of such a segregation, as she removes the scene of eating from the Wellwood dining table and emphatically transfers it to the scene of killing.

Agnes' pre-emptory disposal of Tom's birds is perceived by the Bloomfields as a presumption of Wellwood authority and an appropriation of Wellwood property, as Agnes has destroyed Master Bloomfield's playthings and interfered with his 'amusements' (51). Agnes employs no euphemism for her destructive act: Agnes says if Tom is given more birds, 'I shall *kill* them, too' (50, emphasis mine). Ultimately, Agnes' humane destruction of the birds – the bits of sentient meat considered by the Bloomfields as mere 'soulless' brutes created for human 'convenience' – brings about Agnes' dismissal from Wellwood House; but Brontë does not let her heroine leave before Agnes herself, however reluctantly, has been compelled to eat unwelcome food and forced to spill innocent blood (51). Agnes' destruction of the birds recalls the stain of her heightened color on arriving at Wellwood. As Brontë uses her 'dyed' skin to harken the onset of Agnes' initiation into physicality, Agnes' induction into the Wellwood civilizing process ends with the death of the birds.

When Mrs Bloomfield discharges Agnes from Wellwood, she returns for a time to the tranquillity of the Grey parsonage. Agnes recalls her stay at Wellwood House as a time when her body was fed, but not her soul; Agnes says: 'Kindness, which had been the food of my life through so many years, had lately been so entirely denied me, that I welcomed with grateful joy the slightest semblance of it' (41). Once more peaceably at home, Agnes garners 'new stores' from her family's company, absorbing from them the spiritual nourishment from which she says she had 'fasted so long' (55).

Notes

[1] Brontë depicts Agnes' desire for moderation in all things: in matters of religion (90), wealth (82), intellectual pursuits (172), or personal appearance. It is proper, according to Agnes, to care for one's outer appearance only to the extent of seeming neither 'shabby [n]or mean' (192-93).

[2] Richard Grey is 'respected by all who knew him' (1), Vicar Richardson is a 'decent' man (82), Edward Weston is 'a very respectable man' (215), possessed of a 'respectable house' (211). When Weston speaks to the poor, like Nancy Brown, he does so in a 'quiet dacent [*sic*] way' (102).

[3] While *Agnes Grey*'s dining table at Wellwood suggests the banquet table of Satis House in *Great Expectations* as sites where the protagonists confront the power of the marketplace, Agnes, unlike Pip, recognizes in the inedible food the

emptiness of gentility. See Ronald R. Thomas, *Dreams of Authority: Freud and the Fictions of the Unconscious*, and Dorothy Van Ghent, *The English Novel: Form and Function*.

⁴ Elizabeth C. Hirschman, 'Possession and Commoditization in *Fatal Attraction, Blue Velvet*, and *Nine and 1/2 Weeks*', cautions that food can be used to establish a sacred interpersonal bond or 'used instrumentally by one character to possess and control another' (19). The mixed messages conveyed by the proffer of food places the responsibility for assessment on the eater, as Agnes acknowledges in her struggle to eat the tough meat she correctly interprets as offensive in offer as well as taste.

⁵ Claude Lévi-Strauss, in *The Origin of Table Manners: Introduction to the Science of Mythology: 3*, points out that roast meat has an affinity with the raw, as customarily the outside of the roast is cooked, but the inside still has the color red (482). Mr Bloomfield's regret that the good, red, gravy of his roast was gone, would, according to Lévi-Strauss' theory, connote the Bloomfields' move from a station of decent prosperity to one of decadence.

⁶ While the Wellwood bells summon Agnes to an awakened life of duty, labor, and moral responsibility, the stopped clocks of Satis House mark Pip's entry into what Van Ghent calls the timeless 'de-animated' space of someone else's dream (128).

Works Cited

Armstrong, Nancy. *Desire and Domestic Fiction: A Political History of the Novel*. Oxford: Oxford University Press, 1987.

Auerbach, Nina. *Communities of Women: An Idea of Fiction*. Cambridge: Harvard University Press, 1978.

Austen, Jane. *Pride and Prejudice*. Ed. R. W. Chapman. London: Oxford University Press, 1932.

Brontë, Anne. *Agnes Grey*. *The Shakespeare Head Brontë*. Eds. J. J. Wise and J. A. Symington. Oxford: Basil Blackwell, 1931.

Dickens, Charles. *Great Expectations*. Ed. Angus Calder. Harmondsworth: Penguin, 1978.

Hirschman, Elizabeth C. 'Possession and Commoditization in *Fatal Attraction, Blue Velvet*, and *Nine and 1/2 Weeks*'. *Semiotica* 86.5 (1991): 1-42.

Lévi-Strauss, Claude. *The Origin of Table Manners: Introduction to a Science of Mythology: 3*. Trans. John and Doreen Weightman. New York: Harper & Row, 1978.

-----. *The Raw and the Cooked: Introduction to a Science of Mythology*. Trans. John and Doreen Weightman. New York: Harper Colophon Books, 1964.

Michie, Helena. *The Flesh Made Word: Female Figures and Woman's Bodies*. New

York: Oxford University Press, 1987.

Nicholson, Mervyn. 'Eat – or Be Eaten: An Interdisciplinary Metaphor'. *Mosaic* 24.3-4 (1987): 191-209.

Thomas, Ronald R. *Dreams of Authority: Freud and the Fictions of the Unconscious.* Ithaca: Cornell University Press, 1990.

Van Ghent, Dorothy. *The English Novel: Form and Function.* New York: Holt, Rinehart, and Winston, 1965.

Chapter 5

Anne Brontë's *Agnes Grey*: The Feminist; 'I must stand alone'

Bettina L. Knapp

George Moore wrote that *Agnes Grey* (1847) was 'the most perfect prose narrative in English. . . . [It] is a narrative simple and beautiful as a muslin dress' (Harrison and Stanford 227). Although somewhat exaggerated, Moore's statement nevertheless captured certain of Brontë's literary qualities. *Agnes Grey*, however, is also a feminist novel preoccupied not only with moral problems, but social ones as well. Brontë's voice was raised against paltry salaries, poor working conditions, and offensive treatment accorded governesses; against society's denigration of working women; against the legal status of married women who had to give over their dowries and fortunes to their husbands, thereby reducing them to slave status and keeping them virtual prisoners of their own homes. In *Agnes Grey*, Brontë pleaded for self-fulfillment for women and equality of the sexes.

That *Agnes Grey*, as Moore noted, is a novel 'simple and beautiful as a muslin dress', is rigorously perceptive: 'simple' in its depiction of personalities, each delineated with the deftness and expertise of a craftsman; 'beautiful' in Brontë's interdisciplinary use of nature as a backdrop reflecting the protagonist's moods. Darkness, bleakness, storm clouds, or wind-swept seas convey feelings of sorrow and solitude; ordered and planned gardens, walks, groves, and parks express uniformity and systematization and thus safety; cruelty toward people or animals mirror rage and anger, as well as fear of sin and damnation. Events are planned to create suspense and reach a climax, expanding the depth and breadth of the *learning* experience that was, for Brontë, the goal of her writing.

Moore's metaphor of the 'dress' is equally insightful. Characters, nature, and incidents are all used to clothe or cover what the modest and puritanical Brontë seeks to mask: her private *feeling* realm. Love and hatred, serenity and anger, superiority and inferiority, kindness and meanness, generosity and egotism, dependency and independence are projected onto her characters with deftness and dexterity. By concretizing these feelings, Brontë may unconsciously be facing both sides of her personality, thus beginning to divest herself of what she considers to be her ungodly traits. She might find it easier to manipulate characteristics, such as arrogance and self-centeredness, in her protagonists by categorizing good and evil rather simplistically under two polarities. Thus if Evil seems implicit in a character, it can be condemned and rejected. Observed from a psychological point of view, *Agnes Grey* depicts a medley of warring polarities, reflecting its author's highly complex psyche and her feminist goals.

Written in the first person, *Agnes Grey* tells the story of the naive, idealistic, and inexperienced nineteen-year-old daughter of a poor parson who, to help her family financially, takes a post as governess. Her first employers, the Bloomfields, are tradespeople, the parents of three undisciplined, cruel, willful and egotistical children. Humiliated after failing to teach them properly and to redress their callous ways, Agnes is summarily dismissed. Determined to prove herself, she takes another job as governess to the four Murray children of Horton Lodge. Although each in his or her own way is a conceited and spoiled tormentor and prevaricator, the governess remains with the family for nearly four years, to discover that Mrs Murray is flighty and a social climber, prone to playing favorites among her children, and encouraging her daughters to seek wealth and title rather than love from a future husband. Agnes' ire and disdain for Mr Hatfield, the vicar of the parish, are unsparing. His hypocritical and materialistic motivations are set against the humble altruistic, and noble comportment of the curate, Edward Weston. After the conventional peripeteias and time lapses, Agnes marries Weston and they and their children live happily ever after.

The Feminist: 'All true histories contain instruction'

Subdued, but not passive; reserved, but not weak; patient, but not without fire – Brontë had been deeply preoccupied not only with moral problems, but social ones as well. Regarding the plight and working conditions of the unmarried girls and women who are obliged to go out into the world and earn a living, Agnes constantly battles to eradicate dishonesty and misbehavior and to raise the standards, salaries, and treatment of female employees. The intent of her narrative – to instruct – is clear from the opening sentence of *Agnes Grey*: 'All true histories contain instruction; though, in some, the treasure may be hard to find and when found, so trivial in quantity that the dry, shrivelled kernel scarcely compensates for the trouble of cracking the nut' (61). Experience, Brontë realizes, is the best of teachers: it broadens and deepens the individual and brings insights into the outer world and oneself: 'How little know we what we are/How less what we may be' (Wise, Vol. 1 239).

Like some other didactic feminist novels of the century, such as Maria Edgeworth's *The Parent's Assistant* (1796-1800), Harriet Martineau's *Deerbook* (1839), Mary Taylor's *Miss Miles; or, A Tale of Yorkshire Life Sixty Years Ago* (1890), and Elizabeth Missing Sewell's *Amy Herbert* (1844), Brontë also preached women's education as the first step toward her economic independence and self-respect. For Brontë, perhaps even more so than for the other feminists of her day, instruction became a vocation – a mission in the religious sense of the word – and not merely an avocation.

Brontë was determined – as is a missionary – to reform the plight of the governess who was not only underpaid for her services, but looked down upon and badly treated by her employers and, as a result, by their children and the other servants in the household. Searching for ways to help the growing number of unmarried women find adequate, if not always fulfilling situations, she used the novel as her way of altering society's negative view of the working woman in general. Because of the fact that there were a decreasing number of men in the 1840s, more women remained celibate and thus dependent upon family or charity. The literature of the day was filled with the problem of the spinster, of the woman without a dowry who had little or no hope of finding a suitable husband, of the uneducated girl who could look forward to no more than being a housemaid, a cook, laundress, milliner, seamstress, or factory worker. The well-educated girl might become a tutor, teacher, or secretary, and of course, girls could emigrate to New Zealand, Australia, the United States, or elsewhere, as many of them did. Charlotte Brontë's friend, Mary Taylor, considering the lot of the unmarried woman in England to be outrageous, emigrated to New Zealand.

As more women sought employment, competition grew increasingly acute and good jobs were extremely difficult to obtain. Salaries were concomitantly lowered to such a point as to be hardly sufficient to house, feed, and clothe an unmarried woman. The Bloomfields, Agnes Grey's first employer, although wealthy, paid her only 25 pounds a year; the Murrays, 50 pounds, out of which Agnes paid for her clothes, laundry, postage, stationery, and journeys home, which amounted to 27 pounds a year.

Although novels focusing on the plight of the governess became popular in Victorian England, *Agnes Grey*, unlike the Countess Marguerite Blessington's highly romantic narrative, *The Governess* (1839), is written unsentimentally, from the head. Readers learn of the trials and tribulations of the governess, and of her social status, in a relatively objective and factual manner; they will be invited to peer into the protagonist's heart, but via a strategy of events, relationships, and situations as analyzed by Agnes. Despite humiliations and wrongs meted out to her – resulting in her withdrawal into the intimacy of her room to weep – emotions are released consciously and in private, never irrationally or in public. What was the lesson a governess had to learn? 'To stand alone', that is, to be independent, despite the coldness, the calumnies, and the degradation employers might foist upon her.

Life's Educational Process: 'Seasoned in adversity'

A chill in the air, cold, and icy surroundings pervade the atmosphere from the moment the protagonist leaves her warm and loving home to the time she arrives at her first post as governess at the Bloomfield estate, where she is welcomed by a grave, forbidding, scornful Mrs Bloomfield, whose 'frigid formality' sets the tenor for Agnes' painful adventure. Although terrified at first, Agnes is determined to fulfill her mission as governess/educator. Because her Christian evangelical upbringing had taught her to dedicate her life to doing good works, discipline, self-control, and a highly developed sense of morality are her governing principles.

When a sense of sin and imminent judgment are implicit in the events narrated in *Agnes Grey*, terror and anguish prevail in the protagonist's daily existence, encouraging her to become more rigid in her manner and increasingly doctrinaire in her point of view. When positive Wesleyan values take over, and salvation through faith in Jesus Christ holds sway, Agnes is hopeful for the future and focuses on character building, though perhaps nearly equally rigorous in method. No less an authority than John Wesley, the founder of Methodism, stated in reference to children's education: 'Break their wills betimes, begin this work before they can run alone, before they can speak plain, perhaps before they can speak at all. Whatever pains it costs, break the will, if you would not damn the child' (Gérin 72).

Most important for Agnes, as for Brontë, were moral comportment and the enactment of good deeds coming from the heart. What the protagonist had not counted upon were the changes taking place in England's educational theories and systems, possibly inspired by Jean-Jacques Rousseau's *Emile* (1762). Mrs Bloomfield, an adherent to the new approach, had misinterpreted the theories of Rousseau, who had advocated learning by experience and observation, physical exercise, the mastery of useful trades, the development of judgment, and hard work – all of which were to be carried out by a warm and loving preceptor and in a pleasant and joyful atmosphere. The uninformed Mrs Bloomfield, understanding only that she must spare the rod, forbade Agnes to reprimand, punish, or curtail her children's freedom in any way, unheedful of Rousseau's dictum that a warm, loving, and positive environment must be created. Tom, aged, seven, Mary Ann, six, and Fanny, four, were encouraged by their mother to express their feelings and needs freely and indulge their every whim. In no way was Agnes allowed to thwart their desires. Problems became overt from the very outset. Denied all authority, forbidden to punish the children or even discuss their faults with anyone but Mrs Bloomfield, Agnes was powerless to deal with these unruly young people under her supervision.

Tom, the problem child, was bright but intellectually lazy. Because he was the only boy and the strongest of the three, each time the spirit of rebellion overtook him, he encouraged the others to follow suit. Having decided to refuse to study, for example, he convinced his sisters they should close their books and put down their work. The result? All were backward in their reading and writing skills. Agnes, persevering and determined, pitted against her enemy, the children, forswore giving up: 'by dint of great labour and patience . . . [she] managed to get something done in the course of the morning'.) Nevertheless, with each passing day Agnes found herself struggling against the children, thus making instruction increasingly arduous. She was clever enough, however, to realize that a teacher, unless prepared to carry out her threats and promises, must never resort to such strategies to enforce her will. The only effective means she had of taming these 'wild' children was to play on their fear of their father. The mere mention of his name called them to obedience.

Despite Agnes' educational setbacks and the many insults and humiliations she suffered at the hands of her employers, her faith in her ability to overcome obstacles increased. By making the children aware of their sins, gently and with 'perfect kindness', she was convinced that, in the end, she would surmount their spirit of opposition. Her weapons, in addition to 'Divine Assistance', would be 'Patience, Firmness, and Perseverance'. Agnes' glorious method was not, however, always effective; Tom, in particular, frequently refused simply to listen. When ordered to do something, he would just stand before Agnes, 'twisting his body and face into the most grotesque and singular contortions'. The other children, understandably, would burst out laughing. Their 'yells and doleful outcries' were certainly intended to provoke Agnes. She however resisted the temptations: 'I might inwardly tremble with impatience and irritation, I manfully strove to suppress all visible signs of molestation, and affected to sit, with calm indifference'. There were moments, however, when Agnes, at wits' end, realized that 'In vain I argued, coaxed, entreated, threatened, scolded', trying to dominate the 'absurd perversity' of the children. When Agnes finally lost control of herself – and this was a rarity – she sometimes shook Mary Ann violently by the shoulders, or pulled her long hair, or put her in the corner. Reacting to such punishments, and attempting to seek revenge upon her tormentor, the vindictive Mary Ann, knowing that her governess hated shrieks, would let out 'loud, shrill, piercing screams that went through [Agnes'] head like a knife'. In vain did Agnes wait for any 'symptoms of contrition', any feelings of regret.

Mr Bloomfield's comportment toward Agnes was as rude and as crude as was that of his offspring. Unlike the gracious and courteous Victorian families depicted so frequently in fiction. Mr and Mrs Bloomfield were mean, defiant, self-centered, and unfeeling toward others, and even toward each other. They were oblivious to the concerns of their employees, especially the female ones. Indeed, Mrs Bloomfield's brother, a 'scorner of the female sex', adopted a 'supercilious insolence of tone and manner' that offended Agnes on several occasions. It was he, she felt, who encouraged the children's 'evil propensities'. On one occasion, when Agnes found Tom torturing little birds, she tried to make him stop the mutilation, but he was deaf to her wishes. Out of desperation, and seeking to end their suffering instantaneously, she killed the birds quickly with a stone. Tom's cruelty toward animals, she reasoned, was symptomatic of his outlook on life.

Agnes' moral rectitude and her conviction that her understanding of right and wrong was the correct one, gave her the strength to commit a mercy killing, thus ending injury of a sentient creature. No animal, including a bird, she told the children, was 'created for our convenience'. Nor does anyone have the right to torment anything or anyone for his amusement. Quoting from Matthew, she said: 'Blessed are the merciful, for they shall obtain mercy' (7). When informed of the incident, rather than chastise her son for his ferocity, Mrs Bloomfield blamed Agnes for her reprehensible act. Indeed, her 'aspect and demeanor were doubly dark and chill' as she informed the governess that after midsummer, Agnes' services would no longer be required.

Not only were the Bloomfields completely oblivious to the meaning of shame, Agnes noted, but they were devoid of any and all kindness, affection, or feeling. Coldness alone permeated their manner, congelation their feeling principle. Before her departure, Agnes accorded herself only one luxury: at night, in weakness, she yielded to 'an unrestricted burst of weeping'.

Loneliness and alienation had marked Agnes' first experience away from home. She might have more accurately predicted her fate as she left her warm and loving home on that raw and dreary day for the Bloomfields'. Riding in the gig, ascending and descending hills and vales, she looked back frequently to her village and its spires. She considered the 'slanting beam of sunshine' to be a propitious omen. Yet it was 'a sickly ray', and 'the village and surrounding hills were all in sombre shade'. Nature's dark and solemn aspects, she might have realized, were in the ascendance. Then, suddenly, when she could no longer see her home and the surrounding moors, a stinging sensation struck her. Cut off from family and friends, and all of her loved ones, Agnes realized she would be forced to face *reality* for the first time; henceforth, her life would be shorn of that wonderful childhood world of fantasy and fiction.

Self-worth: 'A wide, white wilderness'

Agnes' second venture into the outside world may again be interpreted through nature. Was it an ominous sign that, on the day of her departure, a 'strong north wind' blew and the 'continued storm of snow drifting on the ground and whirling the air [was] wild [and] 'tempestuous''? Darkness and congelation again prevailed, as it had on the day of her departure from the Bloomfields'. Another element, however, imposed itself in her second foray into the world away from home; the whiteness of the landscape introduced a note of purity and beauty into the scheme of things.

Less naive now, Agnes had learned to be both optimistic and pessimistic, neither one to the exclusion of the other. She was, therefore, resigned in part to the icy reception, the materialism, and the corruption she was certain would greet her at the Murrays'. Still, her evangelical side would urge her to reform people's comportment in the hope of inculcating into them a sense of morality and integrity. Despite feelings of utter 'desolation' that forever invaded her when thrust into a new environment, she sought to rectify what otherwise could have led to a crucial imbalance within her. Her strong willpower enabled her to reestablish some semblance of harmony within her psyche and keep her feelings and actions in check. Only on retiring to her bedroom did she allow her repressed emotions full sway. On cold days, warmed by a small 'smoudlering fire' in the hearth, she would allow herself the pleasure of a good cry, after which she said her prayers and went to bed.

The Murrays differed significantly from the Bloomfields. A 'blustering, roistering country squire', Mr Murray, a bon vivant, devoted his time to fox hunting and farming. Unlike the cold and distant Mrs Bloomfield, the 46-year-old Mrs Murray 'was a handsome, dashing lady' who enjoyed parties and fashion. Agnes' teaching obligations would also be dissimilar. Although her teaching hours were increased, she was disappointed because *real learning* was not the parents' objective. She was directed to cram as much Latin grammar, arithmetic, and other disciplines as possible into the heads of the two boys, while the girls were to learn the social graces and sufficient rudiments of the arts to enhance their attractiveness to young men of high society.

Difficulties with regard to Agnes' teaching methods began almost at the outset. The Murray boys were as headstrong, violent, and unprincipled as those of her former employer. Their mischievous natures were also indulged by their mother as were their 'malicious wantonness' and frequent falsehoods. That music, singing, dancing, French, and German were to be taught the three girls with the sole purpose of enhancing their charm, refinement, polish, and social graces ran counter to Agnes' straitlaced views. The cultivation of the mind was designed to increase one's knowledge, and was not to be viewed only as an ornament to be added to one's accomplishments. Agnes believed such an education was hypocritical – a sham. Increasing her discomfiture was the fact that Mrs Murray had forbidden her – as had the Bloomfields – from exercising her authority. 'Persuasion and gentle remonstrance' alone were acceptable.

Agnes still considered herself 'an alien among strangers', but her increased maturity had made her more aware of the differences that prevailed between her, as employee and employers and their children. To her surprise, her greater self-esteem had served to make her even more vulnerable to insults, slights, denigrating mannerisms and remarks. Unwilling or unable to believe the evidence, she could not accept the fact that she had been hired for the sole purpose of performing a function. Her hurt chafed from the very start, from the moment she noted that Mrs Murray, so intent upon seeing to the happiness of her children, 'never once mentioned' any thought of Agnes' needs or welfare.

The differences between Agnes' values and those of the Murrays also served to widen the line of demarcation between them. She felt 'abused' and put-upon because she was never consulted in matters of judgment, yet her sense of commitment and her faith in her ability to succeed instilled in her a powerful sense of obligation that drove her on. She was determined to inculcate higher standards into her young wards, to teach them to moderate their desires, to temper and bridle their instincts, and above all, to sacrifice their personal pleasures for the good of the others.

Only with Rosalie Murray, the beautiful, tall, and slender sixteen-year-old daughter, did Agnes build a semblance of a relationship. At first 'cold and haughty' to the 'poor curate's daughter', Rosalie grew to 'respect' Agnes and, in time, even become attached to her. Agnes at first found Rosalie's conceited and frivolous behavior most shocking. Anathema to her was the young lady's need to attract young men in order to conquer hearts only to reject them. The pleasure she derived from this kind of 'game' was heartless, Agnes told her; one must never trifle with the feelings of others. That Rosalie's marriage to a titled and wealthy young man failed after but one year – she was no longer able to abide her husband and he became utterly indifferent to her – was, to Agnes' mind, an example of Divine intervention.

The Ministry

Agnes' indignation was aimed not only at her employers and their progeny, but at those involved in the ministry. Mr Hatfield, the vicar, who observed *all* the rules and regulations outwardly, represented everything that was detestable in the established church. His sermons and hellfire orations were designed to inspire fear and not love to the congregation. He saw 'Deity as a terrible task-master, rather than a benevolent father' and was unable to abide dissent. Total obedience to *his* interpretation of church law has to be observed to the letter. Personal thought was not permitted. Repugnant to Agnes were his exhibitionism, his hypocrisy, his attempts to ingratiate himself with the wealthy and influential parishioners, and his contempt for the poor (Ewbank 64). In one of Brontë's gnomic depictions, she writes as follows of Mr Hatfield:

> [He] would come sailing up the aisle, or rather sweeping along like a whirlwind, with his rich silk gown flying behind . . . mount the pulpit like a conqueror ascending his triumphal car; then sinking on the velvet cushion in an attitude of studied grace, remain in silent prostration for a certain time; then, mutter over a Collect, and grabble through the Lord's Prayer, rise, draw off one bright lavender glove to give the congregation the benefit of sparkling rings, lightly pass his fingers through his well-curled

hair, flourish a cambric handkerchief . . .

In sharp contrast to the vicar was the curate, Mr Weston, who visited the cottages of the poor and the sick, ministering to their needs and comforting them. His readings of the Bible filled his flock with feelings of warmth and belonging: 'He that loveth not, knoweth not God'. He neither condemned his parishioners nor aroused fear in them as Mr Hatfield did. The curate's reasoning was that 'He that is born of God cannot commit sin'. Mr Weston's approach to the suffering and those in want was not limited to words alone, but included deeds as well. He sent his parishioners food and coal when these were in short supply, paying for such gifts out of his own meager salary.

The more Agnes saw of Mr Weston and learned firsthand of his kindness, the deeper ran her feelings for him. Unlike Mr Hatfield or the Murrays, Mr Weston showed great concern for her well-being, his delicacy and tenderness toward her manifesting themselves in an exquisite little scene. One day, as Agnes was returning to the Murrays', she saw a clump of primroses that reminded her of those that grew at home; the glow of warmth and love she associated with her family was so strongly felt that she had a sudden urge to pick them. Try as she might she failed to reach them. About to despair, she heard Mr Weston's voice behind her. Startled at first by his unexpected presence, she graciously accepted his offer to pick them for her. Unaccustomed to such attention, she deemed his gesture to be an added jewel to adorn his already exemplary character.

After leaving the Murrays' employ, Agnes did not see Mr Weston again. She busied herself by founding her own school not far from her home. One day, as if destiny had seen fit to instill joy into her life, she chanced upon the curate. After renewing their friendship, Agnes introduced the curate to her mother and family. In due course he proposed marriage and she accepted. They had three children and lived in bliss thereafter.

Conclusion

Although a novel with a message, its heroine being the purveyor of truth, morality, education, and reform, *Agnes Grey* is far from being cut and dry. Nor is it maudlin or self-indulgent. Its crisp sentences are to the point, and endowed with rhythmic and imagistic variety. The strategies aimed at eliciting pity from the reader and creating suspense are neither cumbersome nor artificial. On the contrary, the seemingly effortless and harmonious change from narration to description, to commentary, to confession, lends subdued and unaffected drama to the sequences. Events and characters encourage the reader to probe and evaluate the protagonist's self-conscious, analytical, but paradoxically passionate, personality. Commitment and intransigence, rectitude and rigidity, are weapons that help Agnes cope with her feelings of alienation, solitude, and profound humiliation. Pain, conveyed internally, never overtly, is presented as a fact of life to test the power of her evangelical missionary qualities. Agnes' religious convictions gave her the strength to bear the ignominies, insults, and wayward ways of those with whom she had come into contact.

Rather than underscoring their aesthetic reactions to *Agnes Grey*, mid-Victorian critics focused on the moral issues at stake. The reviewer for the *New Monthly Magazine* preferred *Agnes Grey* to the novels of her sisters, Emily and Charlotte, because 'its language is less ambitious and less repulsive, it fills the mind with a lasting picture of love and happiness succeeding to scorn and affliction, and teaches us to put every trust in a supreme wisdom and goodness' (Evans 381). Along a similar vein ran the comments of the reviewer for the *Atlas*: *Agnes Grey* 'is a tale of everyday life, and though not wholly free from exaggeration (there are some detestable young ladies in it), does not offend by any startling improbabilities. It is more level and sunnier. Perhaps we shall best describe it as a somewhat coarse imitation of one of Miss Austin's [sic] charming stories' (Evans 381).

Audacious and courageous, Brontë's heroines – in *Agnes Grey* and in *The Tenant of Wildfell Hall* – stand their ground, fight for the obligations of employers to respect and to pay their employee/ governess a fair wage, for the right of a wife to keep her fortune in her own name and struggle against the financial dominance of a husband, for the abolition of lascivious and pernicious comportment, regarded as a sickness able to *contaminate* others, and for the rejection of the double standard.

Brontë's unsentimental, skillfully built, and suspenseful scenes, the self-control in her writing, the smooth, ordered, classically constructed sentences, the subdued effect of rhetoric, and the insights into the psyches of her characters, drawn for the most part from observation were remarkable, given her age and experience. It is little wonder that George Moore again wrote: 'If Anne Brontë had lived ten years longer she would have taken a place beside Jane Austen, perhaps even a higher place' (Harrison and Stanford 227).

Works Cited

Brontë, Anne, *Agnes Grey*. Ed. Angeline Goreau. London: Penguin, 1988.
Evans, Barbarea and Gereth Lloyd, *The Scribner Companion to the Brontës*. New York: Scribner, 1982.
Ewbank, Inga-Stina, *Their Proper Sphere: A Study of the Brontë Sisters as Early Victorian Female Novelists*. London: Edward Arnold, 1966.
Gérin, Winifred, *Anne Brontë*. London: Allen Lane, 1959.
Harrison, Ada and Stanford, Derek, *Anne Brontë*. New York: Archon Books, 1970.

Scott, P. J. M. *Anne Brontë: A New Critical Assessment.* London: Vision and Barnes and Noble, 1983.

Sinclair, May, *The Three Brontës.* London: Hutchinson Co. Ltd., 1912.

Wise, J .J. and J. A. Symington, eds. *The Shakespeare Head Brontë.* 19 vol. Oxford: Basil Blackwell, 1931.

Chapter 6

Narrative Economies in
The Tenant of Wildfell Hall

Garrett Stewart

What turns structure into content? This is the oldest hermeneutic question in – and of – the book. What pressures exerted by shape grow legible as meaning? A new volume about Anne Brontë, in her own literary context and ours, would be missing a main chance if, from the perspective of current paradigms in narrative study, it neglected to confront one of the most typically Victorian innovations in – and one of the deepest continuing resistances to – her strongest novel: the literally off-putting structure of narrative recess in *The Tenant of Wildfell Hall*. Immediacy is put off by writing, confrontation held off by text, presence everywhere deferred. So? But I mean *in* the story, not just by its very nature as text. Or, finally, I mean in the former as a reenactment of the latter. The question, then, about what presses structure back into plot becomes an inquiry into what trans*forms* the organizing principles of structure into words, what distributes their weight across the plan of the text via the legible girders of its representation?

Narrative Accountability

Criticism has only very lately warmed to the narrative form of this Brontë novel. Nor has it traditionally been sure whether to classify the text as epistolary or nested, or both. Yet the structure remains frank enough in its laminated displacements to defy overlooking. It is so openly odd that its eccentricity is what one used to call decentered, less an aberration than an allegory of normal reading. For a long while in the critical literature, though, its structure of postponed directness (a letter instead of an oral anecdote about a read journal rather than a passionate confessional outpouring) was considered either an inadvertence or a gross miscalculation. But why should its slippery embedding seem such a dramaturgic sore spot of flubbed immediacy? To put it differently, how can the novel be blamed for failing to achieve at its center the directness it so markedly sets out to avoid, an avoidance it then replicates (at a gratuitous outer level of framing) as if for reasons of external ratification? No answer can come except inductively, from the narrative ground up. Toward an initial floor plan of *Wildfell Hall* and its cumbersome superstructure, then, let me first walk through its transmissive main corridor – and receding narrative thresholds – as simply as I can.

Out of her life's greatest sustained pain in the alcoholic degeneration and death of her brother, a Yorkshire writer of the late 1840s sets down a searing indictment of human abuse, fictionalizes it as a brutal marriage plot, rescues it at the last minute with a happy second wedding, and further distances the sponsoring grief and mourning by publishing it as the pseudonymous novel of one Acton Bell. That is only the beginning of the distanciation: its outer form, so to speak. Inside the story, the account of the cruel and self-destructive drinker is disclosed only to the suffering wife's own private diary. This text is then read once in violation of her wishes by the inflamed husband himself, and then again once after their separation – and at her behest this time – by a new suitor, in order to explain her necessary coolness toward his advances. This later recipient of her text, tendered a thrilling narrative in not quite cold comfort for banned sex, is none other than the novel's own narrator, over whose shoulder we read the many chapters of the diary, making do as he does with lurid melodrama instead of fleshed passion. So that his captivation by the journal stands in for something like the reader's own sublimated fascination with the book's heroine and her hair-raising tale. Subsequent to this protracted climax in a revelatory scene of reading, the denouement eventually brings the new couple together after the long-expected deathbed agonies of the first husband. The narrator-hero did not have to make do with just reading about his beloved after all.

Yet, as noted, Brontë goes very much out of her way so that even his invited rather than forced reading of the heroine's diary, offering as it does the highpoint of his journal-based first-person memoir (our main narrative), is further distanced in turn by the undermotivated but overdetermined rewriting of the whole story in a series of letters dispatched a full two decades later. These are sent by the narrator to an importunate city friend (his brother-in-law) who has been awaiting a delayed return for a lengthy personal reminiscence on his own part at their last meeting. The text as we have it thus constitutes a command performance: impersonal, perfunctory, but (I will want to show) definitive. The surprise in all this layering and terracing of narrative pretexts is not so much that numerous critics have found the bulking embedded diary an egregious contrivance as that these same critics have mostly blinked at the absurdity of what we might call the second-generation frame story (Markham to Halford), complete with its Herculean labors of composition and transcription, weeks on end of lengthy letters in recompense for a spontaneous oral narrative long ago delivered. By what logic might the two strata of framings, one blatantly more far-fetched than the other, be interlocked? If there is such a logic, it may well go to the heart of the entire Victorian fictional agenda. That is what I meant by definitive. But I anticipate still.

In a book that reads like a swan song for two decades of rigorous narrative analysis across previously entrenched disciplinary borders, part of a dialogue that its author helped to inaugurate, Gerald Prince has recently surveyed the question of *Narrative as Theme* in a number of French novels whose foregrounding of the storytelling motive have been grist for much previous theorization. Had he turned to British fiction, Prince would not necessarily have taken up a novel like *The Tenant of Wildfell Hall*, however, since it is not the narratability of the story that is thematized so much as the manner of its transmission, both as to form and effect: the handwritten diary serving, at the innermost communicative layer, as roundabout love-letter.[1] This is where structuralist narratology can expect reinvigoration only from the adjacent considerations of reception theory and textual analysis: widening to consider, that is, the generation and dissemination of the narrative product(ion) as well as registering its internal relays of meaning.[2] So under the adjusted rubric of 'reading [rather than narrative] as theme', and with a closer investigation of the microlevel of linguistic texture by which reading is channeled and inflected, we proceed with *The Tenant of Wildfell Hall* as a Victorian test case in a dynamics (rather than thematics) of narrative conveyance. Often rooted in tacitly economic models of transactional exchange, this is a dynamics whose ultimately transferential negotiations repeatedly transpire at the level of single phrasings, their syntactic and phonetic grain. To take up this texture of interchange requires that we first return from theory to criticism – if only to work our way back.

Otherwise appreciative commentators from novelist George Moore to Brontë biographer Winifred Gérin, whatever their degree of admiration for the central story of *Wildfell Hall*, have regularly regretted its diary structure as lumbering, implausible, and, by being undramatic, counterproductive. Ultimately, the heroine's exonerating story would – opinion once appeared unanimous on this point – have carried more dramatic charge if its purport had been conveyed to the narrator, Gilbert Markham, in a lengthy scene of emotional outpouring and checked affection from the long-suffering heroine, Helen Huntingdon, who would return his love if only she could. To baffle this impact with a diary has seemed to many critics a baffling move on Brontë's part. It comes off as a pallid borrowing (or at best a send-up) of her sister's mediated narrative in *Wuthering Heights* – and without the clear purpose of ironic perspectivism. No explanation seems decisive, let alone satisfying. Certainly one cannot assume that Anne is so unhinged with trepidation over going public with the already fictionalized family tragedy lying behind the autobiographical material (Branwell Brontë's own adulterous scandal and drunken decline) that she has overdone the protective sheathing thrown up around it. The whole mechanism is just too ponderous and forced. Poetic license is one thing, but narrative poetics seems spoiled by the transgressed common sense. Such is the complaint. It amounts to this: What possessed Anne Brontë to think that the exchange and reading of a text (in the case of the diary, to say nothing of the laborious renarration to Markham's brother-in-law Halford that enfolds and retranscribes it) could possibly be as compelling as its story would be in a less mediated form?

Introducing an earlier Penguin edition of the novel, Winifred Gérin suspects an ill-considered indebtedness on Anne's part in the nested diary structure: 'Its weakness lies in the structure, in the clumsy device of a plot within a plot. (Did not Emily Brontë use the same in *Wuthering Heights*?)' (13). George Moore had been even more condescending. Though ranking Anne Brontë very high on the list of English novelists, he had earlier set the tone of dissatisfaction with *Wildfell Hall* in his complaint about the awkwardness – and lost opportunity – of Brontë's decision to embed a written narrative rather than mount a melodramatic revelation scene. He suggests that 'almost any man of letters' would have advised Brontë instead to produce an 'entrancing scene . . . of the telling' with the two principals on hand, advice which would have come in no uncertain terms: 'The presence of your heroine, her voice, her gestures, the questions that would arise and the answers that would be given . . . would preserve the atmosphere of a passionate and original love story'. Instead, for Moore, ' The diary broke the story in halves. . .' (216). Can Anne Brontë really have needed a 'man of letters' to school her in the opportunities made available by the imagined presence of a female narrator in revelatory distress? Can she have doubted for a minute that she was squandering all the tremors of immediacy? If not, then why do it? In pursuit of what compensatory intent?

One rejoinder (around which the reactions of this essay begin to gather) is that these stories are only *meant* to be as engrossing as a novel, a written and read text, which can hardly be a source of complaint for the author's own literary audience – including the critics who think her novel so good it could even have been better. The evidence necessary to demonstrate this claim, that Brontë is in fact flagging her novel as novelistic, crosses provocatively, as we will find, between epistolary frame and the events retailed in the inner diary – while intersecting at the same time the most richly speculative aspects of contemporary narrative theory.

But back to the annoyance so often registered about the diary, in light of the more looming absurdity of the novel itself when repackaged as serial correspondence on demand. Why send the heroine offstage at the crucial turning point, leaving only her words? If one imagines her, like her would-be lover and long-time narrator in the surround of his own yet more voluminous story, to believe that a narrative is best conveyed at the reflective distance of writing rather than in the heat of speech, then why does she not say so? Or why does not Markham in his turn proffer this retroactive defense to Halford against charges of his own oral diffidence? There is one obvious answer. In the Victorian circuits of narrative consumption, it goes without saying. Orality is secondary, entirely at the receiving end: a function of hearth rather than press. This secondarizing of orality is not only what constitutes (and institutes) the genre of the realist novel but what industrializes it: exactly the fact that it comes and goes without saying, a print product, whose power and 'intimacy' (an important formal term for Anne Brontë, as we are to see) derives from rather than transcends this condition of silent exchange.

We are faced in this case, however, with the fended off presence of oral reception as a contrivance rather than a given. It might be tempting to lay some of this at the door of extratextual biography. What if the diary, enclosing as it does the personal family tragedy of the Brontë brother in fictionalized form, is held to written rather than oral circulation for reasons best known, after all, to its author rather than to her audience (by virtue of their sheer fascination with this and all novels) – but its author less as fellow-suffering family member than as sibling novelist? These would be reasons having to do primarily with the attempted silencing of the story by the accomplished and censorial sister Charlotte. For it was Charlotte, having failed to suppress the confessional (however novelized) story of their wastrel brother, who later sided, after Anne's own death, with the hostile reviewers in finding *Wildfell Hall* given over to gruesome and distasteful material. Allowing that the 'choice of subject was an entire mistake', Charlotte was quick to note it as a mistake against which she had in vain struggled to persuade her sister ('Biographical Notice' 317). Charlotte was, as it happens, equally unsuccessful in suppressing the work of her other sister, Emily, and Anne could not have forgotten their battles over *Wuthering Heights*. In her 'Editor's Preface' to the 1850 joint edition of *Wuthering Heights* and *Agnes Grey*, Charlotte looks back on her attempts to intervene and revise Emily's conception of the novel. In so doing, she portrays a scene of oral report and debate typical of the Brontë sisters in the throes of composition: 'If the auditor of her work when read in manuscript shuddered under the grinding influence of natures so relentless and implacable', it was, alas, of no avail, and 'Ellis Bell would . . . suspect the complainant of affectation' – as Nelly might Lockwood, for instance, if he were anything but the porous and uneditorializing voyeur he is.[3] Since the structure of *Wuthering Heights*, with its direct oral recitation of brutal events by a female narrator, as later transcribed by an affectless male conduit, in no way served to mollify Charlotte's discomfort at its 'audition' as recited story, one might, I suppose, wish to take Anne's Brontë's extra displacement of the female narrative in *Wildfell Hall* – from voice to script – as a strategic further retreat from the vulnerability of delivering one's unseemly tale aloud.[4] Indeed, Helen's diary in *Wildfell Hall* is specifically called a 'thick album or' – important afterthought – 'manuscript volume', as if to remind us that by the time it reaches us, publication has done just what it is mechanized to do: placed between authorship and the private audition of a manuscript the diffusive impersonal format that makes for a public reception (129).

If I have momentarily digressed into biography, it is with little risk run. The reason why such a biographical detour does not begin to derail a psychostructural analysis of the novel is that any suspected personal allusion to the tensions of intimate reading in the Brontë household only serves to reduplicate what is already the manifest arc of the whole transmissive experience as a reading event. If the heroine's imputed private motives for the deliberate nonaudition of her story become in this way almost an in-joke on Anne's part against the remembered onslaughts of her sister, the personal emphasis nevertheless epitomizes the protective barrier elsewhere erected by writing (or pseudonymous print) in the venting – even when mostly inventing – of personal trauma. Whether or not a story's grievous extremes of feeling are entirely made up, that is, rather than borrowed more or less directly from survived experience, the realist novel operates as the buffer zone between someone else's (imagined) real pain and your own (in every sense) realization of it. To borrow the founding sanction of the eighteenth-century novel as posited by Catherine Gallagher, this is why Nobody's story, being conceivably anybody's, becomes everyone's in the reading. This is indeed, to speak again economically, as Gallagher does in her own terms, and as Brontë does more baldly, the story's only true currency as minted adventure.[5]

But before watching the novel execute this sense of things in all but perverse detail, we can benefit from the latest critical energies marshalled to address the longstanding crux of the story's central frame. The interpretive variance on this is so wide one would think it exhaustive. Not quite. But both the earlier chorus of complaint against the novel's structure and the more recent scramble to thematize it are, like the structure itself, entirely instructive. Even critical agendas soft on formalism – and certainly far afield from narratology or reception theory – are drawn to Brontë's embedded diary as a lightning rod for their own preoccupations. Structure is repeatedly seen to engineer ideology, whether in its socioeconomic or its sexual bias. In a class-based analysis of the jockeying valences of yeomanry and squierarchy in the social schemata of all the Brontës' novels, for instance, an insistently Marxist reading has found the 'structural inversion' of *Wildfell Hall* patently symptomatic, so that what 'is officially an interlude becomes the guts of the book, displacing the framework which surrounds it' (Eagleton 136). But this does not operate, as it does in *Wuthering Heights* to fuse social and moral dimensions of the work in a critique of the leisured genteel reader (Lockwood). Rather, in this socioeconomic reading, structural design locates the exposé of degenerate squires and lords (and a self-narrating heroine from the same social sphere) at the heart of a story that is merely dutifully copied and transmitted by the gentleman-farmer to whom the lady of the manor finally condescends in marriage.

From a more literary-historical than materialist perspective, the use of framing structure to bracket and manage enormities of moral horror in *Wildfell Hall* is seen by one of the novel's best recent critics as a transformation of the gothic legacy, with demonic turmoil put into recess (and offered redress) by domestic and social continuance.[6] Concerning a related mode of diminishment by distance, and in regard to the parallels between the male frame narrators in *Heights* and *Hall*, Brontë's novel has been been read as a parody and critique of the valorized Shelleyan furor in the former's core story (Chitham 8). Accepting this proposition but taking it in a different direction, yet another critic comes down hard on the very fact of Markham's aired letters as opposed to Lockwood's private diary, finding that they replicate the conditions of 'publication' and thus betray to social consumption his own wife's private past.[7] Value judgments aside, this view has at least the virtue of putting structure before content in a hermeneutic reassemblage of the text – even though it too quickly folds its notation of 'publicity' back into an ethics of characterization rather than a dynamics of response.

But we have only begun to intercept the recent analytic crossfire. For over a decade now, the critical fortunes of Anne Brontë's framing structure have been a litmus test in the feminist transformation of Victorian studies. Rethinking the whole sweep of classic realism, gender critique was quick to see the power plays involved not only in received novelistic formulas but in traditional fictional structures. At times, though, results can seem either dizzily equilibrated or downright paradoxical, here empowering, there effacing to the woman's story, the same novel now quiescent, now seditious. In the case of *Wildfell Hall*, the most straightforwardly sensible of recent gender analyses can fend off George Moore's unimaginative objection by noting that whatever a 'man of letters' (Moore's phrase, you will recall, for the accomplished narrative tactician) might have done, this 'woman of letters' knows the power of the lettered text. One result is that the '*mise en abyme* or the book within the book' can only show that 'Anne Brontë unerringly grasped the radical implications of allowing her heroine to speak for herself within the thoughtful confines of the written page' (Berry 72-73). As if refusing the dead metaphor of voice in characterizing such a diary as a way to 'speak for herself', however, other feminist critics emphasize mediation – and its politics. A more 'problematized' (and to some extent improbable) reading finds the framing structure of *Wildfell Hall*, muting the woman's story by textual distance, as a 'silencing of the powerless' – this from the same critic who nevertheless argues that the 'displacement' (overshadowing) of the larger narrative by the gruesome truths of the diary does constitute in its own right a subversive break with conventional social understandings of domestic relationships (Jacobs 208). Other responses seem also to suggest that the woman's story is somehow recontained by the male narrator of the frame, even if in the service of restoring a positive rather than a negative stereotype of Victorian female intensity exemplary rather than deviant, yes, but no less serviceable to patriarchal maintenance. Surveying the 'doubly retrospective' nature of the narrative framing and the critical dismay over it, the subtlest account in this line stresses the two levels of corrective emphasis involved in the inset diary: first, the reading that reforms the trivial and self-involved Markham, chastening his arrogance and sense of male privilege by the negative example of Huntingdon and his peers; and, second, the sheer transmission on his part that signs on to Helen's view of things in hindsight, though in the simultaneous interests of his own recouped male 'authority' as well (Langland 120).[8]

Where does all this leave us in our reading of Anne Brontë's novel as novel? If taken literally, the question answers itself. It leaves us reading, leaves us in the midst of it – whatever else the characters are doing or may, constructed otherwise, have done. In fact, they too are often reading, and that is where we take up the novel again on its own terms, take it in. The improbability of our own reading is thus a vaunt of structure that becomes a factor in the plot. If Anne's story, over Charlotte's objections, but only in this sense like all Victorian narratives, is in good part about the very fact of going public, we need to look first at the outer rim of her narrative as its true social interface. There, and more explicitly in *Wildfell Hall* than in any other novel of the period, the contractual economies of narrative fascination are laid bare: so bare as to seem almost swamped by the flood of metaphoric exaggeration. The narrator's addressee, the citified Halford, despite what Markham reminds him (and thus tells us) about his friend's native reserve, has originally given Markham a 'very particular and interesting account of the most remarkable occurrences of your early life' (9). When Markham was too tired to respond in kind with an oral recitation of his own at the time, and excused himself by saying he had nothing comparably interesting to relate, his interlocutor not only became peeved and sullen at the time but has harbored a grudge ever since, we are to think, casting a pall over their subsequent correspondence.   Months later, with Markham housebound alone during rainy weather, buried in reveries, old letters, and his voluminous musty journal, the time seems right to make amends with a more than full response. This is one of three things: silly, strategic, or parabolic. Or a little of each.   Either Halford is a petulant boor obsessed with emotional *quid pro quo*s or else Markham is protesting too much the demands made upon him for the redemption of his narrative debt, doing so in order to mask his own need to tell. Or else if narrative is contriving to emphasize twice over the satisfactions of formal written textuality, crafted and meticulous, by contrast with casual oral reminiscence, then the novel seems bent on generating a double parable of its own reception. Can we possibly believe that Halford would have preferred a tired, rambling account of Markham's past, with a hazy paraphrase of the heroine's desperate diary, itself containing as it does the harrowing melodramatic core of the narrative – would have preferred this to the several hundred-page transcription of highly accomplished literary writing that the plot unbelievably provides him? Was not the novel per se, under whatever disguise and by any other name, well worth waiting for? At this early point at least, the sanguine purchaser of the new Acton Bell novel, for one, has every reason to hope so.

The novelistic valence of these London-bound mailings is, however, unconvincingly sidetracked into a concern not for justifying, against all probability, their indefatigable length and writerly flair, but rather for defending their authenticity as strict report. So that Markham closes his prefatory cover letter (and metatextual cover story) by assuring Halford as follows: 'Among the letters and papers I spoke of, there is a certain faded old journal of mine, which I mention by way of assurance that I have not my memory alone – tenacious as it is – to depend upon in order that your credulity may not be severely taxed in following me through the minute details of my narrative' (10). If we fall for this windy notion of a fact-checking source text, or even notice it as anything more than a transparent convention, we are primed to appreciate the redoubled veracity attached to the unedited inclusion, deep within his epistolary reminiscence, of another more privileged journal: namely, Helen's diary, reproduced verbatim this time, stretched out across 28 chapters of its own rather than merely referred to for confirmation. But epistemological veracity can scarcely be expected to settle an issue that has always seemed, to the novel's detractors at least, dramaturgical instead. Well before we arrive at the inner diary, then, we are prepared for its deficit in presence by a full-blown prototype of narrative compensation.

Here Brontë is also building on the inferences of her own previous novelistic success. Along with questions of narrative immediacy, the economic subtext of rewarded reading was made explicit in *Agnes Grey* (1847), where it also emerged (though less showily) from a diary format of minimal structural impact. Folding this earlier novel as precedent into the debate over *Wildfell Hall* helps respond to complaints about, as well as assess the defenses of, the latter's ungainly frame narrative. Again, the question toward which we are driving with *Wildfell Hall* : What did Brontë hope to gain, what compensatory leverage, by deferring omniscient immediacy twice over? And before seeking corroborating evidence from *Agnes Grey,* we can quickly review what seems inescapable so far. At the manifest expense of unmediated emotional exchange for her extended revelation scene, stretching the inner diary alone to virtual novel length (four chapters longer than all of *Agnes Grey*), Brontë has, for one thing, done little more than translate it more openly into its own condition as a written narrative. She has thus converted the most interested party on the dramatic scene, the riveted Markham, into an immobilized reader, extrapolating from his position into that of another reader reading (our surrogate, Halford) and, through him, to our own direct response – all this in order precisely to secure, rather than in any way to abdicate from, the charged force of disclosure.[9] At the same time, Brontë has generalized our identification with Markham in part by underspecifying the site of his reception. It becomes merely the space of domestic reading. In the undescribed space of 'my room', that is, Markham, sitting down before the table, 'opened out' the manuscript – which he calls in the language of windfall profits 'my prize' – and, in a further loaded phrasing, 'delivered myself up to its perusal' (128). The ceding of consciousness is total: a wholesale giving over to the gift received. Moreover, in the process of relaying Helen's story later to Halford, by postal delivery, he does to Helen's manuscript what he has done to the longer narrative that contains it, dividing it up by chapters and bestowing upon them titles of his own. Or, in other words, novelizing it: 'It begins somewhat abruptly, thus – but we will reserve its commencement for another chapter, and call it – [The Warnings of Experience]' (128).

As regards not this inner 'manuscript volume' of Helen's diary but the later 'faded' one of his own that records his reading and copying out of her text, and from which his letters to Halford draw both substance and credibility, it is worth noting that Brontë's previous novel had turned the matter around – dropping the epistemological issues into place as an afterthought. Postponing all questions of authentication, Brontë's first-person narrator in *Agnes Grey* establishes the lesson and the license of Victorian narrative in her very first paragraph. I mean its pedagogy and its intimacy. 'All true histories contain instruction', the novel begins, making the familiar eighteenth-century claims for fiction as chronicle: detailing the facts from which all truths must be adduced. But in some 'true histories' (including fictionalized autobiographies like the present one, about the lessons to be learned from the victimage of governesses at the hands of incorrigible charges and their indulgent parents), the nugget of 'treasure' may be 'so trivial in quantity' that 'the dry, shrivelled kernel scarcely justifies the trouble of cracking the nut'. It is as if Conrad had this passage in mind, or those many like it that speak of a significance less emanated than extracted, when bringing Marlow forward with a narrative agenda meant to contravene it, Marlow who believed that 'the meaning of an episode was not inside like a kernel but outside, enveloping the tale which brought it out like a glow brings out a haze' (67). Indeed, Brontë seems to have thought better of her own strategy for her next confessional 'true history', which found a narrative form equivalent to the structural consequences of Marlow's later credo: a frame tale that displaces and diffuses the inference of history into the field of its transmission and response. In this sense Markham has it just right, counting not on the nugget of wisdom but on the treasured 'prize' of the whole involved event of reading.

In Brontë's debut novel, however, Agnes closes her first paragraph by consoling herself that the anonymity of the title page, as well as the distance of years, shields her truths from embarrassment, giving her leave to 'candidly lay before the public what I would not disclose to the most intimate friend' (1). On we read. 25 chapters of harrowing servitude and mistreatment and final conjugal reward later, we hear only at the very close about the means by which this text has in fact been 'laid before the public'. Only when it is over, in short, is its mediated nature brought forward by the slipping cognitive inference of a single comma splice: 'Here I pause, My Diary, from which I have compiled these pages, goes but little further' (144). After the first waver of an odd vocative sense, as if 'My Diary' as volume is being apologized to for the writer's desertion of it, the private text seems posed instead almost in apposition to an inscribing subject. At the same time, in this quicksand grammar, the verb 'pause' takes on a transitive thrust ('Here I cease my diary') that tapers into the ensuing blank of all inscription. Such a flickering glitch of punctuation aids in minimizing (by confusing) the barrier between transcribed and transcribing 'I' as well as between an edited personal record (vouching for authenticity of detail) and a cogent mimetic fiction of the sort we thought we had been settling for under the licensed directorship of the fictional first person. On reflection, then, is it not more likely that Brontë was drawing on and rethinking her own novelistic structure of 1847, with its courted complexities of witness and distance, rather than borrowing from her sister Emily's, in her decision the next year to foreground in *Wildfell Hall* the textual basis of narrative without in the least foregoing its 'intimacy' – indeed to contrive a scene of reading (rather than an immanent confessional presence) so intensely involving that no textual distance could dampen it? But this would of course be largely to affirm again, as had *Agnes Grey* done in its own way, the immediacy of institutional as well as private reading, the printed novel as well as the confessional holograph.

Even the internal details summoned from Agnes' diary contribute to a structural logic of transmission that the next year's novel will more emphatically theatricalize. One of the moments of idiot meanness suffered at the hands of her spoiled charge, Miss Murray, has the governess Agnes mocked in her efforts to escape from her petulant companion into a yearned-for immersion in news from home, urged all the while by her charge to 'put away that dull, stupid letter' (53). Scale is, twice over, the letter's problem: 'You should tell the good people at home not to bore you with such long letters . . . and above all, do bid them write on proper note-paper, and not on those great vulgar sheets' (52). To the truly petty and uncultured bourgeois, engrossment itself, as well as bulk, is vulgar. Then, too, by displacement onto another version of the full-sized page, this scene installs the printed sheet's inserted justification for itself when Agnes explains simply that 'the longer their letters are, the better I like them' (52). So speaks the popular Victorian novelist from behind the see-through veil of her persona, about the appeal of expatiation per se.

Indeed Markham in *Wildfell Hall* reads a 'missive' – in any case a transmitted text – that is a good deal longer than the whole of *Agnes Grey*. He is never bored for a minute. Nor does he expect that his 'narratee', Halford, will be anything but tantalized by the epistolary frame tale that includes and extensively contextualizes Helen's manuscript. Hence Markham can relax into the flourishes of sheer rhetoric, letting the writerly ambitions of Anne Brontë come through his dispatched obligation to tell. A far cry from the ferocious oscillations and fervid grip of Emily Brontë's style or the syntactic bravado and studied euphonies of Charlotte's, Anne's prose detonates its peculiar verbal effects from the mined underturf of routine phrasings. From amid the otherwise inert circumlocution already quoted from Markham's justificatory rhetoric at the start ('in order that your credulity may not be too severely taxed'), the dead metaphor of 'taxed', for a levied strain on belief, and even the etymological hint of 'credit' in 'credulity', look ahead to the more unmistakable signals of narrative material as an economy of exchange, soon to be driven not only home but over the top.

At the close of the prologue (the first signed and dated letter to London), the demanding Halford, rendered vivid only as a placeholder for all narrative craving, the man of constitutional reserve who nonetheless requires a story as the fulfillment of a bargain, is in this way first and foremost a representation of the urban(e) book-buyer, true statistical destination for the marketed fiction of the rural novelist. Whatever he has done in advance to deserve a story – in this case, and against his predilections, by telling one of his own – the novel opens, as in a sense all novels do, with the bargain already struck. Between the 'not naturally communicative' recipient of a novel-length story (34) – mute by the very 'nature' of the fictional institution's one-way circuit of dissemination – and its participant witness (the narrator) lies the debt of plot as a promissory note. Despite the epistolary fiction of direct address, Markham writes momentarily of (as well as to) his brother-in-law as a third-person novelistic character, 'my crusty old friend', for 'I am about to give him a sketch – no, not a sketch, – a full and faithful *account*' (10; emphasis added). Nothing has transpired between this gesture and the opening of the next chapter, nothing that we know of, to reassure Markham that Halford is satisfied. Maybe we are to assume a posted note of encouragement. But that too, expressing a taste for narrative, would go without saying in this Victorian text. In any case, and free of explicit validation from Halford, the language of calculated worth is at this point transferred to the supposed grateful recipient, since 'I perceive, with joy, my most *valued* friend, that the cloud of your displeasure has passed away... and you desire the continuation of my story' (22; emphasis added). The recipient is given no voice, just a presumed desire fulfilled in the moment of its imputation. Everyone is now content simply to read on from here on, you and I and Halford alike, without having our attention further solicited or coddled or thrust upon us in any way – except for an occasional moment of rhetorical address. As the 'sketch', nay full 'account', begins, we are drawn in as readers by being, like Halford, etched out of the picture – or should we say factored in by subtraction? So it is that in this opening protracted apostrophe (in the form of epistle), Halford seems confirmed in his role as nothing more, nor less, than a proxy for the Victorian public at large.

A book-buying as well as story-reading public, we must quickly add. 'Account': even that deadest of metaphors from the epistolary prologue will not go away. By the end of the first chapter, with one scene-setting stretch of narrative prose behind him, Markham the recountant, if you will, throws open the full vault of his fiscal tropes, cashing them in with spendthrift abandon. Having called the chapter 'the first installment of my debt', he then goads the figure into an almost baroque conceit: 'If the coin suits you, tell me so, and I'll send you the rest at my leisure: If you would rather remain my creditor than stuff your purse with such ungainly heavy pieces – tell me still, and I'll pardon your bad taste, and willingly keep the treasure to myself' (20). Whereas a single metaphoric fillip in the term 'treasure' did the trick in *Agnes Grey* for the invocation of narrative yield, there is an entirely new premium on fiscal figuration in *Wildfell Hall*, imposed by a dominant discursive system of credit and recompense.   Given the structure of debt rather than desire in this case, the economic figure swells to a kind of imaginative usury of returned interest, forcing a repayment with compound interest.   An overdue narrative exchange seems in this way to have been unilaterally renegotiated to the mutual satisfaction of both parties. The idiomatic 'piece' – a term crossing between literary production and legal tender – is the least of it. Even Markham's valediction over his signatory mark, 'Yours immutably', borrows from the figuration of precious metal to suggest the unalchemizable state of essential and unalloyed substance.

But one must stand back. Our interest is not drawn primarily to the way Brontë has strategically prearranged a narrative debt so as to justify an extravagant return. Nor to the means by which she has pressed the notion of confessional accounting and accountability into a full-scale system of textual exchange value. More to the point, one comes to sense these metaphors as deriving from a kind of narratological unconsciousness in the normative prosecution of nineteenth-century fiction. *Wildfell Hall* issues in this way from a Victorian discourse of print interchange, dependent on a general circuit of investments and withdrawals that takes shape as a more or less intimate mode of emotional give and (up)take. The novel as genre circulates as a coin of exchange that has to do, therefore, with an underlying psychoeconomy of narrative. And this is a discursive economy, in Brontë's novel, that gets most potently explored in passages far afield from this opening local pocket of figuration. Far afield, and often only by indirection. We never see Halford's reactions at the site of reading, though we are made to wonder about them by Markham's explicit querying. Inside the story, however, at the recessed borders of its enframed reading scene (Markham of Helen's journal), we funnel through to a full-scale analysis of narrative process as a transactional dynamic. Inner and outer frames thus gloss and interrogate each other in respect to the transferential relays of reading. Markham to Halford: I know how much you want this, so here goes. Helen to Markham: I know that nothing else permitted to us will do, so here is my story as a text. At both levels, the Victorian public is both figured in disguise and conscribed by exemplum.

Affective Transaction

What remains for consideration are the internal displacements of such structural force staged by the plot and contoured by its prose. Right from the start Brontë's story works overtime – and not always underground – to sketch the parameters of its own public consumption as novel. After considering the place of reading and its deflections in Markham's outer narrative, we will turn to a sustained crisis of reading in one relentlessly delimited episode that lends early shape to the grotesque conjugal mismatch recounted by Helen's diary.

Like the phonetic ambiguity of 'frame(d t)ale' in the ears of students, so that they cannot be counted on to tell the framing from the framed (a classroom pitfall slow to dawn on me over the years), *Wildfell Hall* shuttles between the outer and inner logics of reception with reversible inference. Even if we set aside the outer frame of epistolary diffusion as a transparent ruse, the plot comes bearing down on Helen's diary with a steady preparation that unfolds four implied modes of textual dynamism: 1) transmission, 2) disclosure, 3) vicarious identification, and its opposite in 4) self-defense. These features of transparent reading (or in the last case its occlusion) are quick to emerge from the tale of Markham's initial infatuation with the Hall's new tenant, who in her mystery embodies all narrative impetus – the very aesthetics of the undisclosed – through an otherwise stiff periphrasis depicting her as 'the fair unknown' (43). Epistemophilia runs riot, and the desires that fuel or frustrate narrative penetration emerge under those four coordinated aspects as follows:

1) In a gesture of transmission, Markham's first gift to Helen is a copy of Scott's narrative poem *Marmion*. He is mortally offended that she expects him to accept payment, since the economy he has in mind is another one entirely. Within the very plot, then, narrative fiction is a mode of intimacy long before it is reciprocated by her private journal in the form of 2) disclosure. The first time Gilbert learns the given name of the new tenant, Mrs. Graham, whose surname is itself an alias, he does so from the fly leaves of books in her library at Wildfell Hall, in other words from her *ex libris* (94). In like fashion, it will later be from the perusal of another long text bearing her signature, as author rather than mere owner this time, that the narrator-hero will find out *who she really is*. The missing ingredient so far, of course, is the morbid content of such a disclosure in her marriage to the sadistic drunkard. The first leak toward filling in this lacuna comes with a scene of oral rather than textual exchange in Markham's outer narrative, connecting there with his own surcharged 'readerly' curiosity about the newcomer. The scene in question, extending over the whole of the third chapter, has Markham, at home, pretending to be caught up in another kind of journal than a private diary, in this case a printed magazine, while in fact overhearing Mrs. Graham's refusal to let her son take wine with cake. Told by Markham's mother that she is in danger of making a milksop out of the boy, Helen is unmoved, and a debate on the gendered rearing of children ensues. From Markham's point of view, this access to Mrs. Graham's attitudes toward the cultural forms of masculinity, as if he were encountering them in the text at which he absently peers, do the usual work of textual disclosure by, in turn, prodding nothing less engaged than:

3) Identification. For this circumscribed glimpse into the mysterious woman's past springs a leak as well in the self-contained envelope of Markham's narrative, when his own response to her image of proper masculinity throws him back on the shaky confirmations of male narcissism and its rhetorical shoring up. Her would-be suitor wants to be seen as a manly man in the mysterious Mrs. Graham's eyes, of course, and is therefore troubled, once he looks up from his supposed reading to join the debate, by her refusal to be persuaded by his own example. He finally turns in some desperation, well outside of the framed events, to his correspondent Halford as readerly touchstone, whose addressed presence we have all but forgotten – and whom Markham apostrophizes in closing the chapter with 'I was by no means a fop – of that I am fully convinced, whether *you* are or not' (36). With Halford only silently holding down the reader's place, it is of course up to us to decide – just as the male readers among us must decide about ourselves on the same basis, identifying or not with Markham's own self-doubts. Prose has

effected this slippage from absented interlocutor to implicitly queried reader across an ambiguous fold of grammar (and Markham's own italics), for it is as if the addressee himself is being arraigned for foppery ('whether *you* are [one] or not') as well as for withholding immediate conviction in our narrator's evident virility.

But there is still more to note in the tactical (and in Victorian domestic arrangements so entirely natural) accomplishments of this early chapter. We continue in our breakdown of fictional negotiations played out in advance of the novel's distended reading scene (Markham alone all night with Helen's diary) by monitoring yet more closely the hero's textual fortification in this early episode, his taking shelter under cover of a book in the posture of 4) Self-defence. Cautious resistance is the opposite of permeable empathy or identification, of course, and reading can just as easily ward off the real world as bring an invented one closer. To secure this suggestion, the whole scene of masculine investment in a discourse of gendered experience, though gradually drawing Markham into the argument about protective child-rearing after all, has begun with his effort to remain no more than 'apparently immersed in the perusal of a volume of "Farmer's Magazine"' (29). This is a domestic game two can play (as Helen well knows from experience in her bitter marriage, we are to find). So that when her son first tries to pull Gilbert into the conversation, she fends off his inclusion in the same vein: 'You are troublesome to Mr. Markham: he wishes to read' (29). The spectacle of seated immersion in a book is repeatedly what we would have to call stand-offish in this novel. The open page of a buttressing text is soon used again by Markham, for instance, as a defensive hedge against his mother's badgering. 'While she thus remonstrated, I took up a book, and laying it open on the table before me, pretended to be deeply absorbed in its perusal' (110). The point of both episodes – in view of the 'absorbed' reading to come, the involving diary that swallows up a large stretch of the novel's own air time – lies in the fact that the superficial screen of simulated reading is effective as a defensive maneuver only because of deep cultural assumptions about the ability to become lost in a book. Founded on these, Brontë's novel soon moves to study their confounding.

These are assumptions about reading that are to be reversed and travestied, turned more sadistic than reciprocal, in the inner plot of Helen's diary, with its melodramatic degeneration of the scene of reading in the chapter 'First Quarrel'. But not, as we have begun to see, before other figurations of reading have built up pressure behind that central scene. Among these preparations, other media have been maneuvered into comparison with the question of writing and its reception. There is, most prominently, an ekphrastic dimension of this text (begun, after all, as a 'sketch') that enhances its metanarrative impact. Helen is an artist in oils, supporting herself through a gift for painting that, in her amateur phase, was appreciated by her suitor, Huntingdon, only when he discovered her infatuated portraits of himself hastily drafted and unsuccessfully erased on the backs of finished sketches. As in the diary whose later 'secret thoughts' she is afraid he will read for a second time in order to assess her impressions of his escalating debauchery (367), the imprint has been quite literal from the start, for 'the pencil frequently leaves an impression upon cardboard than no amount of rubbing can efface' (156). That these pictures of Huntingdon should emerge from attempted suppression as the double of the diary, itself a synecdoche for the representational energy of the novel as a whole, seems confirmed by the anonymity of Helen's later commercial painting. Having left her brutal husband and set up her tenancy of Wildfell Hall under a false name, she markets her pictures of the same hall under a double pseudonym, its and hers, fictionalizing the very site she has rendered with such delicate precision. Helen explains that since she wishes to conceal her 'present abode' from those who 'might possibly recognize the style in spite of the false initials I have put in the corner, I take the precaution to give a false name to the place also' (47). So with the *Hall* as textual representation, euphemized as fiction and distributed under the *nom de plume* of Acton Bell. Like so much else at stake in the novel, so-called woman's work is put in play across the slippery internal borders of the telling and the told.

Besides reading and painting as the domestic pastimes of the Victorian female, gone to market only under duress and the protection of an alias, there is music: third avatar of hemmed-in feminine accomplishment. Music emerges in *Wildfell Hall* as part of a domestic and feminized ambience associated directly with versification. Brontë's own poetry had been included in *Agnes Grey* as an instance of the 'effusions' (106) that relieve her anguish (equivalent to Helen's therapeutic diary in *Wildfell Hall*). These are explicit literary exercises that Agnes shares with 'the reader' (106) of her larger prose production. Verse makes its way into the plot of the later novel, however, only through the backdoor of musical lyric, a piece to be performed by Annabella Wilmott in the chapter immediately following Helen's embarrassment over her secret portraits of Huntingdon. It is 'a little song that I had noticed before, and *read* more than once, with an interest arising from the circumstance of my connecting it in my mind with the reigning tyrant of my thoughts' (165-66; emphasis added). The laborious circumlocution lingers over the fact of projection and identification in her 'reading' of the sheet music: a familiar pattern of tortuous mental concentration in this novel. In her present overwrought condition, Helen chooses a musical dead metaphor to describe the way in which her 'half unstrung' nerves make her peculiarly vulnerable to the lyrics when 'so sweetly warbled forth' (166).

Everything is readied for our own aural hypersensitivity to these same lyrics. In the event, we seem invited to read not only between the lines but between the words. In any case, we arrive at a curious minor crux in Brontë studies. Describing the 'laughing eye' of the rakish lover, the lyric passes to 'that smile! whose joyous gleam / No mortal languish can express' (166). Tackling this curious diction, Winifred Gérin drops into a footnote to explain her demurral from received opinion: 'The noun "languish" here carries the sense of "a tender look or glance" –

OED, citing Alexander Pope (1688-1744): "The blue languish of soft Alia's eye." There is no need to follow some modern editions of *The Tenant* and emend "language'" (502, n. 2).   Certainly not, especially since the quaint if not archaic sense permits a 'warbled' legato elision in performance that spells out the subjective 'mortal anguish' that Helen's anxiety over Huntingdon's tyrannical charm half anticipates, even as the wish-fulfillment of the song pushes a stanza later in the opposite direction, imagining how 'the future' may 'pay the past / With joy for anguish, smiles for tears'.   By the reprise of 'anguish' and 'smiles' in immediate proximity, and whatever the erotic reward of the fates, our ears have been fully repaid for the suspicions of the previous phrasing. Writing, reading, reading aloud, singing: in each and any case, not unlike the phantom traces left by pencil on cardboard, language circulates through and behind the surface of meaning with the return of its own phonetic repressed.[10] In such cases, registration can scarcely be too narrowly gauged.[11] Concerning such subvocal ironies as 'mortal l/anguish' in *Wildfell Hall*, the effect is not negligible even in its contingency.   In a novel that so carefully orchestrates its embedded acts of reading and textual audition, no instance of this dense – even contrapuntal – orchestration can be too minuscule to count for the fleeting variation on a theme.

So, too, with an extended scene of reading (or its mean-spirited interruption): an episode of textual mediation circumscribed within the plot as a reinscription of its own engaged (or blocked) encounter by the Victorian reader. What we come upon in this light is the novel's negative rather than positive *mise en abyme*.   This scene of reading in (rather than of) Helen's embedded diary, a text later devoured with passionate interest by its privileged interpreter, Markham, details what in fact amounts to a wholesale collapse in the vicarious outreach of reading: a gnawing provocation rather than an empathetic evocation.   For this inference, too, a certain amount of specific background pressure has been built up within the framed narrative of her diary.   We have been reminded in a timely fashion that the concentration necessary for reading is not always easy to come by. Helen first falls prey to the slick charms of the rakish Huntingdon, that is, in a fit of discontent over rural life after her heady sojourn in London. As chief symptom of her defenselessness, she has not even the fortifying consolations of the library. 'I cannot enjoy my books, for they have not the power to arrest my attention' (130). This malaise is indeed the first danger signal in the chapter called 'The Warnings of Experience'.   Inverting the self-cautionary warnings against what we might call consumptive reading familiar in the nineteenth-century novel, here is instead a self-advertisement for the magnetic charge of reading. The promoted admonition could not be clearer. It is those not open to books who are most prone to the emotional misjudgments often diagnosed between their covers. For Helen's lapse of literary attentiveness she will indeed be punished, after the very marriage to which it renders her vulnerable, by an ongoing worry and distraction that comes to a head in the chapter 'First Quarrel' around precisely the unavailable therapy – and the distorted tropology – of reading.

What was once her 'new-sprung distaste for country life' (130) takes a drastically exaggerated form in the demeanor of her loutish husband, who 'is getting tired – not of me, I trust, but of the quiet life he leads' (208). The symptom of this restiveness and 'ennui' (208) is yet again an indifference to books, an imperviousness to their lure. Living only for the moment, Huntingdon can abide only quotidian print, so that 'he never reads anything but newspapers and sporting magazines' (208). But he knows the power of a good erotic story to divert attention – and to infuriate where it cannot titillate. His 'favorite amusement' is in this way to 'tell me stories of his former amours, always turning upon the ruin of some confiding young lady or the cozening of some unsuspecting husband' (208). This is the standard subcultural fare of Victorian light pornography, and the Brontë heroine will have none of it. At first she remonstrates, but then she tries going silent, as if to turn the assaulting narrative into sheer text rather than aggressive interlocution. But she only turns herself into a text instead – and, worse yet, a misinterpreted one, for 'he *reads* the inward struggle in my face, and *misconstrues* my bitterness of soul for his unworthiness into the pangs of wounded jealousy' (208; emphasis added). Huntingdon becomes the deluded hermeneut of his own auditor's supposedly mediated desire. In the process, Helen's dead metaphors of linguistic decipherment flow straight from her deadened hopes. The bride-to-be who, just two chapters before, could not wait until mere correspondence with Huntingdon would be replaced by conjugal presence, so that they might 'exchange our thoughts without the intervention of these cold go-betweens, pen, ink, and paper!' (200), has now only inked paper, her own or that of published print, to comfort her in what a later chapter title calls the 'dual solitude' (36) of mutual avoidance.

In the pivotal scene we were considering, as soon as the self-serving turpitude of Huntingdon's autobiographic stories has abated, Helen sneaks back to the protective custody of her letters and books. All the while Huntington 'could not force himself to read' (211), using a book only as a missile to hurl at his disobedient spaniel. Unmentioned by title, this book, reduced to sheer material object, hits his wife instead, 'rather severely grazing' her (writing?) hand. She returns to her own reading in disgust, and he cannot abide it. 'What *is* that book?' he whines. 'I told him'. Not us. All we know is that is 'very' interesting, like books in general, but that for her too, as for Markham's reading acts in the surrounding tale, its interest can easily be lost by worry or defensiveness. As Helen notes in her diary about this first affective deadlock with her husband: 'I went on reading – or pretending to read, at least – I cannot say there was much communication between my eyes and my brain; for, while the former ran over the pages, the latter was earnestly wondering when Arthur would speak next . . .' (225). In our fourfold anatomy of the reading template in this novel, the processes of transmission, disclosure, and identification are all disabled in this case by the overbearing need for defensive cover – exactly the impairment not suffered by Brontë's readers as they are absorbed in these very pages. In Helen's brief personification allegory of the senses, 'communication' is almost a dead metaphor for transit (as in rooms that 'communicate'). Textuality's process of conveyance, though not reversible, does come in two stages, marked by the passage from utterance toward its intentional recipient and, once arrived, from signifying page to its processed signifieds. It is the second stage that is short-circuited here by distraction and anxiety. And all that is left for Helen is to continue transcribing her anguish in the mute pages of her diary, an act of record she figures as the need to 'confess' her growing contempt to 'silent paper' (243). All, that is, except for a further spoilation of textual experience in the defensive manipulation of silent script. The fly-leaf of a book that once disclosed to our curious narrator the name of the mysterious tenant is the same mode of blank text on which Helen later intercepts the adulterous dallyings of Lady Lowborough in her own parlor. In 'putting into her hand the book I had been trying to read, on the fly leaf of which I had hastily scribbled' (310), Helen delivers her message of contempt in bound but uncopyrighted script. Even in the thick of sexual intrigue in this novel, writing and reading are the very conduits of lust and its rebuking. And not just writing and reading, but their materialization within the covers of printed volumes, extrapolated thereby to the Victorian literary institution as it traffics in the same desires, indulged and corrected by turns.

Of this deep structural implicature there is an ingenious witty anticipation *en route*. Concerned to warn her mistress about the adulterous threat of Lady Lowborough in the house, the servant Rachel seems inexplicably upset. Indirect discourse sidles up to one of the novel's few – and fleeting – moments of comic relief, not just momentarily puncturing the tension but opening an escape valve to the story's own bracketed narrative status as framed tale within a frame tale. Here is what we get of the filtered interrogation scene, as Helen tries to determine what troubles her maid: 'Was she unwell? No. Had she heard bad news from her friends? No. Had any of the servants vexed her?' (297). The upsetting possibility of physical decline, commiseration for the distress of others, or pity for one's own mistreatment – the three primary affective registers in the plot of this novel as a whole – are summarily ruled out. '"What then, Rachel? Have you been reading novels?"' (297). No, she swears. But we have. And the one we are reading right now is about to swerve into the most lurid of adulterous melodramas. For readers to recognize the suggestion of just this encompassing site of their own absorption in Helen's character, including this moment of gentle sarcasm, is only to recommit to the charter of classic fiction and its entailed empathies. If somebody is not in dire straits, then maybe Nobody is: once again Catherine Gallagher's name for the permeable essence of a fictional personification. Furthermore, if Rachel had been able to throw herself into a novel or two, of course, she would have been the envy of a mistress almost never able these days to clear her own head for reading. Instead of the free communication with other minds through textual transmission, Helen's 'locking herself in the library' (349) is more often the sheer seeking of shelter rather than a mediated commerce with the world. As the plot thickens, the very conditions of the Victorian fictional readership are everywhere violated by cruelty and perverted to a shrinking from otherness. In the psychoeconomies of narrative empathy, this is the true default incident to imaginative bankruptcy and its sadistic fallout. When Helen later 'took up a book and tried to read', she found that 'my eyes wandered over the pages', so that it was 'impossible to bind my thoughts to their contents' (387-88). At this point we are only one chapter away from Markham's frame-breaking remarks to Halford about his own reactions to reading just this story. Once again, with no power for reading, Helen has 'recourse to the old expedient' and added more lines of output rather than intake to 'my chronicle' (388). The suggestion abides that writing in Victorian domestic life is mostly necessitated by the temporary suspension of reading in a cultural circuit of textual immersion for which Halford has begun this whole novel by making such (presumed) aggressive demands. Contemplating this hint, Victorian readers might well be ratified in their fascination to think that writers write mostly when, and because, they cannot enjoy the tenderer mercies of reading.

In the long run, the 'silent paper' of Helen's 'chronicle' is never given voice. Once received in manuscript by Markham, however, it is read with unstinted curiosity well into the night. And just like his own letters to Halford, containing it and much else, the diary reading is interrupted in progress, impossible as it is to take in (like a novel) at one sitting. This interruption is staged to occur – in Markham's contingent (rather than constitutive) case, that is – because, once his candle has guttered out, he must await the illumination of a new dawn. What come to light there, among other things, are his own reactive motives in reading on. He finds in the diary the lifted veil of his very desire, the potential chance of consummation, the wish-fulfillment scenario of triangulated passion overcome at last by the humiliating degeneration of the rival. For all the searing misery of the tale, he feels a 'selfish gratification' (397) in reading on. Embarrassed though he is over his own motives, Markham, in short, wishes Huntington dead. However repulsed or embarrassed in turn we may feel at this candid admission, we of course do too. In its reverberations for the novel's framing structure, the force of this confessional gesture is difficult to overstate. The death of the villain, if only in good time, is in every novel reader's interest. Yet as an audience looking for a more satisfying domestic closure, we are chastened in advance for our investment in the heroine's release – as well as punished later, along with Markham, by the prolonged harrowing account of Huntingdon's last hours, faithfully attended by his wife and reported in further letters to her brother, shown in turn to Markham, copied in turn to Halford, and ours at a modest price. Held off for as long as possible and relished in the grotesque contours of its object lesson, the scene of Huntingdon's last tortured days is the true heart and soul of the novel for Brontë. Focus of its dramatized religious treatise on divine forgiveness, this is a spiritually agonized death scene unprecedented even in the mortuary annals of Victorian fiction – and too painful to have wished visited upon any character, even a scurrilous villain. To read the denouement in this way, as an inferential scene of further reading, is no doubt prompted by the way in which a link between the narrator's feelings and those of his presumptive audience has already been made explicit. Thus Markham's question to Halford as the diary is wound up, epitomizing the mechanics of readerly identification: 'Well, Halford, what do you think of all this? and while you read it, did you ever picture to yourself what my feeling would possibly be during its perusal' (402). Again that limp, stuffy diction, 'perusal', usually associated in this novel with the showy and shallow skimming of a text, rather than the throes of fascinated participation. We expect the question to be rhetorical, so obvious is the affirmative answer. But Markham pushes ahead as if there were serious doubt, as if his function as interested party as well as conduit has been forgotten, or let us say as character rather than narrator, in the toils of his own role as retranscriber of the diary. 'Most likely not', he adds to his presently unanswerable question. But can there be any way for a reader, even the undemonstrative Halford, not to bear in mind the invested primary recipient of the journal or at the very least to replay such feelings in the strictly textual economies of the imagination's own engaged – and not altogether attractive – reading? Can we forget for long that a reader there before us (in every sense) is not only voyeuristically, like us, but not even disinterestedly steeped in the mortuary (rather than theological) nuances of Huntington's ordeal? Only if we feel at least a little guilty about our readerly interest from here out do we apprehend the full depth of our commitment until now – in precise contrast to Huntingdon, whose incapacity for reading left only one way to plumb and so prove his soul: deathbed trauma. By negative association with the tenor of the villain's spirit, then, reading works to authenticate a soul ready for saving, an inwardness held apart and inviolable, hence infusable at a distance by sympathetic texts. Reading is therefore the proving ground not only of the protestant work ethic but of the spiritual subject tested by private hermeneutics rather than received dogma: Brontë's devout version of the middle-class aesthetic of reading.[12]

And it is primarily reading that must now carry the plot itself to closure. What follows upon Huntingdon's death in *Wildfell Hall* to ensure and ennoble the next marriage is a further waiting period, during which Helen selflessly returns to Huntingdon's deathbed and Markham learns of the yearned-for and suddenly all too horrific decline through her second-hand letters. We come again upon the deep affinity in this novel between the economy of narrative exchange and the social psychology of paid leisure in the consumption of popular fiction. Once shown to Markham, these supplemental texts offer a vicarious relay of event which this time lacks no 'communication' between page and brain, for 'I devoured those precious letters with my eyes, and never let them go till their contents were stamped upon my mind' (444). Then, in a passive grammar whose impersonal instrumentality extends the idea of the 'stamped' with the suggestion of an almost automatic secondary impress or printing, we hear that 'when I got home, the most important passages were entered in my diary' (444) – as if with no conscious intervention. And hence, thanks to that diary, stamped out as our novel. Here is the destination of all Brontëan melodrama: the true 'silent paper' of passionate expressive writing communicated from the site of trauma through a chain of more, then less, familiar or intimate relays – from brother to lover to friend and brother-in-law to general public – so that the harrowing set piece of the death agony, more openly mediated in form and at the same time more inescapably gripping in effect than anything before it, brings to a climax a prototypical Victorian novel on the brink of its recuperative marital closure. No one has to imagine the feelings of anyone else when reading this, Brontë the tacit phenomenologist would suggest, since, by projection and introjection, they are all our own to inhabit.

Let me put the case as clearly as I can. None of this is, first and foremost, what one should call Brontë's theme. She did not, for instance, invent the novel's scenes of defensive reading – the book as curtain or shield – to ramify some guiding idea. These scenes are more properly thought to derive, instead, from the very texture of mediated experience in Victorian domestic settings, a travesty of its finer distractions. Nor, put positively, was the activated and conveyed power of narrative developed as a concerted motif in *Wildfell Hall*. Rather, it was the story's whole motivating dynamic, the condition of any such narrative as a Victorian novel: a thing of realist grip and overriding immediacy, a transparent 'sketch' whose images of lives lived and died are vicarious events that no signs of mere marking, no marks of sheer signification, can screen out. Circulation, transaction, investment: these are the very medium of Victorian print culture, but only when tapped by concentration, only when replenished from within the reading mind. This is the culture of reading into which this one novel inserts – by performing twice over – its own exchange value, operating entirely within the psychic economies of disclosure and receipt, inscription and participation, or in other words within the convertible urgencies of lent interest.

A further psychological detail clinches the issue, tightens it to a reflexive textual irony. In a last spurt of frustrated vanity, Markham peevishly regrets the torn-away last leaves of Helen's manuscript volume. There, had she left them intact, he might have read directly about himself in Helen's words, might have 'watched the progress of her esteem and friendship for me' (396) – all those shifts of feeling that the reader, too, has only been able to deduce from her seemingly mercurial behavior in the novel as we have had it. For the character himself, however, the motive is no more attractively selfless than Huntingdon's wishing to study the impressed pencil sketches of his visage through her smitten eyes. The novel is out to arrest and redirect this narrowly narcissistic investment in the mind of others, however, at the same time that it wishes in countless ways to suggest that its readers should always be finding lines of identification between themselves and any such literary text, always reading ourselves in.

At just the point when the last letters from Helen are read into second-generation epistolary evidence in the outer frame, we are reminded not so much of Markham's continuing presence to the inner story (rather than its events) as, one step back and world's away, of Halford's – the one character (because barely one at all) whom we have always been in danger of forgetting, the sheer locus of reading. Or should we say the one character in whom we forget ourselves by reading on? So that Markham is speaking to me now, as well as to my faceless effigy in Halford, when, on the way to the novel's final framing gesture of epistolary valediction, he sets into quotation the beginning of Helen's correspondence from Huntingdon's deathbed with a telling grammatical swivel between her reported past ('I read') and, let us say, the prospective present tense of my reading: 'I read it and so may you' (423). Once again the lag of transcription is melted away in the heat of identification. I am there, nowhere and everywhere, waiting like Halford not so much to be told as to read along, to go through it with the hero. We may advert again to Gallagher's terms in sensing how this novel about autobiographical reading retraces, by its forced conduits, not only the conditions of its own production as masked autobiographical writing but the transactive authenticity of reception. Though announced at a flat fee, the commercial novel as nobody's story (even when it is somebody's in thin disguise) is always on auction to the highest bidder, rewarding to exactly the degree of its emotional outlay at the receiving end. And that receiving agent has its own inner life confirmed *in advance* by the logic of avid narrative interest. Why else is Halford made to ground the whole apparatus of exchange by a precedent disclosure that requires no content for its force and that sets in motion a chain of social entailments that only reading can redeem? The structurally empty center is the proof of fullness. Only if we have something in us that might be brought out are we ready for the intake of reading. To internalize with any real intensity the characters of a text, you need character of your own. Only then can you disappear, like Halford, lost in a text.

Reading takes you out of yourself. The truism is given local habitation, or more to the point local eviction, by the metaphoric capstone of Markham's plea in separating from Helen after he has read of her sordid marriage. In language that directly anticipates the final deathbed debates with her husband about the possibility of unbodied reunion for forgiven souls after death, Markham asks if it could possibly be 'a crime to exchange our thoughts by letter?' (408). He goes on to imagine a prose eroticism beyond the body that may sound less far-fetched than otherwise from a character who has spent much of a long novel thrilling through the night to a passionate stream of pages. Here is his rhetorical brief for epistolary exchange: 'May not kindred spirits meet, and mingle in communion, whatever be the fate and circumstances of their earthy tenements' (403). The loosed soul need not honor the restraints of its body, whether that 'tenement' be its mansion or its hovel, and so may seek contact and transaction beyond the confines of its mortal tenancy. But to put this metaphor of a soul unhoused by the two-way transit of verbal communication alongside the notion of an overdue prose accounting, the sublime over against the mundane, is to reveal the spiritual and the fiscal as part of the same exchange economy. In this way the tropes of tenancy and rent may seem elevated to the novel's ultimate psychoeconomic metaphors for its own textual lease on the reader's attention, its transferential relay of private imaginative property. And where we choose to reside for awhile, there may we find a hermeneutic residuum. I can best sum up the point this way. As if respecting by the indirection of its title the anonymity of Helen Huntingdon, to say nothing of her pseudonym as Mrs. Graham, the novel that followed the flatly eponymous *Agnes Grey,* and that might well have been called in the same vein either *The Mysterious Mrs Graham* or *The Fair Unknown,* is named by way of a self-instanciating circumlocution after all. For the novel's name works to textualize not its title figure this time but, instead, its entitled premises. In reading on and in, you too become an occupant of the let space set before you. Thanks to Markham's broadcast reminiscences, or in other (though the same) words, thanks to Anne Brontë's novel as a published vacancy, we are each of us for an allotted period the tenant like Halford, all attention and nothing else, of a *Hall* of mirrors by any other name.

Notes

[1] Gerald Prince (1992) does allude to Barthes' emphasis on 'contractual' narrative (18), which of course bears on what he would call a 'theming' of the outer frame structure of *Wildfell Hall.* Further, Prince's remarks on the privileging of inscribed over oral tale-telling in Flaubert, in his chapter 'Written Narrative' (65-76), might have shed light on critical debates over the supposedly sacrificed vividness of Helen's diary.

[2] Though he makes direct use of Peter Brooks (1984) in connection with Stendal and the scandal of narrativity, Prince's work (n. 1) does not broaden out into the general psychopoetics pursued by Brooks either there or in his subsequent commentary (1994), where the transferential modeling of the narrator/narratee relationship is further explored.

[3] Reprinted in the Norton Critical edition of *Wuthering Heights,* where there is further emphasis laid on the 'mere hearing of certain vivid and fearful scenes' as they 'banished sleep by night, and disturbed mental peace by day' (321).

[4] Mostly in connection with the close bond between Emily and Anne, this is a dimension of 'viva voce critique of each other's manuscripts' discussed (apart from any direct connection with the diary format of *Wildfell Hall*) by P. J. M. Scott (1983).

[5] See Catherine Gallagher (1994), especially 162-74, on the novel's place in a Humean discourse of sympathy as related to fiction's unique transgression of private property rights.

⁶ Jan B. Gordon's (1994) is both the most closely read and the most theoretically inflected treatment of the novel. Tracking the lines of discursive exchange (from gift books to gossip) at the level of plot and structure, Gordon pursues a tacit fusion between the psychopoetics of Peter Brooks, in his emphasis on 'transaction and transference' and the deconstructive emphasis of Barbara Johnson's epistolary address, drawn from Poe and Derrida (742, n. 8 and 12 respectively). Building on her own sense of the novel's gothic legacy (720), Gordon sees Huntingdon, for instance, as 'the demon of the anti-text' in his invasion of Helen's privacy through the veritable rape (my term) of her diary (729-30).

⁷ P. J. M. Scott, whose treatment of the frame is the fullest I have seen, going beyond the interest of 'Chinese boxes' (112) in *Wuthering Heights* for which he credits Chitham (112). Yet Scott's sense that 'Gilbert Markham is publishing his own love's annals and his wife's journal, to his brother-in-law "Halford"'(111) folds this back into the social psychology of gossip and indiscretion in the novel, rather than tilting it outward (as I am attempting) toward the implied reader's sympathetic reception.

⁸ When Langland first suggests that the frame is there to 'authorize [Markham's] version of events and his interpretation of Helen Graham' (122), bent on converting 'the Fallen Woman and runaway wife of Victorian convention', this sounds like he is seizing the reins of narrative power. But he is only doing so in order to sanction the 'model of excellent womanhood that the novel proposes' in its own inferred sympathies. In this recuperative hermeneutic, the outer narrator is complicit with the narrated subject (Helen) and his own narrator (Brontë) – but only insofar as he has been schooled in their values by the diary she now transfers for our perusal. On the educative function of the diary, as it in fact must precede the interpretive one, see 134-37. Citing other critics besides Langland, Elizabeth Signorotti (1995) seems dubious about the argument that 'Markham's narrative enclosure legitimizes Helen', and prefers instead to think that 'Markham's revealing epistle taught Halford further the means by which Victorian men maintained power over women' (21). In a yet more recent feminist reading that reverses the sense above (n. 9) that Markham's going public with Helen's story is a betrayal, Rachel K. Carnell (1998) draws on Habermas' theories of the public sphere to suggest that Helen has humanized Markham for a return to just that communal arena in his epistolary relation with Halford, forging a commonality ('a bond of affective humanism' [17]) out of private turmoil. One is forgiven for finding the widely differing conclusions of feminist commentary on this novel at times indigestibly divergent.

⁹ Operating in tandem with interpolated attention through direct address, this is the mode of extrapolated inference which organizes many a scene of reading in the examples of Garrett Stewart (1996), where space did not permit more than a passing mention of *Wildfell Hall* in my chapter on Charlotte and Emily Bronte.

¹⁰ This from the novelist who has, just a few chapters earlier, ventriloquized

through her own heroine-diarist a virtual 'deconstruction' (by spelling out) of the Dickensian tag name. Concerning a dreary suitor preferred by her aunt to Huntingdon, so that she was always 'sounding his praises in my ears' (134), Anne takes revenge through her own ear in overexplicitly disclosing him as 'Mr Boarham, by name, Bore'em as I prefer spelling it, for a terrible bore he was' (134). Compare Dickens' schoolmaster M'Choakumchild in *Hard Times*, of whose name not a word more needs saying. Brontë, of course, has a stake in stressing the sensitivity to word sounds of her own reading and writing heroine.

[11] Such was the burden of the commute between micro- and macro-reading in my study of conscripted attention in Victorian fiction: that even the ideological orientation of the audience begins perforce in the coils of linguistic decipherment, the techtonic rock-bottom of all shifting narrative prose.

[12] What I am suggesting is that the particular narrative structure (rather than mere presumption) of a given Victorian fiction can wildly complicate the general schema advanced by Deidre Shauna Lynch (1998), a work meant in part to answer Catherine Gallagher's argument that reading about strictly fictional characters derives its paraeconomic force from their emotional lives being more permeable to sympathy than those of real people, unimpeded by the restrictions of normal propriety – and property rights. Lynch insists instead, or as well, that the imputed existence of such an inner life in the first place, for real and imagined people alike, is only a gradual cultural construction of eighteenth-century market economies and their literary armatures, bent on the individuating (and maximizing) of purchasing drives. For Lynch, the 'inside stories' of subjectivity, harboring the 'inward territories of the unavowed' (213), represent a concerted evolution in the very idea of 'character' as we know it, reciprocally generated and trained in the reading act in such a way that reading redounds to the plausible interiority of civilian subject as well as literary figment. 'We value the characters who, as we say, have taken on lives of their own, even though our faith in their singularity and autonomy is difficult to reconcile with our knowledge that a character exists to be read, that the legibility of the literary character makes it a social experience' (205). It is this condition of legibility, one may say, that the characters of *Wildfell Hall*, undiscussed by Lynch, take into their own hands. 'At the same time, the plot of animation on which we draw to discuss character in these terms indexes our wish to make our novel reading the occasion for our own romantic escapes from the social' (205). And it is that escape which Anne Brontë's plot everywhere frustrates or ironizes. Her fiction also tacitly serves to derive a modern sense of literate subjectivity from the very origins of the novel form in a secularizing of God's providential masterplot. In the transferential dynamics of *Wildfell Hall*, the reciprocity of reading and interiority is therefore less assumed *a priori* than submitted to laboratory testing. Markham is made to sustain his own interiority of response through reading, just as Helen is able to manifest hers only by becoming the heroine of her own diary. Denying himself the culture

of the book, Huntingdon pays a higher price yet to vouch for a soul worthy of damnation, let alone salvation. Instead of being premised on an established bourgeois myth of inwardness, therefore, Brontë's framing mechanics, turned dynamic as we read, might be thought instead to enact the very 'inwardizing' of consciousness in textual encounter.

Works Cited

Berry, Elizabeth Hollis. *Anne Brontë's Radical Vision: Structures of Consciousness.* Victoria: English Literary Studies Monographs, 1994.

Brontë, Anne. *The Tenant of Wildfell Hall.* Ed. Stevie Davies. Harmondsworth: Penguin, 1996.

-----. *Agnes Grey.* London: Wordsworth Editions, 1994.

Brontë, Emily. *Wuthering Heights.* Ed. William M. Sale, Jr. and Richard J. Dunn. New York: Norton, 1990.

Brooks, Peter. *Reading for the Plot: Design and Intention in Narrative.* New York: Knopf, 1984.

-----. *Psychoanalysis and Storytelling.* Oxford: Blackwell, 1994.

Carnell, Rachel K. 'Feminism and the Public Sphere in Anne Bronte's *The Tenant of Wildfell Hall*'. *Nineteenth Century Literature* 53.1 (June 1998): 1-24.

Chitham, Edward, ed. *The Poems of Anne Brontë: A New Text and Commentary.* London: Macmillan, 1979.

Conrad, Joseph. *Heart of Darkness and the Secret Sharer.* New York: Signet, 1983.

Eagleton, Terry. *Myths of Power: A Marxist Study of the Brontës.* London: Macmillan, 1975.

Gallagher, Catherine. *Nobody's Story: The Vanishing Acts of Woman Writers in the Marketplace, 1670-1820* . Berkeley: University of California Press, 1974.

Gérin, Winifred. 'Introduction'. *The Tenant of Wildfell Hall.* Harmondsworth: Penguin, 1979.

Gordon, Jan B. 'Gossip, Diary, Letter, Text: Anne Brontë's Narrative *Tenant* and the Problematic of the Gothic Sequel'. *ELH* 51.4 (Winter 1984): 719-45.

Jacobs, N.M. 'Gender and Layered Narrative in *Wuthering Heights* and *The Tenant of Wildfell Hall*'. *Journal of Literary Technique* 16.3 (Fall 1986): 204-19.

Langland, Elizabeth. *Anne Brontë: The Other One.* London: Macmillan, 1989.

Lynch, Deidre Shauna. *The Economy of Character: Novels, Market Culture, and the Business of Inner Meaning.* Chicago: University of Chicago Press, 1998.

Moore, George. *Conversations in Ebury Street.* 1924. London: Chatto & Windus, 1979.

Prince, Gerald. *Narrative as Theme: Studies in French Fiction,* Lincoln: University of Nebraska Press, 1992.

Sale, William M., Jr. and Richard J. Dunn, eds. 'Biographical Notice of Ellis and Acton Bell (1850)'. *Wuthering Heights.* By Emily Brontë. Norton Critical Ed.

New York: Norton, 317.

Scott, P. J. M. *Anne Brontë: A New Critical Assessment.* London: Vision, 1983.

Signorotti, Elizabeth. "'A Frame Perfect and Glorious": Narrative Structure in Anne
Brontë's *The Tenant of Wildfell Hall*. *Victorian Newsletter* 87 (Spring 1995):
20-25.

Stewart, Garrett. *Dear Reader: The Conscripted Audience of Nineteenth-Century British
Fiction*, Baltimore: Johns Hopkins University Press, 1996.

Chapter 7

'I speak of those I do know': Witnessing as Radical Gesture in *The Tenant of Wildfell Hall*

Deborah Denenholz Morse

In Anne Brontë's *The Tenant of Wildfell Hall* (1848), witnessing is a radical gesture, an act that defies the authority of the patriarchy. Brontë's book – the story of an intelligent, high-minded married woman, Helen Graham, who escapes her alcoholic, philandering upper-class husband to support herself and her young son on her earnings as an artist – serves to bear witness in multiple senses of that term. The meaning of witnessing enlarges as the text progresses, from seeing good and evil played out in the domestic sphere to recounting that vision in order to understand it oneself, and ultimately, to educate others, be they characters within the narrative or readers of the novel itself. To bear witness is to give a firsthand account of what is seen, and not only Anne Brontë herself, but also her heroine Helen Graham and other characters in the novel testify to the truth of what they have perceived. That testimony in Brontë's case is of course written as the novel itself, and in the instance of Helen, much of her testimony is also written, in her own diary and in the framing letter from Gilbert Markham, the man who eventually becomes her second husband. Finally, reading as well as writing becomes a mode of witnessing, as Markham reads Helen's diary before inscribing it as truth into his own private journal, which he then writes down once again in a letter to his brother-in-law Halford. We as readers of Anne Brontë's novel are drawn into the role of witness, as we judge what we read, the truth of Helen's words – and of Brontë's.

Within the written narrative frames of the novel, Helen and others witness to the truth of what they actually see, rather than subscribing to social codings of manners and mores, in particular to the gender ideals of Regency culture, the era in which most of the novel's action is set. The admirable characters in the novel demand openness and vision, rather than the masking and blindness endemic to society's upper classes. The definition of witnessing enlarges further still in the text to signify the legal term assigned to one who provides evidence or testimony in a courtroom. The readership of the novel is asked to judge in lieu of a society that provides no forum for legal redress when women and children suffer the domestic abuses that are chronicled in the novel. As Laura Berry claims in her fine article on *The Tenant of Wildfell Hall* and *Wuthering Heights*,[1] both of these novels are, in an important sense, infused with the same concerns about child custody and the virtual incarceration of wives that filled parliamentary debates both before and after the 1839 Infant Custody Bill. Brontë is concerned with truthfully depicting the injustices of patriarchal culture that are encoded in the very laws of the land. Her book provides the evidence that a married woman could not give in a court of law, since she would be femme covert or 'covered by' the body of her husband, subsumed in his identity. Brontë focuses on the dissipated behavior of upper-class men of the late Regency period in order to reflect with some temporal distancing upon the continuing inequalities of her own mid-Victorian time.

Finally – and for Anne Brontë, most significantly – to witness is to stand up for Christ, to testify to the truth of the Word made flesh. Brontë herself is witnessing to God in the very writing of her book, as her heroine Helen witnesses in the writing of her diary within the novel. The mind of Anne Brontë reflecting upon her own desires and passions – as well as upon her firmly held Christian beliefs – is in part embodied in the mind of Helen as she painstakingly writes the diary that forms the center of the novel both literally and figuratively: both Brontë herself and Helen stand up for Christ, writing their testaments of belief. Brontë's pervasive use of the Bible as the undergirding structure of her novel points to the sacred Word as the legitimating source of her own words, a Law that is above the laws of man and an authority that frees women from the strictures upon them that are imprisoning them under English law. As Stevie Davies asserts, 'Helen's words build on the Word' (Davies xiii).[2] Therefore, as Brontë's own words become infused with the divine force of the Word, her story of resistance to patriarchal law and custom is legitimated, her words constituting a new vision of social and moral possibility.

These testaments are deeply feminist in their critique of male dominance. They are radical documents that witness to a passionately held belief in what the critic Marion Shaw terms 'spiritual egalitarianism' (127), the equality of all Christian souls, male and female, before God. From the outset, Brontë makes it clear, in the 'Preface' to the Second Edition, that she is redefining the writer's art, demanding that it be unfettered by gender expectations:

> in my own mind, I am satisfied that if a book is a good one, it is so whatever the sex of the author may be. All novels are or should be written for both men and women to read, and I am at a loss to conceive how a man should permit himself to write anything that would be really disgraceful to a woman, or why a woman should be censured for writing anything that would be proper and becoming for a man. (5)

When Winifred Gérin stated in her biography of Anne Brontë that some critics had 'denied to the bravest of the Brontës those very qualities of forthrightness and independence which made her novels and poems so startling to the readers of her day and age' (Gérin v), it is Anne Brontë's urgent voice Gérin seems to hear, testifying her belief in a more egalitarian and truly Christian society.

The narrative frame of *The Tenant of Wildfell Hall* implicitly calls all readers as witnesses.[3] The story begins with a letter from the prosperous farmer Gilbert Markham to his friend Halford (his brother-in-law, as we learn at the novel's close); Markham's letter invites Halford (and the reader) to witness past events. The letter itself is an assertion of truth – a witnessing to – events recorded twenty years before in the diary of the novel's heroine, Helen Huntingdon, who is now Gilbert Markham's wife. Markham's letter documents Helen's long-ago diary entries, which he copied at that time into his own private journal. This journal is a personal text witnessing the truth of Helen's own written words, which he has inscribed as truth into his most personal record. The letter to Halford is also an apologia, Markham's attempt not 'to apologize for past offences, but, if possible, to atone for them' (9). Melvin Watson asserts that Halford's identity as brother-in-law 'makes no difference' (108), while Rachel Carnell argues in a recent essay that the Markham-Halford relationship is significant primarily as a figure of the social bond between two educated, propertied men. I suggest, rather, that Markham writes as an act of intimacy and good fellowship between men and brothers-in-law who are temporarily estranged, that he writes to create renewed faith between brothers.[4] In this gesture, Markham demonstrates that he is a generous man, one who has learned something about the necessity of forgiveness and the need to show good will toward men. He writes to 'atone' (9) for what has appeared to Halford as an unwillingness to respond to his own proffered intimacy, 'an unparalled proof of friendly confidence on that memorable occasion', as Markham jokes. The word 'atone' further suggests the Christian connotations of this witnessing, through which Markham at once testifies to his belief in Helen, in the Word, and in Christ's Atonement.

In witnessing Helen's story, the middle-aged, re-educated Markham writes his support of married women under English law.[5] He, like Brontë herself, implicitly questions the legitimacy of laws that usurp women's right to the custody of their children in the face of mistreatment by reprobate fathers, that assign all the wife's earnings to the husband, that give the husband legal right to the body of his wife, even if he abuses her. As Davies eloquently states: 'Helen can call neither her home nor her name her own' (xi). At the novel's close, it is significant that Markham lives and raises his own children at Staningley, his wife's estate, and cedes his own paternal acres at Linden-Car to his reformed younger brother Fergus. Although Carnell sees this gesture as essentially conservative, 'crucial to the stability of the bourgeois public sphere' (18), I think Brontë's intentions here are perhaps more radical. Both in choosing to inhabit his wife's house and in having a younger brother inherit in defiance of primogeniture (and a brother whose very name evokes the rebel Celtic poetic tradition and Brontë's own humble paternal Irish descent), Gilbert Markham symbolically demonstrates that he does not want to be implicated personally in the injustices of English property laws.

A greater rebellion against patriarchal inheritance may be embodied in Helen herself. It is possible that Helen is illegitimate, although she is ultimately an heiress by the end of the novel. In his tour de force book of literary puzzles, *Is Heathcliff a Murderer?*, John Sutherland convincingly argues that Helen is the child of old Squire Lawrence and some unknown woman, 'one of her debauched father's byblows' (77). One might, indeed, dispute even Sutherland's ingenious and logical argumentation; Helen writes in her diary of 'the old hall where he [her brother Frederick Lawrence, the young squire] and I were born and where our mother died' (370). Even so, Sutherland's perception illuminates *The Tenant of Wildfell Hall*. The possibility that Helen is illegitimate focuses a number of struggles she encounters in the text, attempts to legitimate Woman's experience within the 'illegitimate' laws of England, laws that control a woman's right to her property, to her earnings, to her children – and even to her own body. That Helen Graham finally inherits not her husband's nor her father's property but her guardian uncle's – at the bidding of her stalwart Aunt Maxwell nee Lawrence, whose dowry provides the inheritance – serves only to reinforce the sense of the new feminized order that is redefining legitimate inheritance in England.

As Brontë transforms the story of Woman under patriarchy, she re-envisions some of the key stories that underlie English literature and culture: Genesis, *Paradise Lost*, the Arthurian saga. As Davies claims, '*Wildfell Hall* is a feminist manifesto of revolutionary power and intelligence. Helen "Graham" or "Huntingdon" or "Lawrence" stands as an image of unaccommodated woman, in a landscape of biblical texts as well as moorlands and pasture, in which we plainly see that the daughter of woman has nowhere to lay her head' (Davies xi). In particular, the story of the fallen woman is reinterpreted in Brontë's text, reimagined as the story of a motherless girl neglected by her father and later, as a wife and then a mother, abused by her husband. This fallen woman uses her imagination and her indomitable will to plan her escape from her brutal husband, and then to create a life for herself and her young son in the haven of her birthplace, Wildfell Hall, where she will support them both through the fruits of her labor as a professional artist. As Elizabeth Langland states: 'In brief, *The Tenant of Wildfell Hall* rewrites the story of the Fallen Woman as a story of female excellence' (*Anne Brontë* 119). In this new story, Woman is not responsible for the Fall; she is neither sinful Eve to the yet unfallen Adam nor betraying Guinevere to the faithful Arthur. In Brontë's revised cultural narrative, the pastoral Grassdale Manor is already inhabited by a fallen angel, Arthur Huntingdon, who has made it a hell on earth as he drinks and whores and carouses with his libertine friends. This Arthur is very far from being a stainless knight, but is instead first a rakish and then a brutish man whose only goal is the pleasuring of his senses, a man more akin to the utterly sensual Tristram that Tennyson will create more than a decade later in his *Idylls of the King* than to the Christ-like King Arthur. Arthur Huntingdon's son, the Arthur of the next cycle, is redeemed by his mother from a similar fate and lives to marry a new Helen and to live again at a benign Grassdale. His story re-inscribes the quintessential English legend from a feminist perspective.

As a number of critics have pointed out, *The Tenant of Wildfell Hall* also reinterprets an eighteenth-century literary tradition, in particular the epistolary novels of Richardson. Juliet McMaster focuses on the Victorian critique of Regency values, 'certain dominant manners and mores of the preceding generation' (353), while Davies is concerned with the refocusing of authority through the change in narrative mode, from Clarissa's letters to Helen's diary. The theme of a libertine pursuing an innocent young girl who views herself as the means of his salvation is revisioned by Brontë. I would add to McMaster's and Davies' analyses that whereas in *Clarissa*, the heroine is raped and dies, in Wildfell Hall, Helen lives and her husband dies an agonizing death from mortification of a wound – significantly acquired by being thrown from his horse while engaged in one of his predatory sports, hunting. Janet Kunert comments: 'the desired retribution falls upon the body of the male, who has oppressed the heroine by the physical fact of maleness rather than by moral superiority; his mental torment is a result of physical torment. The male's sexually derived dominance is imaged . . . by the horse which he cannot control and which is consequently the agent of his injury'.[6] Rachel Carnell suggests, moreover, that 'Helen escapes Clarissa's fate in part because she is able to teach Gilbert the one thing that Clarissa never manages to teach Lovelace: how to read his moral obligation from her narrative of distress' (16).

Helen's experience is also different from Clarissa's in relation to the vulnerability of her body to rape, although Helen is threatened with rape at one point in the novel. Unlike Clarissa, however, Helen is fully conscious, keenly aware that she is in danger, and that her would-be rapist, the degenerate seducer Hargrave – is completely overwrought: 'I never saw a man so terribly excited' (358), she comments with distancing acuity. Brontë pointedly has Hargrave use the male-defined language of chivalry to defend his brute intentions toward Helen: "'. . . let *me* protect you! . . . I worship you. You are my angel, my divinity!'" (359-60). This language serves as commentary upon the riveting chess game that Hargrave earlier plays so intently with Helen, a game that clearly figures the battle for her body and soul; he tells Helen that "'it is those bishops that trouble me . . . but the bold knight can overleap the reverend gentleman'" (300).

Yet Hargrave does not succeed in his efforts at seduction. Against his suggestion that she can quell her conscience by pleading feminine passivity – "'if your conscience upbraid you for it, say I overcame you and you could not choose but yield!'" – Helen defends herself with her palette knife, an instrument of her female art. It is significant that Helen has transformed the library into her own studio, the location in which she produces the landscape paintings she hopes will provide her with the money to escape Grassdale's tortures. She has created her workspace, the place in which she generates rebellious female art, within a library that is filled with books written by men. Moreover, all these books are owned, as the library itself of course is owned – as she herself by law is owned – by Huntingdon. Her defense of her person with a tool of her art symbolizes the strength and power of female art, and its ability to reconstruct civilization out of the coarsest brutalities.

Helen Graham is an artist, like her creator, the novelist and poet Anne Brontë. Helen's narrative is, on one level, a story of the female artist, as Sandra Gilbert and Susan Gubar argue. Brontë reimagines the story of the female artist – the woman constructed by her society as 'unnatural', a woman who creates rather than procreates – in part by making her a mother. When Helen is driven from her husband's home at Grassdale Manor by his philandering and drunkenness, it is her responsibility to her child that motivates her decision to escape from Huntingdon's tyranny: 'I could endure it for myself, but for my son it must be borne no longer' (352). Once safely harbored, symbolically, at her birthplace Wildfell Hall, having taken her mother's name of Graham and assumed the new identity of a widow, she writes of the income she is earning from the sale of her paintings: 'I am working hard to repay my brother for all his expenses on my account. . . . I shall have so much more pleasure in my labour, my earnings, my frugal fare, and household economy, when I know that I am paying my way honestly, and that what little I possess is legitimately all my own; and that no one suffers for my folly – in a pecuniary way at least' (397-98). As Julia Gergits points out: 'Ironically, she is incorrect in assuming that what she earns is "legitimately all" her own; legally everything she earns is her husband's property. Caught up in the illusion of escape, she forgets just how tightly she is bound to Arthur Huntingdon' (116).

Huntingdon destroys the implements of her art because he has discovered that they are the means for her to support herself and their son, and thus to liberate herself from being 'a slave, a prisoner' (366). In a critical scene, Helen witnesses Huntingdon reading her diary, which he has 'forcibly wrested' from her just after she has written about Hargrave's attempted rape and Huntingdon's disowning of his marital bond ("'My wife? What wife? I have no wife . . .'" [355]) that instigates Hargrave's outrage, since Huntingdon offers Helen to "'any one among you, that can fancy her'" (355). Huntingdon discovers Helen's plan of escape through reading her diary; he proceeds to burn her painting materials and takes away her money and jewels as well. But Huntingdon does not take into account the resiliency of the female artist. With the help of her brother and the servant Rachel, with whom Helen has a lifelong friendship, Helen escapes to

Wildfell Hall, where she resumes her painting in a new studio. As she is disabused of her early faith in Huntingdon, and of her belief that she can – as she assures her Aunt Maxwell – depend on 'his natural goodness' (149) despite the 'thoughtlessness' (177) she at first deprecates, Helen comes to rely on Christian principles to curb wild Nature. She was attracted to Huntingdon in the first place because of his rebellious Romantic qualities, in particular the erotic promise that relieves her from the company of the aptly named Mr Boarham and the restraints of her aunt's too prosaic views on marriage. When Aunt Maxwell tells her that she has heard Huntingdon spoken of by Helen's uncle as "'a bit wildish'", Helen asks for a definition of this phrase, and is answered, "'It means destitute of principle, and prone to every vice common to youth'" (135-36).   She learns through bitter experience what 'a bit wildish' signifies, and finally understands fully the dark results of men's unbridled nature.   As Gilbert and Gubar state: 'Helen pays for her initial attraction by watching her husband metamorphose from a fallen angel into a fiend, as he relentlessly and self-destructively pursues a diabolical career of gaming, whoring, and drinking' (81-82).

As she is reeducated, Helen's understanding of the role of female savior to men that cultural ideals of womanhood have enjoined upon her is also changed. Before her marriage to Arthur, Helen declares to her aunt that "'if he has done amiss, I shall consider my life well spent in saving him from the consequences of his early errors, and striving to recall him to the path of virtue – God grant me success!'" (150). Ultimately, at her husband's deathbed, she realizes that only he can save himself by imploring forgiveness from the one Savior.   When Huntingdon desperately implores her – "'Helen, you must save me!'" – she knows that she cannot assume the role of savior: 'And he earnestly seized my hand, and looked into my face with such imploring eagerness that my heart bled for him, and I could not speak for tears' (441).

Helen's new vision profoundly affects her art. Her paintings reflect her maturing consciousness as they move from the beatific vision of Nature and human nature embodied in her early, conventionalized allegorical painting and decorative miniatures to increasingly realistic portraiture, and finally to representational landscapes that strive for the authenticity of verisimilitude until, as Margaret Berg states, 'Helen, like Anne, is committed to a more literal and objective recording of external reality' (14).[7] The adoring portrait of the handsome, sensual young Huntingdon that she paints during her early days of worshipping his beauty and erotic energy is, significantly, turned 'with its face to the wall' (48) in Helen's Wildfell Hall studio, and Helen writes pragmatically that 'the frame . . . is handsome enough; it will serve for another painting' (393). Helen's art – like Anne's – now witnesses to the truth of her perceptions.

An early painting of Helen's that is described in detail is a conventionalized allegory of young womanhood that she is painting during Huntingdon's courtship. The work depicts 'an amorous pair of turtle doves' near 'a young girl . . . kneeling on the daisy-spangled turf, with head thrown back and masses of fair hair falling on her shoulders, her hands clasped, lips parted, and eyes intently gazing upward in pleased, yet earnest contemplation of those feathered lovers – too deeply absorbed in each other to notice her' (159). Huntingdon sees Helen and the painting, and springs through the window – significantly, with gun in hand. While he has been slaughtering animals, engaged in predation, Helen has been depicting an idyllic Nature. Huntingdon comments on the painting:

> 'Very pretty, i'faith!' . . . and a very fitting study for a young lady – Spring just opening into summer – morning just approaching noon – girlhood just ripening into womanhood – and hope just verging on fruition. She's a sweet creature! but why didn't you make her black hair?'
>
> 'I thought light hair would suit her better. You see I have made her blue-eyed, and plump, and fair and rosy'.
>
> 'Upon my word – a very Hebe! I should fall in love with her, if I hadn't the artist before me. Sweet innocent! she's thinking there will come a time when she will be wooed and won like that pretty hen-dove, by as fond and fervent a lover; and she's thinking how pleasant it will be, and how tender and faithful he will find her'.
>
> 'And perhaps, suggested I, 'how tender and faithful she shall find him'.
>
> 'Perhaps – for there is no limit to the wild extravagance of hope's imaginings, at such an age'. (160)[8]

Although Helen chooses to believe in Huntingdon's good nature at this point despite his jaded remarks, she soon comes to recognize the truth about uncurbed natures. Davies states, 'Anne Brontë's novel is a powerful and disputatious sister-novel to Emily Brontë's *Wuthering Heights*' (ix). However, this 'kinship' also serves as critique by Anne's reformist, explicitly Christian text of Emily's Romanticism as it is embodied in *Wuthering Heights*. Anne does not imagine the touchstone of Romantic thought – experience liberated – as the heady dash out on the moors of Catherine and Heathcliff that Emily visions in *Wuthering Heights* nor the yearning for transcendence that Catherine's "'I will be incomparably beyond and above you all'" voices to the uncomprehending Nelly Dean. There is no shepherd boy's vision of 'Heathcliff and a woman yonder, under t' nab' at Wildfell Hall's close, no promise of an earthly paradise in which ghost lovers profanely wander and the Romantic Agony is vibrantly consummated.

In Anne's novel, civilization is necessary rather than corrupting, and the heroes of this novel are those who are 'guides' through the 'weary mazes' (325) of this world rather than 'tempters' who lure others on to sin. The heroes are like Helen Graham, who serves as nurturer and moral teacher to her son Arthur and to Gilbert Markham, as Gilbert later does to Halford and to his own and Helen's children, 'the promising scions that are growing up about us' (488). If there is a corollary to the story of Helen and Gilbert in Emily's novel, it is the story of the second Cathy and Hareton, of civilization brought with a book and a kiss of forgiveness. In both stories, passion is ultimately tempered, but in Anne's text the precepts are more explicitly Christian.

The Romantic primitive, in *Wildfell Hall*, is embodied in the increasingly bestial actions of Helen's alcoholic, philandering husband Arthur Huntingdon and his degraded companions at Grassdale Manor. There is no Heathcliff in this text, with his erotic glamor and the agonized faithfulness that impels him over twenty years' time. Moreover, civilization itself is viewed as a good, rather than Wordsworth's 'shades of the prison house' that 'close upon the growing boy'. Civilization is the key that will unlock the prison of degradation that the wholly 'natural' man will inevitably create for himself and others. Books – especially the Bible – are the vehicle of this civilizing process, which is enacted in Anne Brontë's book itself, the work of an artist who insistently incorporates the Word within her own words in order to provide a story that morally educates us through Art while creating her own feminist testament.

Helen, enmeshed in a marriage with the degraded brute Huntingdon, increasingly comes to view untamed nature not with joy, but with fear. Eventually, she names spring as 'the dreaded time', 'the rutting season' in which her husband spends his seed not in fertile rural scenes but in the most decadent haunts of the city, and then brings his cronies back to the pastoral-named Grassdale Manor and transforms it into a scene of debauchery. The formerly innocent and idealistic Helen comes to know that Nature – and human nature, including her own – must be confronted as they in truth are, not as one might wish them to be. She is increasingly aware that the evil tendencies in human nature must be rooted out, and the good seeds encouraged to flourish. As most critics have noted, Brontë's book argues for the singular importance of childrearing in creating a moral human being, one who has self-discipline as well as imaginative empathy.[9]

Indeed, one of the first acts of witnessing we encounter is the fervent discussion of childrearing at the Markham's party, in Chapter Three, 'A Controversy'. Marion Shaw argues in her thoughtful essay, 'Anne Brontë: A Quiet Feminist', that it was Anne's intimate exposure to Branwell's alcoholism and tragic demise that most influenced her portrayal of the destructive effects of 'the upbringing of children, particularly the upbringing of boys. What constitutes true manliness and womanliness in the formation of Christian character during childhood, and what mistakenly passes for these attributes, bring forth Anne's most heartfelt and independent views in her novels' (126). Throughout *Wildfell Hall*, Brontë argues for an ungendered and Christian upbringing for children of both sexes. As she does in her earlier novel *Agnes Grey*, in *Wildfell Hall* Brontë delineates the damage wrought by an idea of manliness that dictates the trampling of 'petticoat government' (*Agnes Grey* 105) and teaches a boy 'to despise his mother's authority and affection' (*Wildfell Hall* 32) while it celebrates the 'manly' virtues of licentiousness, drunkenness, and predation.

In the scene in question, Helen has brought her young son Arthur to a party at Linden-Car, the Markhams' farm. The widow Mrs Graham – as Helen is known in the first section of the story, which tells of her life in the months immediately following her escape from her husband – has just told the gathering that little Arthur '"detests the very sight of wine"'. She has described her method of making him hate alcohol and spirits by taking it '"by way of medicine when he was sick, and in fact, I have done what I could to make him hate them"'. All of Mrs Graham's listeners criticize her actions. Educated to believe that boys should be tough and experienced, they are convinced that she is coddling Arthur; as Mrs Markham avers: '"The poor child will be the veriest milksop that ever was sopped! Only think what a man you will make of him, if you persist"'.

Gilbert argues for an upbringing that will, in his view, lead to stalwart manliness. At this point of the story, he is newly acquainted with the pretty, sober Mrs Graham, but nevertheless tries to convince her that '"if you would have your son to walk honourably through the world, you must not attempt to clear the stones from his path, but teach him to walk firmly over them – not insist upon leading him by the hand, but let him learn to go alone"'. Helen insists that she will herself be her son's guide: '"I will lead him by the hand, Mr Markham, till he has strength to go alone"' (31). Helen goes on to question: '"And why should I take it for granted that my son will be one in a thousand? – and not rather prepare for the worst, and suppose he will be like his – like the rest of mankind, unless I take care to prevent it?"' When Gilbert takes her statement personally – '"You are very complimentary to us all"' – Helen explains that

> 'I know nothing about you – I speak of those I do know – and when I see the whole race of mankind (with a few rare exceptions) stumbling and blundering along the path of life, sinking into every pitfall, and breaking their skins over every impediment that lies in their way, shall I not use all the means in my power to ensure for him, a smoother and a safer passage?' (32)

Helen seems here to be like the Warrior Greatheart in Bunyan's *Pilgrim's Progress*, a text that was central to her sister Charlotte's art as well. Like the St. John Rivers Jane reimagines as Bunyan's Greatheart at the end of *Jane Eyre*, Helen assumes responsibility for other Christian souls as a part of her Christian duty; unlike St. John, she begins with her own child and herself, and extends her circle slowly, while he must restlessly proselytize with missionary zeal in India, in pursuit of his own 'incorruptible crown'.

As Helen speaks of 'what I do know – and when I see', she is witnessing to the truth of her experience in the hell of her marriage with the dipsomaniac, profligate Arthur Huntingdon, a fact that neither the first-time reader of this passage nor the others at the party know. She feels compelled not only to act according to this truth, but also to voice the lessons she has learned. When Gilbert goes on to support his mother's assertion that Mrs Graham will make "'a mere Miss Nancy'" (33) out of young Arthur and to argue for gendered nurturance, Helen completely overwhelms him with the force of her logical argumentation. She claims:

> 'I would have both so to benefit by the experience of others, and the precepts of a higher authority, that they should know beforehand to refuse the evil and choose the good, and require no experimental proofs to teach them the evil of transgression. I would not send a poor girl into the world, unarmed against her foes, and ignorant of the snares that beset her path: nor would I watch and guard her, till, deprived of self-respect and self-reliance, she lost the power, or the will, to watch and guard herself; – and as for my son – if I thought he would grow up to be what you call a man of the world – one that has 'seen life', and glories in his experience, even though he should so far profit by it, as to sober down, at length, into a useful and respected member of society – I would rather that he died tomorrow! – rather a thousand times!' (34-35)

Helen's horror of what she has seen at Grassdale causes her to speak in rather disturbing hyperbole. However, her scarifying experiences have made clear for Helen that worldly codes of manliness are in truth license in the guise of liberty, that to be a 'man of the world' is the opposite of being a child of God, and that the man who claims to have "'seen life" and glories in his experience' is becoming a devil who works against the Life and the Glory of God. Her speech thus witnesses to an ideal of ungendered nurturance. Although Helen is presented in the novel in all possible roles of womanhood – maid, wife, mother, widow, ostensible fallen woman/mistress, the heroine of *The Tenant of Wildfell Hall* is most overtly a mother. Helen, in her maternal role, fervently argues for a new mode of childrearing that acknowledges the minds and spirits of male and female children are equal, and equally susceptible to influences from the fallen world of experience. Moreover, Brontë testifies her belief that all children of either sex are bound to obey the 'precepts of a higher authority' – moral laws that take no account of gender.

While Helen's words provide witness to her experience in this scene, there are other modes of witnessing that require action as well as speech. A later scene of witnessing occurs when Helen finds herself an unwilling observer of what Huntingdon calls 'a regular jollification' (270) in the ironically titled chapter 'Social Virtues'. As Helen watches the drunken sports of her husband and his friends, she is dismayed by 'the riotous uproar' with which they enter the drawingroom and join the ladies. After watching the besotted misogynist Grimsby pour cream into his saucer and put six lumps of sugar into his tea, the ridiculous, childish actions of the men become more rowdy and ultimately violent. Lord Lowborough, a reformed member of the circle who now abstains from drink, has just been derided by his wife Annabella for joining the women in the drawingroom before the other men, implicitly accused of unmanliness in his avoidance of what Annabella views as male camaraderie. Lord Lowborough departs in great – and justified – distress at his wife's reproof. 'Such scenes as this are always disagreeable to witness. Our little party was completely silenced for a moment' (271), Helen writes. She then tries to make Annabella see her mistake in berating rather than praising her husband's temperance, but to no avail. When Lord Lowborough rejoins the group as the men enter, he asks his wife bitterly, quoting her own words back to her, '"which of these three 'bold, manly spirits' would you have me to resemble?"' Helen tries to support Lord Lowborough's abstinence by first arguing with Annabella and then courteously offering '"a hope his lordship will condescend to sit down with us, such as we are, and allow me to give him some tea"' (276).

Helen finds that her voice alone does not suffice. She forces herself physically to intervene when Lord Lowborough is abused, as the ruffian Hattersley demands that Lowborough drink with them all, and 'there followed a disgraceful contest' (276). When Hattersley asks for aid on his side, the debauched Huntingdon is helpless with 'imbecile laughter'. No one will help Lowborough, who is fighting desperately. He asks Annabella for a candle: '"I shall take no part in your rude sports"' replied the lady, coldly drawing back, '"I wonder you can expect it"' (277). In a signal moment, Helen tells us that '"I snatched up a candle and brought it to him. He took it and held the flame to Hattersley's hands till, roaring like a wild beast, the latter unclasped them and let him go"' (277). In taking up the candle, Helen has acknowledged her support of Lowborough's defiance, his rebellion against the codes of manliness that promote the anarchy at Grassdale. Symbolically, she takes up the light against the darkness, and although in this context the candle might seem only a part of the general hellfire at Grassdale Manor, Helen's defense of Lowborough is an act of resistance on her part as well as his.

Helen's witnessing of Lord Lowborough's reform is a touchstone for the novel. Lowborough is a dark, near-Byronic figure who ends up renouncing all his former 'manly' vices and addictions, divorcing his adulterous wife, and marrying a woman of 'genuine good sense, unswerving integrity, active piety, warm-hearted benevolence, and a fund of cheerful spirits' (457). A key scene in relation to Lowborough's reformation occurs just after he has learned of Annabella's liaison with Huntingdon. Lowborough confronts Helen, and she admits that she has known of his wife's illicit connection with her husband for two years. Lowborough accuses her: "'You knew it!'" cried he with bitter vehemence. – "'and you did not tell me! You helped to deceive me!'" Although Helen defends herself from the last accusation – "'My lord, I did not deceive you'" – she later writes in her diary that 'I felt like a criminal' (341). Although she did not at first speak to Lord Lowborough about his wife's infidelity, she acknowledges to him in this scene – and later, again, by writing of the encounter in her diary – that she was misguided: 'I confess I was wrong . . . but whether want of courage or mistaken kindness was the cause of my error, I think you judge me too severely' (342). Helen's explanations of her own feelings and the warning she has only recently given Annabella instigate some responsive sympathy at last in the wretched Lowborough: "'You too have suffered, I suppose'", to which Helen replies, "'I suffered much, at first'" (343).

Helen's empathy with Lowborough's crisis takes a compelling turn that extends the boundaries of witnessing in Brontë's text. As Lowborough grapples with the knowledge of his wife's betrayal, Helen lies awake most of the night, imagining the sufferings of the man she can hear but cannot see:

> I know not how she passed the night, but I lay awake the greater part of it listening to his heavy step pacing monotonously up and down his dressing-room, which was nearest my chamber. Once I heard him pause and throw something out of the window, with a passionate ejaculation; and in the morning, after they were gone, a keen-bladed clasp-knife was found on the grass-plot below; a razor, likewise, was snapped in two and thrust deep into the cinders of the grate, but partially corroded by the decaying embers. So strong had been the temptation to end his miserable life, so determined his resolution to resist it. (346)

Helen's description of the tortures that Lowborough endures – in particular, his refusal to commit suicide – define a new heroism that she is quick to appreciate at its full value, commiserating with his agony and longing to assuage it. Helen writes that 'My heart bled for him . . . now I forgot my own afflictions, and thought only of his'. She realizes that all his friends mock him as a cuckold, that he 'is an object of scorn to his friends and the nice-judging world.

The false wife and the treacherous friend who have wronged him are not so despised and degraded as he, and his refusal to avenge his wrongs has removed him yet farther beyond the range of sympathy, and blackened his name with a deeper disgrace' (346-47). Although Lowborough is judged by the world to be unmanly both for the supposed lack of sexual force that has driven Annabella to Huntingdon and for Lowborough's refusal to engage in a duel to 'avenge his wrongs', Helen declares that he is a worthy exemplar in God's sight. In one of the most eloquent passages in the novel, Helen describes her imagined witnessing of Lowborough's painful heroics of survival, identifying his struggle with her own experience of suffering:

> He knows that God is just, but cannot see his justice now: he knows this life is short, and yet death seems insufferably far away; he believes there is a future state, but so absorbing is the agony of this that he cannot realize its rapturous repose. He can but bow his head to the storm, and cling, blindly, despairingly, to what he knows to be right. Like the shipwrecked mariner cleaving to a raft, blinded, deafened, bewildered, he feels the waves sweep over him, and sees no prospect of escape; and yet he knows he has no hope but this, and still, while life and sense remain, concentrates all his energies to keep it. Oh, that I had a friend's right to comfort him, and tell him that I never esteemed him so highly as I do this night! (347)[10]

The only member of Huntingdon's dissolute cronies other than Lowborough who eventually reforms is Lowborough's tormentor in the 'candle' episode, Ralph Hattersley. Although most of Lowborough's reformation occurs offstage, the very moment that decides Hattersley's altered mode of life is portrayed in great detail. In this scene, the method of reformation is instructive: After trying to convince Hattersley that his reckless mode of life is deeply affecting his wife and children, Helen provides as evidence two letters written by her beloved friend Milicent to her husband, 'one dated from London and written during one of his wildest seasons of reckless dissipation; the other in the country during a lucid interval' (380):

> The latter was full of hope and joy, yet with a trembling consciousness that this happiness would not last; praising his goodness to the skies, but with an evident, though but half-expressed wish that it were based on a surer foundation than the natural impulses of the heart, and a half prophetic dread of the fall of that house so founded on the sand – which fall had shortly after taken place, as Hattersley must have been conscious while

he read.

Almost at the commencement of the first letter, I had the unexpected pleasure of seeing him blush; but he immediately turned his back to me and finished the perusal at the window. At the second, I saw him, once or twice, raise his hand and hurriedly pass it across his face. Could it be to dash away a tear? (380)

It is significant that Hattersley's reformation begins in the earlier scene in which he agrees to witness to Helen's truth in the aftermath of Hargrave's attempted rape of her as she paints in the library she has reconstructed as studio. The full significance of witnessing to the truth is represented in this dramatic scene. Reviled by the misogynist Grimsby and accused by her husband, Helen turns to Hattersley, the husband of her best friend Milicent. Helen appeals to Hattersley to speak the truth of what happened between her and Hargrave, and he agrees to be her witness – an event that marks the beginning of his own moving reformation. Afterwards, Helen writes in her diary:

What could possess me to make such a request of such a man? There was no other to preserve my name from being blackened and aspersed among this nest of boon companions, and through them, perhaps into the world; and beside my abandoned wretch of a husband, the base, malignant Grimsby, and the false villain Hargrave, this boarish ruffian, coarse and brutal as he was, shone like a glow-worm in the dark, among its fellow worms. . . . Could I ever have imagined that I should be doomed to bear such insults under my own roof – to hear such things spoken in my presence – nay spoken to me and of me – and by those who arrogated to themselves the name of gentlemen? (361)

There is a connection among Helen's identity as artist, Helen as diarist of the truth, Hattersley's oath to defend Helen's word, and Milicent's letters to Helen, which reveal Milicent's suffering and Hattersley's shame through the truth of sororal discourse. The letters are a woman's writing – like Helen's diary and Anne Brontë's novel – and through each layer of women's writing, the truth is revealed. Hattersley's reformation comes, indeed, with the force of revelation. He feels his sorrow through the body – Helen sees the strong, burly Hattersley blush and cry – and the knowledge of his past sins takes firm hold upon his soul. As Davies comments: 'Hattersley's tears . . . have a yet larger significance: in Christian iconography, tears are signs of contrition, denoting the melting of the heart so that work of Grace and redemption can take place' (528).

We learn that Hattersley's reformation is permanent. With

acknowledgement of his own sins, he becomes more compassionate; Hattersley is the only friend who bothers to travel to the bedside of the dying Huntingdon, whose gruesome death confirms Hattersley in his new, reformed course. He is a bedside witness, along with Helen, of the painful, lingering death Huntingdon suffers. At the novel's end, we learn that after Huntingdon's horrible demise, Hattersley 'never needed another lesson of the kind. Avoiding the temptations of the town, he continued to his life in the country immersed in the usual pursuits of a hearty, active country gentleman. . . . I need not tell you that Ralph Hattersley, Esqr., is celebrated throughout the country for his noble breed of horses' (457-58).

While Hattersley eventually gets control over the animal within his own nature, as his successful breeding of horses symbolizes, Huntingdon becomes increasingly brutish, defined by his animal nature. The scene that Helen witnesses, as Arthur and Lady Lowborough profess their illicit love in the shrubberies outside Grassdale Manor, symbolizes Arthur's identification with untamed nature and his unwillingness to bridle his animal passions.

The scene intentionally begins with a description suggestive of Romantic iconography: 'the moon rising over the clump of tall, dark elm-trees'. Helen is watching this scene, and she is also looking at Arthur – who is, she surmises, 'so sentimental as to stand without, leaning against the outer pillar of the portico, apparently watching it too' (195). In this scene, the natural world is not a Romantic vision of an inherently benign and divinely infused place, for Arthur in fact is on the lookout for his mistress Annabella, with whom he has a profane assignation in the shrubbery. Helen meets him instead, and rejoices over his having turned over a new leaf, as evidenced in his more temperate drinking. (In fact, he has only temporarily become more abstemious, in response to Annabella's warnings that he will lose his good looks; he is briefly more sober only out of lust and vanity rather than out of any changed moral view.) He sends Helen away from him with the belief that all might still be well with her marriage, and in 'her new-found happiness and revival of hope and love' (296-97), after which she lights up the gathering assembled at Grassdale, making it, as she now thinks, 'a very merry, innocent, and entertaining party' (297).

The bitter irony of Helen's assessment becomes manifest two days later, when she witnesses Arthur and Annabella exchanging lover's vows in the very same shrubbery in which she joyfully met Arthur. In this second scene in the shrubbery, however, Nature is imbued with the Christian sacred as Helen prays to God for strength to endure. In this prayer, Helen witnesses to her belief in God even in the very midst of her agony, testifying to her belief, finally, in the repetition of Christ's own words:

> 'God help me now!' I murmured, sinking on my knees
> among the damp weeds and brushwood that surrounded me, and

looking up at the moonlit sky, through the scant foliage above. It
seemed all dim and quivering now to my darkened sight. My
burning, bursting heart strove to pour forth its agony to God, but
could not frame its anguish into prayer; until a gust of wind swept
over me, which, while it scattered the dead leaves, like blighted
hopes, around, cooled my forehead, and seemed a little to revive
my sinking frame. Then, while I lifted up my soul in speechless,
earnest supplication, some heavenly influence seemed to
strengthen me within. I breathed more freely; my vision cleared;
I saw distinctly the pure moon shining on, and the light clouds
skimming the clear, dark sky; and then, I saw the eternal stars
twinkling down upon me; I knew their God was mine, and He
was strong to save and swift to hear. 'I will never leave thee, nor
forsake thee', seemed whispered from above their myriad orbs.
No, no; I felt He would not leave me comfortless: in spite of
earth and hell I should have strength for all my trials, and win a
glorious rest at last! (303-04)

Fortified with her belief in God and in her own strength and endurance,
Helen easily parries Arthur's attempts to lie about his affair with Annabella. When
he vehemently tries to deny her accusations of infidelity, she cuts him short,
declaring: "'Spare yourself the trouble of forswearing yourself and racking your
brains to stifle truth with falsehood . . . I have trusted to the testimony of no third
person. I was in the shrubbery this evening, and I saw and heard for myself'"
(305). After this speech, Helen finally admits to her diary that her own husband is
'my greatest enemy' (308).

In contrast to Helen's powerful use of words, Huntingdon is ultimately
barely able to sign his own name. Helen has come to nurse the very ill
Huntingdon, and insists that he cannot see young Arthur until "'you have
promised to leave him entirely under my care and protection'". Huntingdon
promises to comply – "'I swear it, as God is in heaven!'" – but Helen has had
more than enough of false witness. She states: "'But I cannot trust your oaths
and promises: I must have a written agreement, and you must sign it in presence
of a witness'". Huntingdon demurs, pleading 'inability to hold the pen' and
declares that 'he had not the power to form the letters' (426). Although his
inability to write is at least in part manipulative, a forestalling tactic, Brontë also
wants to suggest that Huntingdon has lost control over language as a
consequence of his demise into the animal. This scene is also important because
Huntingdon's sickroom at Grassdale becomes a kind of courtroom, a reimagined
place where it is possible for a mother to wrest legal custody of her child away
from a dissolute father. In writing, Huntingdon must cede his authority over his
child to his wife, although the laws of the land write him still as proper custodian

of his son. However, as the faithful servant Rachel and Helen witness, Huntingdon finally 'managed to ratify the agreement' (426).

In her descriptions of the natural world, at certain moments in Brontë's narrative, the rose serves as a kind of witness, a symbol through which Anne Brontë figures and examines the nature of love. The first passage, involving the seducer Walter Hargrave,[11] is prefaced by a scene of seduction in which Helen has been lulled by Hargrave's recent good behavior to trust his restraint. She thus allows him to walk with her in the park at Grassdale on a spring evening, and while they are 'gazing on the calm, blue water', he 'suddenly electrified me' by trying to seduce her with 'all the bold yet artful eloquence he could summon to his aid' (326-27). There is a sense here, as in the chess game scene, that what is at stake is Helen's soul. In this garden at Grassdale, Brontë portrays Hargrave's attempted seduction as a thwarted reenactment of the Fall. After many weeks, he returns and is in another garden – this one at his own home, the Grove – when his sister Esther asks him to get a rose for 'Mrs Huntingdon'. Hargrave returns with a moss rose, which, in his offended state, he tries to give to his sister rather than to Helen. Esther calls him a 'blockhead', takes the rose from Hargrave and gives it to Helen. Innocently, Esther has served as a kind of pander between her brother and the married woman who is her best friend, as the moss rose symbolizes unsanctioned love and nature unrestrained, the unbridled passion that Hargrave later tries to enforce upon Helen when he nearly rapes her in Grassdale's library.

At the close of the novel, Helen's transformed vision of nature is embodied in the Christmas rose, symbolizing a union of nature with Christianity. This scene of proposal can be viewed as a revision of the previous moss rose scene, a kind of witnessing to the love of Helen and Gilbert Markham, with the Christmas rose itself as visible emblem of their love.[12] Unlike the red, luscious, and many-petaled moss rose, the Christmas rose is white, and has only five petals; it is a very simple, pure, and hardy rose. As Helen tells Markham: '"This rose is not as fragrant as a summer flower, but it has stood through hardships none of them could bear. . . . Will you have it?"' (482). Yet Markham does not at first understand Helen's request, and 'she laid the rose across my palm, but I scarcely closed my fingers upon it, so deeply was I absorbed in thinking about what might be the meaning of her words' (483). Ultimately, Helen needs to spell out her meaning, verbally to bear witness to her love: '"The rose I gave you was an emblem of my heart"' (483).

Markham's education from the young coxcomb he was at the novel's outset to the self-deprecating man of the Christmas rose scene is reflected in his self-reprimand, 'Stupid blockhead that I was!'. Markham acknowledges that he needs to learn to read the feminine more perceptively, but in a sense, his very tentativeness argues that he has read Helen's diary narrative well, and that he refuses to enforce himself upon her, to prey upon her as did Huntingdon and

Hargrave. This sense that he should not intrude upon Helen's privacy is evidenced much earlier, as he longs to read the sections of her diary that refer to his relationship with her, but decides 'no, I had no right to see it: all this was too sacred for any eyes but her own, and she had done well to keep it from me' (396). This acknowledgment of Helen's right to her thoughts, her writing – implicitly, to her art – must be read against Huntingdon's previous violent wresting of Helen's diary from her, and his unauthorized reading of its contents as prelude to devilishly burning the very materials of her art.

Markham has come a very long way indeed from the scene of brutality that we witness early on in the novel, in which he knocks Frederick Lawrence off his horse in a jealous rage. This scene of primitive anger, in which Markham, 'impelled by some fiend at my elbow', hits Lawrence with the metal horse atop his whip and looks at the resulting damage to his foe with 'savage satisfaction' (116) is an evidence of fallen natural man uncurbed by moral precepts. This fierce blow to his supposed enemy – Markham thinks that Helen's brother Lawrence is her lover – explicitly follows a scene in which Romantic iconography of moonlit darkness impels Markham to return to the garden at Wildfell Hall and look over the garden wall. Markham thinks that he witnesses a lovers' tryst; the reading of Helen's diary disabuses him of this false interpretation. From being convinced of her guilt and spurning her in consequence, Markham becomes – like Hattersley when he swears to defend Helen's honor – a witness for truth. He ultimately vindicates her name to his sister Rose: 'it was now in my power to clear her name from every foul aspersion' (437). Concomitantly, Markham serves as witness against the malicious slander of Jane Wilson, whom Lawrence has ideas of marrying; Markham tells him that "'her delight was, and still is, to blacken your sister's character to the utmost of her power without risking too greatly the exposure of her own malevolence!'" (417).

Helen's explicitly Christian, civilizing force is aligned with her decidedly feminine brother, Lawrence, whose body is damaged by the phallic whipping he receives from the sexually frustrated Markham. Lawrence's 'slender white fingers, so marvelously like her [Helen's] own, considering he was not a woman' (413) as Markham fondly notes, at last grasp the hand in marriage of the most feminist of the novel's women, Esther Hargrave.[13] Esther, named after the biblical savior of her people, symbolizes a wiser version of the young Helen. Esther is the sister of both Helen's closest friend and bridesmaid, the Christ-like Milicent, and Helen's would-be seducer, the 'tempter' Walter. Esther's feminist values – forged in despite of her elder sister's suffering in an abusive union and her brother's profane disregard of the marriage sacrament in his four-year pursuit of the married Helen – bode well for the next generation of women. The marriage of Esther and Lawrence offers an egalitarian relation in contrast to Helen's own oppressive bond with Huntingdon.

Helen's own Christian and feminist values will eventually recreate even

Grassdale Manor. She and Markham reside with the pious Aunt Maxwell at Staningley, now Helen's property, while young Arthur Huntingdon in time marries Helen Hattersley, daughter of Milicent and the reformed wild ruffian Ralph Hattersley. This second-generation Arthur-Helen union reenacts the first marriage, perhaps symbolically redeeming it and certainly returning Grassdale Manor to a civilized state. Like the prospective marriage of the second Cathy and Hareton at the close of Wuthering Heights, this love relationship does the work of reparation.

Paradise is not regained. Anne gives us neither the savage earthly paradise that Emily's Heathcliff and Catherine inhabit in Romantic ecstasy on the moors of *Wuthering Heights* nor a foreshadowing of the 'erotic faith'[14] expressed in the apocalyptic promise of the storm and shipwreck at the end of Charlotte's *Villette*, written several years after Anne's death. Perhaps the restoration of Grassdale is most akin to the transformation of Ferndean, once a hunting lodge, into the feminine retreat in which Rochester secludes himself after the burning of the patriarchal estate, the battlemented Thornfield, in Charlotte's *Jane Eyre*.

In the final sentence of the text, Markham invites Halford to visit Staningley, to leave the 'dusty, smoky, noisy, toiling, striving city for a season of invigorating relaxation and social retirement with us'. *The Tenant of Wildfell Hall* does not end with the Romantic promise of the return to Eden, but rather with a recognition of the possibilities for community when primitive Nature is restrained by Christian love.[15]

Notes

[1] See Laura C. Berry.

[2] See Stevie Davies' introduction to *The Tenant of Wildfell Hall* (xiii). All quotations from the novel are from this edition.

[3] A number of recent articles discuss the narrative mode of Brontë's text. Most of these essays are in tension with George Moore's *Conversations in Ebury Street*, in which he states that the frame narrative is a mistake, a 'clumsy' break in what might have been a 'passionate and original love story' (216). Another exceptional view is stated by W. K. Craik, who claims that Anne 'is always an unsophisticated writer, a primitive in the art of the novel, gaining her results by very simple methods, which owe little to the techniques she might have learned from others' (39). The most provocative of more recent articles include Elizabeth Langland's essay, 'The Voicing of Feminine Desire in Anne Brontë's *The Tenant of Wildfell Hall* ', N. M. Jacobs' 'Gender and Layered Narrative in *Wuthering Heights* and *The Tenant of Wildfell Hall* ', and Jan B. Gordon's 'Gossip, Diary, Letter, Text: Anne Brontë's Narrative Tenant and the Problematic of the Gothic Sequel'.

[4] This telling of a tale by one man to another as the outer frame of a

narrative concerned chiefly with a woman's experience is presaged by Sarah Scott's 1762 feminist utopian novel *Millenium Hall*, in which a male traveller reports to a friend about his experiences with the emancipated women of Millenium Hall. Within his tale, a number of women tell their own stories, as Helen relates hers in her diary. In 'Maenads, Mothers, and Feminized Males: Victorian Readings of the French Revolution', Linda Shires suggests that

> Gilbert Markham's story documents Helen Huntingdon's rebellion against her husband Arthur, and, in so doing, it recalls several eighteenth-century novels by Mary Wollstonecraft and Charlotte Smith. Yet it differs in that it counsels an inscribed male friend that what he may perceive as overly independent female behavior is a strong woman's only way to maintain integrity in a world where aristocratic male domination can easily slip into abusiveness. It is important that the text addresses a man, for the counter-hegemonic project of the text is not merely to expose a bad marriage but to teach patriarchy the value of female rebellion. (160)

[5] Elisabeth Rose Gruner analyzes women's struggle against the laws constricting the rights of married women and mothers in 'Plotting the Mother: Caroline Norton, Helen Huntingdon, and Isabel Vane'. Laura C. Berry discusses child custody laws in 'Acts of Custody and Incarceration in *Wuthering Heights* and *The Tenant of Wildfell Hall*'.

[6] See Janet Kunert, 'Borrowed Beauty and Bathos: Anne Brontë, George Eliot, and "Mortification"'. Kunert also discusses Janet Dempster's husband in 'Janet's Repentance' (*Scenes of Clerical Life*). One thinks as well of the brutish, wife-battering Bentley Drummle in *Great Expectations*, who is killed when he is thrown from his horse, as narrated in the original ending of the novel.

[7] Margaret Mary Berg's analysis in '*The Tenant of Wildfell Hall*: Anne Brontë's *Jane Eyre*' is more helpful in this respect than Gilbert and Gubar's assertion in *The Madwoman in the Attic: The Female Artist and the Nineteenth-Century Literary Imagination* that 'what distinguishes Helen Graham (and all the women authors who resemble her) from male Romantics, however, is precisely her anxiety about her own artistry' (82). Helen is in fact quite prosaically methodical in painting so that she can escape her cruel husband's dominion, and views her art as a liberating force. Helen is not anxious about her artistry, but about the possibility of discovery and the thwarting of her escape and separation from Huntingdon.

[8] In *The Art of the Brontës*, Christine Alexander and Jane Sellars suggest that Helen's youthful painting is similar to Anne's July 1840 drawing 'What you please', which depicts a 'pretty young girl standing nervously at the edge of a

wood, surrounded by the beauties of nature'. The authors usefully point out that 'the manner of its execution, however, suggests that the subject was probably derived from a print rather than from the imagination. In nineteenth-century British art images of a young girl poised on the edge of womanhood are numerous, very often set in a spring landscape such as this one, to symbolize female youth and virginity'. Alexander and Sellars also link Helen's painting to December 16, 1843 drawing 'Landscape with trees', which 'pictures a glade in a leafy wood with a stunted fir in the middle and a large spreading tree to the side' (142-143).

[9] Rachel Carnell states, however, in 'Feminism and the Public Sphere in Anne Brontë's *The Tenant of Wildfell Hall*: 'Although much has been made of Brontë's challenge in *Tenant* to the rigid, gendered norms of the Victorian age, little has been made of her interest in the proper education of sons' (3-4).

[10] The shipwreck metaphor prefigures that in Charlotte's *Villette*: 'the ship was lost, the crew perished' (94). The writing in this passage is reminiscent of other sacred/biblical passages in *Villette* as well, such as the scene in which Lucy Snowe dreams of the 'well-loved dead' who 'met me elsewhere, alienated' from her, echoing Psalms in her pronouncement '"From my youth up Thy terrors have I suffered with a troubled mind"' (231-232), or Lucy's description of her emotions on the eve of her journey from England to Villette, as she listens to the tolling bells of St. Paul's Cathdral: '"I lie in the shadow of St. Paul's"' (107).

[11] In 'Anne Brontë: A Quiet Feminist', Marion Shaw analyzes the significances of Hargrave's name: 'Mr Hargrave (and his name suggests the destiny he offers: Whore-grave/Heart-grave) would keep Helen as his mistress' (134).

[12] In 'Imbecile Laughter and "Desperate Earnest" in *The Tenant of Wildfell Hall*', Juliet McMaster states: 'So much is confirmed by the memorable image of the Christmas rose which Helen gives to Gilbert at their betrothal, and which is the emblem of their love. Combining the most joyous elements of winter and summer, the Christmas rose also symbolizes an achieved union of delight and pain, passion and duty' (367-68).

[13] This marriage illustrates Linda Shires' argument that rebellious women figured as maenadic are connected to powerful mothers and feminized men in literary works of the 1830s and 1840s in England as a rewriting of the radical energies of the French Revolution. Importantly, Helen is a kind of older sister/mother to Esther, displacing her social-climbing, materialistic biological mother; thus Helen is strongly linked both to her feminized brother Lawrence and to her surrogate 'daughter' Esther.

[14] I borrow the term from Robert Polhemus' great critical work, *Erotic Faith: Being in Love from Jane Austen to D.H. Lawrence*.

[15] The best analysis of this Brontëan tension remains Robin Gilmour's brilliant work in 'The Sense of the Self: Autobiography, the Brontës and the

Romantic Inheritance', in his germinal *The Novel in the Victorian Age*. Although Gilmour is writing of Charlotte's *Jane Eyre*, his interpretation provides equal illumination of Anne's *Tenant*: 'Its interrogation of contemporary Christianity is part of a larger spiritual enquiry which daringly seeks to combine the Romantic quest for emotional fulfilment with the Christian search for salvation and true being. In that quintessentially Victorian enterprise of reinterpreting the Romantic and Christian inheritances, *Jane Eyre* is a key document' (66).

Works Cited

Alexander, Christine, and Sellars, Jane. *The Art of the Brontës*. Cambridge, England: Cambridge University Press, 1995.

Berg, Mary Margaret. '*The Tenant of Wildfell Hall*: Anne Brontë's *Jane Eyre*'. *Victorian Newsletter* (Spring 1987): 10-15.

Berry, Laura, C. 'Acts of Custody and Incarceration in *Wuthering Heights* and *The Tenant of Wildfell Hall*'. *Novel* (Fall 1996): 32-55.

Brontë, Anne. *Agnes Grey*. New York: Penguin. 1988.

-----. *The Tenant of Wildfell Hall*. Intro. Steve Davies. New York: Penguin. 1996.

Brontë, Charlotte. *Villette*. New York: Penguin. 1985.

Carnell, Rachel. 'Feminism and the Public Sphere in Anne Brontë's *The Tenant of Wildfell Hall*'. *Nineteenth-Century Literature* 53.1 (June 1998): 1-24.

Craik, W.A. '*The Tenant of Wildfell Hall*'. *The Brontë Novels*. Methuen, 1968. Rpt. in *The Brontës*. Ed. Harold Bloom. New York: Chelsea House Publishers, 1999.

Gérin, Winifred. *Anne Brontë*. London: Allen Lane, 1974.

Gilbert, Sandra and Susan Gubar. *The Madwoman in the Attic: The Woman Writer and the Nineteenth-Century Literary Imagination*. New Haven: Yale University Press, 1979.

Gilmour, Robin. *The Novel in the Victorian Age*. London: Edward Arnold, Ltd., 1986.

Gordon, Jan B. 'Gossip, Diary, Letter, Text: Anne Brontë's Narrative Tenant and the Problematic of the Gothic Sequel'. *English Literary History* 51.4 (Winter 1984): 719-45.

Gruner, Elizabeth Rose. 'Plotting the Mother: Caroline Norton, Helen Huntingdon, and Isabel Vane'. *Tulsa Studies in Women's Literature* 16 (1997): 303-25.

Jacobs, Naomi M. 'Gender and Layered Narrative in *Wuthering Heights* and *The Tenant of Wildfell Hall*'. *Journal of Narrative Technique* 16.3 (Autumn 1986): 204-19.

Kunert, Janet. 'Borrowed Beauty and Bathos: Anne Brontë, George Eliot, and 'Mortification''. *Research Studies* 46.4 (December 1978): 237-45.

Langland, Elizabeth. *Anne Brontë: The Other One*. London: Macmillan, 1989.
-----. 'The Voicing of Feminine Desire in Anne Brontë's *The Tenant of Wildfell Hall*'. *Gender and Discourse in Victorian Literature and Art*. Ed. Anthony H. Harrison and Beverly Taylor. DeKalb: Northern Illinois University Press, 1992.
McMaster, Juliet. 'Imbecile Laughter and "Desperate Earnest" in *The Tenant of Wildfell Hall*'. *Modern Language Quarterly* 43 (December 1982): 352-68.
Moore, George. *Conversations in Ebury Street*. London: Heinemann, 1930.
Polhemus, Robert. *Erotic Faith: Being in Love from Jane Austen to D. H. Lawrence*. London and Chicago: Chicago University Press, 1990.
Shaw, Marion. 'Anne Brontë: A Quiet Feminist'. *Brontë Society Transactions* 21.4 (1994): 125-35.
Shires, Linda. 'Maenads, Mothers, and Feminized Males: Victorian Readings of the French Revolution'. *Rewriting the Victorians: Theory, History, and the Politics of Gender*. Ed. Linda Shires. New York: Routledge, Chapman, & Hall, Inc., 1992. 147-65.
Sutherland, John. 'Who Is Helen Graham?' *Is Heathcliff a Murderer?: Great Puzzles in Nineteenth-Century Literature*. Oxford: Oxford University Press, 1996. 73-77.
Watson, Melvin R. 'Form and Substance in the Brontë Novels'. *From Jane Austen to Joseph Conrad: Essays Collected in Memory of James T. Hillhouse*. Ed. Robert C. Rathburn and Martin Steinmann, Jr. Minneapolis: University of Minnesota Press, 1958.

Chapter 8

Anne Brontë's Method of Social Protest in *The Tenant of Wildfell Hall*

Lee A. Talley

This article locates Anne Brontë's *The Tenant of Wildfell Hall* (1848) within the rich yet often misunderstood context of the religious influences that helped shape her life to argue that distinctly Evangelical reading practices helped her perform powerful analyses of Victorian culture and informed the narrative structure of the novel. Her maternal inheritance of a particular run of the *Methodist Magazine* furnished Brontë with important source materials and a range of narrative strategies that enabled her to critique the world in which she lived. After setting up the familial and religious context of Brontë's writings, I turn to *The Tenant of Wildfell Hall* to demonstrate how her engagement with early nineteenth-century and contemporary religious debates helped Brontë disrupt received ideas about gender, education, the learning process and the sanctity of the domestic sphere.

The Brontë Family and Religion

When Maria Brontë died on September 15, 1821, she left behind a husband and six children. Her sister, Aunt Branwell to the children, helped Patrick Brontë raise them and taught them her own, strict version of Methodism, a religious approach that was in many significant ways dramatically different from their mother Maria's type of Methodism, which was characterised by its 'persuasive tenderness' (Gérin 32). Anne Brontë, the youngest of the children, not yet two at the time of her mother's death, had the most contact with Aunt Branwell (they even shared a bed) and her Methodism.[1] This influence of a fearful Methodism is clearly evident in Anne's life-long fear regarding her own salvation and her belief that she had accomplished nothing 'to any purpose' in the material world at the time of her death (Gérin 320). Anne's relationship with her Aunt Branwell and their extensive contact and proximity – the other children shared a room together without an adult – helps explain why her relationship to Methodism was so different from that of her two older sisters.[2] Despite this difference, however, Anne also used her maternal legacy of Methodist Evangelical discursive practice to challenge societal conventions, scrutinize the ways in which one learns, and respond critically to her sisters' novels.

Although Patrick Brontë was an Anglican Evangelical minister, he too had extensive contact with and knowledge of Methodism. Indeed, he met his future wife, Maria Branwell, at Woodhouse Grove, a Methodist school for boys in Yorkshire. He lived with his family in a part of Yorkshire full of Methodists with whom he remained friendly even after the Methodists broke with the Church of England in 1813, and was friends with many Methodist ministers. Patrick Brontë also worked in a town whose inhabitants still vividly remembered his most famous predecessor, the dramatic Methodist minister, William Grimshaw (who some believe helped to inspire Emily's creation of Heathcliff in *Wuthering Heights*).[3] Tabby, the Brontë's maid, told the children tales of Grimshaw and other (in)famous Methodists as well. The children were all knowledgeable about the Society of Methodists and its founder John Wesley and, with the exception of Anne, satirized Methodism in their juvenilia, and in some of their adult fiction, most notably Charlotte Brontë's novel *Shirley* (1849), reflecting mid-Victorian sentiments on a religion seen as fanatical.[4]

Most important for the four who survived childhood were their mother's copies of the *Methodist Magazine*, a run that spanned from 1798 to 1812. Although damaged, but not destroyed, by a storm when they were shipped from Cornwall to Yorkshire,[5] a detail interestingly echoed in Charlotte Brontë's novel *Shirley*, where the magazines are 'stained with salt water' (376), the copies of this magazine survived to exert a largely unrecognized influence on all three sisters' fiction, and Anne's in particular.[6] Winifred Gérin writes of how 'from such a source were Anne Brontë's first lessons in reading taken' (Gérin 37).

The magazine's eclectic collection of missionary reports, conversion accounts, descriptions of deathbed scenes, supernatural dreams and occurrences, sermons, biblical and philosophical disquisitions, hymns, poetry and embattled opinion pieces on how Methodists were emphatically not fanatic 'monster[s]' provided the Brontës with an eccentric religious supplement to their well documented secular periodical readings in *Blackwood's* and *Fraser's* magazines.[7] Biting responses to articles such as *The Quarterly Review*'s piece 'On the Evangelical Sects' provided the young Brontës not only with religious history, but also with argumentative models upon which they could fashion their own often controversial opinions.[8] Mostly, however, the magazine offered a wide and powerful range of rhetorical strategies through which they could describe themselves and the world around them. This plethora of narratives gave the Brontë sisters ways of thinking and writing that allowed them to scrutinize and challenge social stereotypes bound to race, class, gender and religion. Although Emily's and Charlotte's works are in large part written against Methodist Evangelical doctrine, Anne's fiction reflects its debt to her maternal inheritance less oppositionally. It is here that one can see Anne's struggles against the Methodism of her Aunt Branwell and her incorporation of her mother's Methodist and literary legacy. Anne's readings in the *Methodist Magazine* and her knowledge of and immersion in both late-eighteenth-century and contemporary religious debates of the mid-nineteenth century enabled her to write boldly and critically about the ways in which education privileged boys, how pedagogy was ineluctably bound up with learning socially appropriate gendered behavior, and how the marriage market could cripple women in an intensely patriarchal society.

The Tenant of Wildfell Hall

Unlike Charlotte and Emily, who deployed the more exotic, imaginative aspects of the *Methodist Magazine* and challenged the beliefs the magazine put forth, Anne Brontë enlisted the more practical and moderate parts of the periodical and worked within Arminian Methodist doctrine in her novel, *The Tenant of Wildfell Hall. Tenant* rigorously upholds the division between mind and body, and stays firmly within the realm of realist narrative techniques. This Brontë novel contains no supernatural elements, no character who recounts extraordinary dreams or nightmares, and no character who radically challenges in any way the recognizable parameters of Englishness of the mid-nineteenth century. Anne's novel is solidly rooted within the domestic sphere and in the motherland. England's imperial ventures, her colonists, and her immigrants are banished from this critical exploration of family relations.

Anne Brontë's Methodist heritage shapes her realistic approach to worldly and philosophical problems. Brontë upholds the division between spirit and flesh to show how sexual passion, or other states that affect the body and mind (such as jealousy or drunkenness) can erode reason. She explores in almost excruciating detail the horrors of a bad marriage in order to challenge the gendered way in which her culture divides the realms of public and private, and girls' and boys' education, and opposes the ways that dominant culture perceives marriage. Brontë most strongly depends on the productions of the *Methodist Magazine* whenever she explores how one learns, and how learning affects knowledge. Habits deemed to be natural and hence unquestioned, because of or by the mandates of society and the consensus of science (or pseudo-science), are shown to be acquired, and hence amenable to moral reform.

Unlike Emily and Charlotte who plundered the *Methodist Magazine* for its exotic elements, Anne makes much of its ordinariness, following instead the faction of Methodists who opposed the distortions of fantasy. In what can be read as a sororal rebuke, she produces for her readers a novel in which 'the bosom that has been used to melt at the tale of fictitious woe, will be touched with the simple relation of real distress; and those who disapprove of romantic flight of imagination, will here be presented with authenticated facts' ('The Shipwreck of the Namur' 111). Charlotte, however, was able to diminish Anne's inventiveness by claiming that her sister's fictions were merely copied, in an obsessive way, from life. She writes that:

> [Anne] had, in the course of her life, been called on to
> contemplate, near at hand and for a long time, the terrible
> effects of talents misused and faculties abused; hers was
> naturally a sensitive, reserved, and dejected nature; what she saw
> sank very deeply into her mind; it did her harm. She brooded
> over it till she believed it to be a duty to reproduce every detail
> (of course with fictitious characters, incidents, and situations) as
> a warning to others. She hated her work but she would pursue
> it. When reasoned with on the subject, she regarded such
> reasonings as a temptation to self indulgence. She must be
> honest; she must not varnish, soften or conceal. (34)

While it is true that Anne witnessed the horrors of Branwell's adulterous
involvement with Mrs Robinson at Thorp Green and that parts of *Tenant* can be
read as a response to that affair, to read the novel solely as a 'reprodu[ction of]
every detail . . . as a warning to others' minimizes its artistry and power, and
undermines the deliberate realism Anne employs in her novel.[9] Like the
Methodist writer 'B.R.G.', Anne Brontë wanted to touch her readers with 'the
simple relation of real distress', believing that it was her 'duty to speak an
unpalatable truth' (30). In her 'Preface' to the second edition of *Tenant*, Brontë
writes that she has no desire to 'limit [her] ambition . . . to giv[ing] innocent
pleasure' reminding the reader that 'such humble talents as God has given me I
will endeavour to put to their greatest use' (30). This Brontë's early Methodist
lessons inform her novel's content and its aesthetics.

Charlotte, however, paints a picture of a religious enthusiast obsessed with
truths she compulsively retells, regardless of the consequences. Anne's supposed
dismissal of reasonable objections to her course of action 'as a temptation to self-
indulgence' marks her for Charlotte as one of those Evangelical hard-liners for
whom the 'reasonings' of worldly brains could never compete with decisions
guided by the Holy Spirit. To withhold truths that might affect the eternal as well
as the temporal condition of her readers would be unthinkable for such a zealot.
Here Charlotte reinforces the cultural repudiation of Evangelical extremism
regarding the need to testify almost hysterically to the horrors of various 'sins'. In
an emblematic article on 'The Pernicious Effects of Intoxication', a contributor to
the *Methodist Magazine* describes it as a 'MOTHER SIN', pointing out shrilly that
'her offspring is [sic] beyond calculation' (468). Many examples of such
proclamations in which one 'sin' quickly leads to so many others would have been
familiar to readers tired of Evangelical enthusiasm in general and jaundiced by
their denunciations of the evils of alcohol in particular. Charlotte's critique of her
sister's extremism thus almost resembles the Anglican minister's response to
Helen's teetotalism in *Tenant* as 'denying the fruits of Providence' (64).

Like many of the contributors to the *Methodist Magazine*, Anne Brontë viewed writing as an important medium through which to speak of earthly experience and to instruct the innocent about the ways of the world. One contributor to the magazine describes life as a 'dangerous voyage' and 'the rudiments of education [as] the stores which [children] will need on their passage' ('On the Education of Children' 373). As a concerned parent, 'it is [his] duty to provide them with necessaries for every possible hazard' (373). In the 'Preface' to the second edition of *Tenant*, Brontë, who creates such a concerned parent in Helen Huntingdon, almost echoes this writer when she asserts that it is 'better to reveal the snares and pitfalls of life to the young and thoughtless traveler', and that there should be 'less of this delicate concealment of facts' (30). She wants to teach the unvarnished truth – not a milder or diluted version of it – to help prepare her readers to live in this world.

Indeed, given her Evangelical beliefs in God's law, Anne goes beyond most secular writers of the time in the importance she ascribes to a moral education. In *Tenant* she boldly violates social convention by writing of domestic abuse, giving her female readers 'stores which they [might] need on their passage' through the marriage market. She too believes that it is equally important to 'store [children's] minds with useful knowledge of the things of time, and promot[e] their happiness in a future state', and presents her novel as a guide for growth in both the temporal and eternal world ('On the Education of Children' 373). *Tenant* not only provides the reader with a compelling romance, but also offers its female readers realistic examples of the ways desire works and can influence one's life. Although Anne writes her novel against both her sisters' passionate and supernaturally inflected fictions, she also refuses to accept the extreme Evangelical injunction against all 'Plays and Romance, those literary ignes fatui' so injurious to 'the understanding' that they invariably lead 'their airy votaries to ruin' (Stevens 82). Her fiction is romantic, entertaining and useful – calculated to teach, not 'ruin'.

Although Anne's strong faith and her belief in the importance of the eternal are crucial for carrying out this agenda, she tempers the more strident Evangelical positions adopted in the *Methodist Magazine*. She wants to impart 'real' lessons, not merely cautionary tales to scare her readers. One contributor to the magazine, after recounting the deleterious effects of a 'worldly', socially acceptable education on a previously pious young girl, pedantically asks that

> before I take my leave of your young readers, permit me to advise them to place on their toilets an hour glass, and a death's head, as necessary mementos, one to remind them of the swiftness of time, and the other of the certainty of death: with a Bible to direct them how to make their calling and election sure, and furnish them with instructions for the journey of life. ('Hints to Young Persons' 626)

Brontë's novel fictionally performs a similar function without ever resorting to such ghoulish or boorish reminders of the 'certainty of death' and the vital necessity of adhering to a moral framework that would lend meaning to earthly life and help ensure 'election' to heaven. Still, the novel also insists on the importance of a Bible to direct and secure these goals. In the two scenes in which Helen and her aunt fight about the eligibility of Arthur Huntingdon, each woman resorts to the Bible to shore up her belief as to whether Helen should or should not marry this already debauched young man.

Part of Brontë's agenda, however, is also to teach her sister Charlotte a lesson about religion. Anne's choice of names for her protagonist is vital, for here, she literally resurrects *Jane Eyre*'s overly zealous Helen Burns to inform Charlotte and the reading public about more practical applications of religious belief. While Helen Burns functioned as an excessively religious foil against whom Jane comes to define herself, Helen Huntingdon transforms Burns' over-zealous focus on the eternal to more material ends. Huntingdon is not the perfect embodiment of Christian eloquence and understanding that Charlotte's Helen is. This woman, a devout Christian, is also passionate. It is, in part, her physical attraction to the handsome Arthur that has her misread the Bible. This passionate misreading beautifully fleshes out the Evangelical distinction between a person's spiritual and corporeal brain, while recasting Charlotte's Helen into a much more human mind and body.

Although both Helens focus on their eternal states, Charlotte's otherworldly Helen presents the reader of *Jane Eyre* with an almost abnormal example of faith. Anne, working with the same Methodist source material, makes much more practical use of the applied ramifications of these types of belief, since they enable the faithful to uphold a slightly critical stance on matters of 'this world'. In countless articles such as 'Practical Reflections on the Shortness of Human Life', and in 'Cursory Remarks on Methodism', Anne would have learned that 'Methodists have hitherto borne a resolute and decided testimony against conformity to the world', and been more emboldened to critique the material world regardless of her readers' responses (402-03). Deciding not to conform to society was difficult indeed, and Brontë explores just how hard it was for female nonconformists with Helen Huntingdon and, later, Esther Hargraves. Despite Helen's religious upbringing, for example, she is willing to see Arthur's 'sins' as venial, alarming her aunt with the alacrity with which she could view them through the lens of 'perverted [worldly] judgment' (166). Although Helen's culpability may not have been as harshly judged by liberal Victorian readers, the 'sins' (gambling, drinking, womanizing) she so hastily forgives would have concerned even the most secular among them. The habits of reprobates like Arthur could spell moral and social ruin for any bride, regardless of her religious beliefs. Not surprisingly, the *Methodist Magazine* explored in detail the grave spiritual problem of marrying someone who was not an equal in faith and practice.[10]

Tenant's Narrative Structure and Its Pedagogical Agenda

Although *Tenant* recounts Gilbert Markham's interest in and courtship of the mysterious Helen Huntingdon and describes Helen's earlier marriage (the impediment to the fulfillment of Markham's desires), the novel is centrally engaged with teaching and learning. Each layer of the text addresses an aspect of pedagogy and knowledge in both secular and religious ways. Anne Brontë's preface, written as Acton Bell, vindicates her novel, telling the press and public that s/he wished to 'tell the truth, . . . [preferring to] whisper a few wholesome truths [in the public ear] than much soft nonsense' (29). Bell asserts that if there were 'less of this delicate concealment of facts . . . [that] there would be less of sin and misery to the young of both sexes who are left to wring their bitter knowledge from experience' (30). Thus, one can see how Anne Brontë is working to instruct her readers so that they can learn without having to experience first-hand what her protagonists do, much like the readers of cautionary tales the magazine published.

The second layer of the text and first narrative frame of the novel proper, Gilbert Markham's letter to his friend Halford, is also shaped as a lesson on the value of openness. Markham writes this letter to 'atone for . . . past offenses' of silence earlier when the two men were discussing their pasts frankly with one another (33). The epistolary narrative that ensues is not just meant to instruct Halford, however, but also recapitulates the lessons Gilbert himself has learned by painting in stark relief his countless misreadings of Helen. As a bumbling misreader of women, Gilbert is Anne's version of Emily's Lockwood. Unlike the young man who refuses to be drawn into the main plot of *Wuthering Heights*, Gilbert is allowed to become a protagonist. Still, he remains secondary to Helen, whose diary and excerpts from 'a certain faded old journal of [his]' make up the primary lessons of the text. As a convert, Gilbert can teach others how to read properly, and how to avoid the bitter reality of some married lives (34).

The narrative structure of *The Tenant of Wildfell Hall* has been under attack since the nineteenth century.[11] But the way in which the text is organized reflects Brontë's commitment to education, and to her firm grasp, as former governess, of how to further steady a learning process. Learning is rarely linear and Anne Brontë's novel reflects the necessarily circuitous route beginning to understand a difficult 'truth' takes.[12] Her narrative strategy frustrates the reader's need to learn about Gilbert's desire or to see the linear unfolding of story. The insertion of Helen's diary not only impedes the progression of the romance plot, but also teaches the journal's reader – Gilbert, Halford, and the novel's reader – about the realities of alcoholism and bad marriages. Eclipsing the love story, Helen's diary meticulously documents her own education in the horrors of her married life; hence, it mimics, once again, the acquisition of knowledge.

In an essay comparing pedagogy to psychoanalysis, Shoshana Felman argues that psychoanalysis provides people with a different and useful model for teaching and learning (Felman 1982). Her insights can be productively applied towards the direction of a knowledge that is faith-based, as part of a belief system – like religion – that regards ignorance as a stepping stone for the advancement of a higher consciousness. All types of 'believers' must necessarily remain comfortable with ignorance, with not knowing. Wesley himself insisted on the acceptance of human limitations in his repeated writings about knowing and types of knowledge that would forever remain opaque to humans. In a letter from 1773 reprinted in the *Methodist Magazine*, Wesley writes:

> For it is hard to think, these walls of flesh and blood can intercept the view of an angelic being. But we have, in general, only a faint and indistinct perception of their presence, unless in some peculiar instances, where it may answer some gracious ends of Divine Providence. Then it may please God to permit, that they should be perceptible, either by some of our outward sense, or by an internal sense, for which human language has not any name. (520)

Wesley is not only comfortable with ignorance, but he also finds it vital to his theology. Not knowing marks us as human, delimited by 'these walls of flesh and blood'. If a person were able to perceive an 'angelic being' (or some divine truth), he or she would still be fettered by a language which, being human, could not possibly articulate that extraordinary experience. Ignorance not only marks the perception of observers such as Gilbert, but it initially shapes the experience Helen as well. Anne Brontë rigorously surrounds the central story within *Tenant* with the walls of human misreading and miscommunication that only Helen's testament (her diary) can dismantle.

The movement from ignorance to enlightenment that occurs first for Gilbert when he initially receives Helen's diary is not a purely linear one, however. His learning is marked by notable errors, sending him back to the beginning and to the person with knowledge. If we were to read this learning process Evangelically, Helen would be converting Gilbert to her way of reading the world for meaning. Shoshana Felman's insights about the role that ignorance plays in the psychoanalytical process offers contemporary critics a secular model that seems less arcane than the older, faith-based system that Anne Brontë utilizes with such skill in *The Tenant of Wildfell Hall*. Felman's remarks about the circuitous nature of the movement from ignorance to enlightenment are thus enormously helpful:

> Proceeding not through linear progression, but through breakthroughs, leaps, discontinuities, regressions, and deferred

action, the analytic learning process puts indeed in question the traditional pedagogical belief in intellectual perfectability, the progressivistic view of learning as a simple, one-way road from ignorance to knowledge. (27)

Brontë's novel, with its emphasis on Gilbert's gradual understanding of Helen's identity and past, also must work through 'breakthroughs, leaps, discontinuities, [and] regressions'. As so many of the magazine's accounts of converting to Methodism stress, ultimate truths are seldom reached in a linear or comprehensible way. Instead, 'backsliding' and the paralyzing effects of torturous illnesses that threaten the very foundations of the believer's faith, must be read as constituting progress of some sort. The convert presents his or her change as proof of an ability to see the world differently – within a changed master narrative. This master narrative can retrospectively assess events that appeared to be setbacks as contributors to some type of forward progress.

Felman's notion of an 'analytically informed pedagogy' that 'has to reckon with 'the passion for ignorance' calls attention to resistances quite similar to those Methodists described in their accounts of the unconverted or by Brontë in her discovery of a readership that repudiated her clear and bold discussion of the domestic sphere. Felman writes that:

> Ignorance, in other words, is nothing other than a desire to ignore: its nature is less cognitive than performative . . . it is not a simple lack of information, but the incapacity – or the refusal – to acknowledge one's own implication in the information. . . . The truly revolutionary pedagogy discovered by Freud – consisted in showing the ways in which, however irreducible, ignorance itself can teach us something – becomes itself instructive. Teaching, thus, is not the transmission of ready-made knowledge, it is rather the creation of a new condition of knowledge – the creation of an original learning disposition. (30-31)

In its careful account of the education of both Helen and Gilbert, *Tenant* insists upon the creation of 'a new condition of knowledge'. Those possessed with 'learning dispositions' can fundamentally reshape themselves, and do so more than a fixated Catherine Earnshaw or Jane Eyre—neither of whom can ever fully free herself from the man she continues to call her 'master'. Yet those who cannot refashion their identities are damned: there is less sympathy for the obdurate ravings of the dying Arthur Huntingdon than there was for an equally delirious Heathcliff, whom even Nelly Dean cannot fail to pity.

Tenant, thus, is structured not just to show us how Gilbert learns about

Helen, but also to show how badly Markham, his family, and community desire to remain ignorant of the truth, preferring instead to believe an easier story, and constantly circle around the truth. The diary's radical disruption of the outer, more comfortable narrative layer with the truth of Helen's past, so crucial to setting up the novel's non-linear pedagogical scene of instruction, is what has outraged so many critics.

George Moore, one of the few early critics who really appreciated Anne's work, laments the injuries done to the romance he wanted to read:

> an accident would have saved her[.] [A]lmost any man of letters would have laid his hand upon her arm and said: You must not let your heroine give her diary to the young farmer. . . [sic]. Your heroine must tell the young farmer her story, and an entrancing scene you will make of the telling. . . [sic]. The presence of your heroine, her voice, her gestures, the questions that would arise and the answers that would be given . . . would preserve the atmosphere of a passionate and original love story. The diary broke the story in halves. (qtd. in Gérin, 'Introduction' 14)

And Winifred Gérin approvingly supplements this quotation with, 'How right was Moore!' Yet Brontë's decision to undercut the 'love-story' such critics demand, is, of course deliberate. However jarring it might seem to some, the narrative shift allows the heroine to present Gilbert with a written text – a secular testament to her virtue. Like scripture, Helen's diary functions as a textual document to which Gilbert can refer to learn and propagate truth.[13] Although the physical presence of the heroine might well 'preserve the atmosphere of a passionate and original love story', it would also work against the deliberately *disembodied* lessons Anne wants both Gilbert and Helen to learn. Gilbert must learn to defer his passion for Helen, and Helen must learn more about decision-making without worldly desires affecting her judgment.

More recently, Terry Eagleton, though recognizing Brontë's design, questions the insertion of the diary on different grounds; for him, it is its romance that is controversial:

> What is officially an interlude becomes the guts of the book, displacing the framework which surrounds it. That structural incongruity has its significance. By enfolding the Grassdale events with a traditional love story, the novel once more dissolves the social to the individual, diverting a confrontation of class-values to an exploration of personal suffering and self-fulfillment. (136)

Yet the love story is not as invidious and individualised as Eagleton contends, for it explores the condition of a woman as very much involving 'a confrontation of class-values'. After all, many of Brontë's Victorian readers would have liked to believe that the types of abuses she documents did not occur in 'proper' English families. Eagleton seems to overlook the possibility of viewing women as a class in their own right, and hence fails to allow that an attention to gender might be crucial to any class analysis as well. Helen's diary is much more than an account of 'personal suffering and self-fulfillment'. It is an exploration of domestic violence; that is an indisputable social event that cuts across class lines. In displacing the framework of the love story, the diary gets to the 'guts' of the novel: a detailed and sustained examination of the often harsh realities of married life, and the ways in which alcoholism can profoundly disrupt parental responsibilities.

Furthermore, as Helen hijacks the novel to vindicate herself by presenting Gilbert with the truth about her life, she is mirroring in a condensed, fictional way Brontë's own project of educating her readers about the very real potential dangers to women of married life. The romance plot, safely lodged within the correspondence of two men, functions as a protective narrative frame for the more disturbing portrait of a marriage between a philandering alcoholic and his non-conformist wife in an intensely patriarchal culture.[14]

Beyond this central lesson, however, the diary also represents Brontë's fictional adaptation of a standard feature of the magazine: the published diaries of the faithful. Safeguarded within the sanctioned pages of the religious community's periodical were innumerable accounts of unconventional and successful women's lives. Many of the female diarists featured in the magazine were as intelligent as Helen Huntingdon, and found innovative ways of studying subjects normally reserved for men. One account, representative of many, but unusual in this particular woman's truly remarkable education, is worth recounting. Elizabeth Bury, born in 1644, had a 'genius [that] led her to studies not common to her sex. She was conversant in Philology, Philosophy, History, Mathematics, Geography, Astronomy, Heraldry, and Music' (Bury 450). She even 'took much pleasure in Anatomy and Medicine, being led to them partly by her own ill health, and partly from a desire to be useful to her neighbours' (450). Like Bury's diary, Helen's diary provides her female readers with an example of possibility. For just as women readers of the 1811 June edition of the *Methodist Magazine* must have marveled at Elizabeth Bury's intellectual accomplishments, so could mid-Victorian readers marvel at the fact of Helen's tenacity and perseverance. Helen resembles Bury in her work. And, similar to Bury's interests in the medical arts, prompted 'by her own ill health', Helen, in order to support herself and her son, is 'forced' to learn about the art world to support herself and her son. *Tenant* can thus also be read as a nineteenth-century testament to the life of single, working mother. Helen's diary testifies to the experience of her 'class' (women) and the very real struggles of middle-class working women. The interruption of the story with the insertion of the diary is vital since its existence points to Brontë's utopian and 'feminist' impulse. The diary is indeed, in many ways, 'the guts of the novel'.

The Tale Proper: Its Sororal and Educational Lessons

The story contained within Gilbert's correspondence begins, like the opening of *Jane Eyre*, at the pagan new year: the end of October and beginning of November (45). Gilbert Markham's mother even invites Helen to a Guy Fawkes Day party on the fifth of November to meet the neighbors (53). Unlike Charlotte, Anne does not invoke the pagan calendar to structure her tale, but rather seems to be trying to domesticate *Jane Eyre*'s narrative into a more worldly and less supernaturally inflected series of events.[15] Helen refuses 'to grace [the Guy Fawkes Day party] with her presence', but her unusual beliefs in child-rearing and temperance – which soon become the talk of the party – certainly begin to unsettle the status quo (59). Like Jane, Gilbert has been told tales of the supernatural from his nurse, but when he sees the overgrown, animal-shaped boxwood hedges that seem to have a 'goblinish appearance that harmonized well with the ghostly legends and dark traditions [his] old nurse had told [him] respecting the haunted hall and its departed occupants', nothing remotely 'goblinish' or supernatural occurs (46). Gilbert has no reveries and sees no vision of the otherworldly. What he does see, 'a tiny hand elevated above the wall', is very different from the supernatural hand that reaches into Lockwood's bedchamber in *Wuthering Heights* (47). The beginning of *The Tenant of Wildfell Hall* evokes the openings of both *Jane Eyre* and *Wuthering Heights* to counter their invocation of the supernatural with very worldly lessons about temperance and gender.

Brontë furthermore appears to use her protagonist as a mouthpiece for her own views; she has Helen use the same images that she would later appropriate for the 'Preface' to the second edition of her novel. For example, Brontë enlists Helen's protestations that she 'would not send a poor girl into the world unarmed against her foes, and ignorant of the snares that beset her path' (57) when she contends that her novel is designed 'to reveal the snares and pitfalls of life to the young' (30). Again, when Helen notes in her diary that she 'cannot wish to go and leave my darling in this dark and wicked world alone without a friend to guide him through its weary mazes, to warn him of its thousand snares' (334), her voice blends with that of Acton Bell.[16]

Brontë and Helen are equally unconcerned about violating socially prescribed gender roles. In response to reviews querying the gender of *Tenant*'s author, Brontë forcefully stated that she was 'satisfied that if a book is a good one, it is so whatever the sex of the author may be' (31). Helen similarly works against culturally dominant ideas of gender by teaching her son Arthur to hate alcohol despite societal encouragement of male drinking; Helen even goes so far in her diary to link certain forms of bad behavior with ideals of manhood. The worst of her husband's teachings to his son are linked to gender, as he 'and his friends delighted to encourage in all the embryo vices a little child can show, and to instruct in all the evil habits he could acquire – in a word, to "make a man of him"' (356). Brontë points out the double standard between 'making a man' and 'being a lady'. The making of a man could involve vice, whereas the making of a proper 'lady' could not. Helen saves young Arthur from sin, but more importantly in terms of the material world, she saves him from the permissive, hyper-patriarchal pedagogy of his father and his friends.

Having already explored a worldly education in her first novel *Agnes Grey* (1847), Anne now turns to more subtle aspects of the teaching of gender. In *Agnes Grey* she challenges the ways boys are reared when she questions the sadistic torture of birds as an activity valorized by the family as a proper past time for a 'fine boy' (17). When Agnes Grey puts a stop to the torture of another nest of birds, Tom 'heap[s] . . . bitter maledictions and opprobrious epithets . . . upon [her]'; yet his uncle proudly exclaims that '"the lad has some spunk in him too. Curse me, if I ever saw a nobler little scoundrel than that. He's gone beyond the petticoat government already"' (38). Not only is the cruel torture of animals granted approbation as 'manly' behavior, but so is the defiance of female authority figures. Unenlightened patriarchy is about power, interpretations of scripture that violate the 'truth', and the primary importance of man's gain. Tom's mother, for example, responds to Agnes' concern for the birds by reminding her 'that the creatures were all created for our convenience' (39). Brontë creates more subtle gender lessons in *Tenant* in her detailed exploration of boys' relationships to their mothers, even having Helen defy the belief that her son should be sent 'to school . . . to learn to despise his mother's authority and affection' (55).

Helen's educational practices are hardly well received by the world around her. In fact, Helen's involvement in her son's education prompts Mrs Markham to exclaim that 'the poor child will be the veriest milk sop that ever was sopped' (54). Helen is accused by Mrs Markham of having made 'the fatal error . . . of taking that boy's education upon [her]self' (55). This will 'spoil his spirit, and make a mere Miss Nancy of him' (55). Brontë, however, insists that the different ways in which boys and girls are educated can only lead to divergent moral as well as educational standards.[17] Helen even sarcastically notes that 'our sons . . . prove all things by experience, while our daughters must not even profit by the experience of others' (57). Yet her involvement with young Arthur's education is deemed as unnaturally feminized by the community.

Helen's teachings are discussed by the community not only as defying the practices of this world, but also as opposed to the teachings of God. The vicar, for example, states that what Helen is doing is not only wrong, but 'criminal! Not only is it making a fool of the boy, but it is despising the gifts of providence, and teaching him to trample them under his feet' (64). He then goes on to discuss how 'temperance . . . is one thing, but abstinence is another' (64). The vicar further asserts, much like public opinion of the time, that Helen's lesson are contrary both 'to Scripture and to reason to teach a child to look with contempt and disgust upon the blessing of providence instead of to use them aright' (65).

Helen's lessons to her son, despite convincing arguments about the use of laudanum and the biological 'predisposition to intemperance', also render her unwomanly in the eyes of others (64). Even the admiring but totally conventional Gilbert states that 'a woman liable to take strong prejudices, . . . and stick to them through thick and thin, twisting everything into conformity with her own preconceived opinions [is] too hard, too sharp, too bitter for my taste' (65). His depiction of her as, to say the least, shrewish also works against attributes traditionally associated with the feminine.   Thus, according to Brontë, conventional interpretations of scripture or gender do not adequately encompass a range of beliefs that account for true deviance.

The community not only views Helen as an inappropriate teacher to her son, but also as an inadequate scholar herself. For according to the popular opinion within the novel (and in mid-Victorian culture), her own education has been sorely lacking. 'On household matters, and all the little niceties of cookery, and such things, that every lady ought to be familiar with, whether she be required to make use of her knowledge or not . . . [Helen] betrayed a lamentable ignorance' (39). Since child-rearing, the direction of servants and household management were considered 'interrelated topics' in the mid-nineteenth century, a Victorian reader would have found Helen's ignorance of household matters completely in keeping with her unorthodox views of child rearing, education, and alcohol.[18]

I would argue that Brontë's belief in and engagement with Methodist Evangelicalism allowed her to challenge the educational practices and gender boundaries that Helen defies. Brontë embraces the Methodist belief that a temporal education could insure the goodness of one's eternal life, but that these teachings could make life in the material world more difficult. As a devout Christian protagonist, Helen welcomes her newborn son, by claiming that 'God has sent me a soul to educate for heaven' (252). She is reiterating almost verbatim the belief that 'every family should be a little nursery for heaven', so often espoused in the *Methodist Magazine*.[19] Helen's teachings also align themselves with another article that describes 'how wrong it is to teach children that education will help them cut an impressive figure in the [temporal] universe' and reminds the reader that 'to know the world is to know its emptiness, its vanity, its futility and wickedness' ('On the Religious Employment of Time' 268). Both articles clearly state the importance of eternal life in sharp distinction to the life of the body or of this world; one even reminds the reader that 'the soul is the man rather than the body' ('An Admonition . . .' 424). Brontë's material concerns about education and its relationship to how one fares in this world point, however, to secular influences as well, and in particular to a canon of literature that has a distinctly female focus: late eighteenth-century educational tracts written predominantly by women.[20]

Helen Huntingdon applies contemporary theories of associationist psychology to the care of her son's soul in her use of alcohol as both medicine and punishment. She conditions him to fear and loathe 'spirits' in order to arrest his potential growth into an alcoholic. She takes advantage of Arthur's body to help shape his soul by using alcohol 'therapeutically': to discipline and medicate. Helen confesses that she is 'determined to enlist all the power of association in [her] service . . . wishing this aversion to be so deeply grounded in his nature that nothing in afterlife may be able to overcome it' (376). Like so many pieces in the *Methodist Magazine* that uphold the distinction between spirit and flesh, and the importance of the latter's weakness, Helen unhesitatingly takes charge of her son's body: she must mortify the flesh to save his soul and teach the young Arthur to understand the evils of drink.

Brontë's use of Methodist doctrine, however, remains selective. She never adopts the more punitive techniques of child-rearing techniques Wesley himself advocated:

> Break their wills betimes, begin this work before they can run alone, before they can speak plain, perhaps before they can speak at all. Whatever pain it costs break the will if you would not damn the child. Let a child from a year old be taught to fear the rod and to cry softly; from that age make him do as he is bid, if you whip him ten times to effect it (qtd. in Gérin 34).

Young Arthur is never 'broken' as Helen raises him. Nor does she endorse the view that 'children are conceived in sin, and brought forth in iniquity, [and that] they are naturally without God, and without hope in the world' (Bogie 27). Helen similarly never suggests that her husband, Arthur, was an inherently bad person 'naturally without God [or] . . . hope'. Rather, she lays the blame of her husband's behavior upon his childhood education: an over-indulgent mother and a 'bad selfish, miserly father, who . . . restricted him in the most innocent enjoyments of childhood and youth, and . . . disgusted him with every type of restraint' (190). In fact, the elder Huntingdon's restrictions represent a worldly refraction of certain Methodist childrearing techniques. If the elder Huntingdon's motives had been less about his own selfish desires and more about his concern for his son's eternal future, it would be difficult indeed to make a distinction between 'worldly' selfishness and strictly Methodist belief systems. Mr Huntingdon senior thus becomes a worldly example of Brontë's working against a Methodist 'spare the rod and spoil the child' method of instruction or child raising. *Tenant's* milder methods of teaching are, I believe, selectively Methodist, and reflect Brontë's belated Arminian legacy of Methodism.

Tenant also explores how class and wealth intersect with the teaching of gender, and how women suffer under these worldly types of instruction. For it is in part the worldly education that Helen receives that makes her believe that she can change Arthur. Her willingness to view his sins as venial disturbs her aunt (her own teacher), because of the 'perverted judgment' of the world (166). Helen, however, also has lessons to learn about her own religious training. While she does not hold on to her religious training's division between venial and mortal sin, she overly embraces the Evangelical 'hate of the sins . . . [and] love [of] the sinner' (166). Helen, youthful and full of hubris, believes that she can teach him. She believes her 'life [will be] well spent in the effort to preserve so noble a nature from destruction' (166), that she can 'save him from . . . the devil and his angels', and that she shall 'consider [her] life well spent in saving him from the consequences of his early errors and striving to recall him to the path of virtue' (167).

Tenant works to instruct readers about the difficulty (and often impossibility) not just of conversion, but of changing another individual's confirmed patterns of behavior. Helen wrongfully believes that Arthur's 'wife shall undo what his mother did' (191). Like the young converts whom the contributors to the magazine felt compelled to warn, Helen begins to 'fall' because of the hubris of believing she can change Arthur. The *Methodist Magazine*'s words depict with a startling clarity not just the youthful sense of possibility that infects Helen, but also the desire that clouds her abilities to reason clearly. One contributor, heeding his readers to remain vigilant, describes scenarios that will become familiar to Helen. He writes:

> with heart panting to be employed in our Redeemer's service ...
> too often we forget to examine our abilities for the work. Hence
> the early efforts of other young converts are frequently fruitless,
> and he often endangers his own safety by his injudicious
> endeavours. . . . He rushes with eager haste into scenes which
> the boldest Christian cautiously avoids. ('On Being Equally
> Yoked' 777)

Although the magazine is only discussing the zeal for conversion, the contributor has already pointed out that that this 'evil' 'has its origin in vanity, from a desire to stand well in the estimation of the worldly' (776). The writer's dramatic, corporeal description of the 'panting heart' also evokes the spectre of worldly passion that has infected Helen. And, as the magazine article warns, someone may belatedly realize, like Helen, that she 'possesses not the partner of [her] life, a sympathizing spirit to partake [her] sorrow or [her] joy' (777).

In recasting the monitory articles that filled the magazine, Brontë was also rewriting *Jane Eyre* by questioning her sister's notion that a well-meaning young woman might completely reform a libertine. Her message to Charlotte, implicit throughout the novel, stands out in one particular scene, when Arthur claims that he will comport himself in order to fulfill Helen's earlier desires to marry a man of 'decided piety' (188). Arthur promises to 'comport myself in such a godly sort that she shall regard me with admiration and sisterly love, as a brand plucked from the burning' (188). Not only does this scene evoke *Jane Eyre*'s Rochester, a literal 'brand plucked from the burning', but Arthur's mention of 'sisterly love' invokes St John, *Jane Eyre*'s other brand, as well. Unlike the reformed Rochester or the martyred St John, Arthur remains a mocker. When Arthur jokes that he will 'come home sighing like a furnace . . . full of the savour and unction of Dear Mr Blatant's discourse', Arthur's words simultaneously mock Charlotte's frequent use of fiery imagery and blaspheme the penitent's experience of church (188).

Tenant also provides the reader with more secular examples of the ways in which women's worldly education deforms them. As Arthur becomes more dissipated, the text returns to the site of pedagogy, focusing on Esther Hargraves' experience with the marriage market when she returns from her first season in London. *Tenant* thus explores how women are educated with the goal of marriage – not intellectual knowledge or spiritual growth – in mind. Furthermore, the marriage market works to narrow the parameters of acceptable feminine behavior. Anne does not Methodistically condemn such a worldly phenomenon, but rather examines the desperation the market engenders in its participants, a desperation that could unsettle the 'natural' division between classes that both Methodists and society at large wished to uphold.[21]

Although Mrs Hargraves is clearly a product of the class-bound patriarchal system of marriage, Helen faults her for trying to disguise her true financial situation in her attempts to have her children make successful 'matches'. Mrs Hargraves is:

> ever straining to keep up appearances with that despicable pride that shuns the semblance of poverty as of a shameful crime. . . . Mrs Hargraves' anxiety to make good matches for her daughters is partly the cause and partly the result of these errors: by making a figure in the world and showing them off to advantage, she hopes to obtain better chances for them; and by thus living beyond her legitimate means and lavishing so much on their brother, she renders them portionless, and makes them burdens on her hands. (243-44)

Helen recognizes that Mrs Hargraves' possibilities are clearly circumscribed by her status as widow, for she well knows the desperate straits that a woman can find herself in under patriarchy, where women are judged primarily on rank, looks and accomplishments. But in Helen's opinion, Mrs Hargraves shows far too much concern for worldly matters. Ironically, her exclusive concern about money and status renders her daughters 'portionless'. These concerns also make her act like someone she is not. In her portrayal of Mrs Hargraves trying to look farther up the social ladder than she 'should', Brontë shows how easily worldly concerns can disrupt 'natural' class-bound social order.

More upsetting to Helen, however, is how Esther's 'blithe spirit is almost broken [by that] unnatural parent' (439). The necessity of marriage distorts class, but also the fundamental properties of one's person. This child would not have been 'broken' by a parent's concern for the eternal status of her soul, but she is almost broken by a parent's indoctrination into a system that is very much a product of the temporal world. Esther's mother, upset at her behavior in London '[brings her] home to school [her] . . . into a proper sense of . . . duty' (380). Esther's duty as daughter is to conform to the acceptable parameters of gender so that she can marry, and no longer remain a 'burden' to her mother and brother (379). Properly gendered attributes are unequivocally tied to the material world of which *Tenant* is often critical. And with only Helen urging Esther to 'stand firm', starkly reminding her that a bad marriage is much like 'sell[ing] yourself into slavery', Brontë shows how powerful and negative types of gender instruction come often from those closest to home: the family (380). Mrs Hargraves' attempt to teach Esther a 'proper sense of duty' is also reminiscent of Arthur's earlier lessons to Helen not to have her 'religion . . . lessen her devotion to her earthly lord' (217). It becomes clear that worldly duties can deform both secular and religious 'souls'.

While remaining suspicious of worldly lessons in a properly Methodist way, Brontë also echoes the earlier, more controversial, irreligious, feminist Mary Wollstonecraft who wrote in *The Vindication of the Rights of Woman* (1792) that

> women are told from their infancy, and taught by the example
> of their mothers, that a little knowledge of human weakness,
> justly termed cunning, softness of temper, *outward* obedience,
> and a scrupulous attention to a puerile kind of propriety will
> obtain for them the protection of man. (6)[22]

Like the women Wollstonecraft discusses, Mrs Hargraves desperately wants her daughter to acquire the protection of a man through properly submissive behavior. In Lady Lowborough Brontë creates a character who embodies Wollstonecraft's theories of women's social education, thus providing the reader with a clear example of how society can deform not just outward forms of behavior, but can corrupt 'internal' belief systems as well: '[Lady Lowborough] knows her power, and she uses it too; but well knowing that to wheedle and coax is safer than to command, she judiciously tempers her despotism with flattery and blandishments enough to make [her husband] deem himself a favoured and a happy man' (241). Lady Lowborough is the well-socialized coquette Wollstonecraft writes about, and Brontë makes her as morally bankrupt as Helen's husband, Arthur. Brontë's incisive commentary on pedagogy of this world is implicit in her careful construction of the two most morally depraved characters in her novel as good at worldly, social events and excessively well schooled in the superficial attributes of their gender.

Unlike Wollstonecraft, however, Brontë depends on conventional Christianity for her critique of educational practices. This Christianity not only provides her with a cover denied to the controversial Wollstonecraft, but it also enables her to keep intact other crucial social variables within her critique. Religion (apart from doctrinal disputes regarding universal salvation), race, and class work together in *Tenant* to form recognizable and unthreatening social divisions, thereby freeing Brontë to overturn received ideas about gender and education. Brontë can rework notions of gender while safeguarding and preserving the other social divisions like class and race, so that readers might easily appreciate the 'reasonableness' of her project. Brontë's project does have revolutionary aspects, but she manages to keep her novel at a safe distance from either the embattled religious opinion pieces of the *Methodist Magazine* or the incendiary, irreligious prose of Mary Wollstonecraft. While Rachel K. Carnell contends that *Tenant* reflects Brontë's interest in and debt to Enlightenment reasoning more so than her probable debt to Wollstonecraft, I believe that Brontë's philosophical legacy is also one she inherited from her mother's magazines. For Wesley's profound interest in Lockean philosophy in particular (he published multiple versions and extracts of Locke's *Essay Upon Human Understanding* in his magazine) created an Evangelical miscellany strongly influenced by rationalism.[23] Brontë's work is both revolutionary and nostalgic; it reflects her private inheritance of Enlightenment philosophy and educational theories as filtered through the lens of the *Methodist Magazine*.

Conclusion

Composed in less revolutionary times, Anne Brontë's *The Tenant of Wildfell Hall* tackles many of the issues Mary Wollstonecraft had raised in her earlier, controversial *Vindication of the Rights of Woman*. Yet Brontë's radical novel of social protest is profoundly indebted to her Methodist legacy and her own intense religious faith. She wrote her novel to reassert, for the benefit of her sisters as much as for a Victorian reading public, the importance of earthly conduct. Concerned about 'how little can the dread of future punishment – and still less the promise of future reward – avail to make [men] forbear and wait', this Brontë created a fiction all about pedagogy and deferral (qtd in Gérin 361).[24]

In her fictional documentation of the recognizable excesses of alcoholism, infidelity, and domestic abuse, Brontë creates a narrative that embodies the processes of waiting and learning in order to teach her readers to persevere and focus on the transcendental. She wrote her novel, she confessed to the Reverend David Thom, to give 'as many hints in support of the doctrine [of Universal Salvation] as [she] could venture to introduce in a work of [fiction]' (qtd. in Gérin 361). Brontë sees this novel as a place where she can articulate the doctrine she 'cherished . . . from [her] very childhood – with a trembling hope at first, and afterwards with a firm and glad conviction of its truth' (qtd. in Gérin 361). Even though she creates a most unregenerate sinner, a Heathcliff-like figure who never atones for his 'sins', and depicts a domestic sphere deformed by ignorance and neglect, her novel is ultimately a project of hope. Brontë uses the romance, a genre permeated with worldly concerns, to speak loudly about social injustice and the temporal doctrine of suffrage. By ending not just with the marriage of Helen and Gilbert, but also with happy marriages for the other female characters as well, she tries to signify the possibility of transcendent fulfillments through modest and very earthly change.

Notes

[1] Elizabeth Branwell was not a Calvinist Methodist. She, too, was Arminian. For more information on the misinterpretation of her beliefs see Barker.

[2] Although Emily's *Wuthering Heights* is known for its parody of Methodism through the almost unintelligible religious patriarch, Joseph, Charlotte's juvenilia and *Shirley* provide a number of sarcastic renderings of Methodist enthusiasm as well. For more information see Cunningham.

[3] William Grimshaw (1708-63) was not only a dramatic preacher, but also actively involved with the religious revival that swept Yorkshire in the late-eighteenth century. John Wesley himself preached at Haworth several times as well in 1757, 1761, 1766, 1772, 1786, 1788, and 1790. See Wise 53. Harrison most vividly explores the connection between Grimshaw and Heathcliff.

[4] For examples of the children's satires of Methodism see Barker 250-51. For a telling extract from Charlotte Brontë's manuscript, 'Julia', see Cunningham 287-91.

[5] For Maria Brontë's description of the storm see Barker 55.

[6] Cunningham, Gérin, and Harrison do recognize this influence, although Harrison's desire to claim the Brontës as part of a legacy twentieth-century Methodists have inherited over determines some of her readings. For a full length study of the *Methodist Magazine*'s influence on the Brontës see Talley.

[7] See 'On Fanaticism'.

[8] See 'On the Evangelical Sects'.

[9] This is not to say that I disagree with critics such as Winifred Gérin who writes that 'less than any other of the Brontë novels can *The Tenant of Wildfell Hall* be separated from the circumstances in which it was composed' (236). I believe it is vital to see *Tenant* as a work of fiction – not as a text with the almost mimetic relationship to reality that Charlotte writes about. Mary Margaret Berg makes a similar point stating that 'Charlotte Brontë effectively reduces the novel from a deliberately designed work of fiction to an obsessive reiteration of personal concerns' (10).

[10] See, for example, Anonymous, 'On Being Unequally Yoked'. This article is particularly compelling in light of Helen's relationship with her aunt. It not only discusses the hubris of believing that one could change another and the despair upon realizing, after marriage, that the relationship is based upon very little indeed, but it also explores in depth the frustration and pain of the 'pious parents' who watched over their charges 'with anxious solicitude and many tears and prayers' (778).

[11] Particularly strong articles that explore the history and importance of *Tenant*'s narrative structure are Carnell's, Gordon's and Shires'.

[12] The learning and acceptance of Helen's past by Gilbert and the other members of their community is marked by denial, desire to believe almost anything else, and difficulty in accepting its truth. The obstacles to understanding reflect the traumatic aspects of Helen's past and both individual and communal needs to deny the reality of domestic abuse. For a book-length study on the ways in which personal and political acceptance of these types of incidents are connected see Herman. For more information on the relationship between trauma, testimony, teaching and learning see Felman and Felman and Laub.

[13] Jan B. Gordon thoroughly explores the meaning of textual exchange connecting the text's use of economic language with desire and religious discursive practices. Lori Paige points out that Helen's diary continues the system of exchange of books that takes place within the novel.

[14] Linda Shires writes about the necessity of Helen's revolutionary story being contained within two men's correspondence; Rachel Carnell continues this exploration asserting that Brontë, in fact, returns to rationalist Enlightenment philosophies and is nostalgic for 'the classical, liberal model of bourgeois public debate' (4).

[15] For more information on how *Jane Eyre* is carefully and deliberately structured according to a pagan calendar see Talley.

[16] Both G. D. Hargraves and Lori A. Paige also note the similarity between Anne Brontë's 'Preface' and Helen Huntington's language on 57. See Hargraves, 497, n. 5, and Paige, 'Diary', 226 and 227, n. 2.

[17] Winifred Gérin makes a similar point in her biography of Anne Brontë stating that 'it is by the defective education given to boys that the vices of men are implanted' (252).

[18] See Mitzi Myers.

[19] See, for example, 'An Admonition to Youth: Sermon on 2 Timothy, II: 22'.

[20] For a strong study on this see Myers.

[21] Methodism's most confusing contradiction is its simultaneous espousal of equality and strict class division. One sermon, originally delivered around 1681 by the Reverend Doctor Annesley that was reprinted in the magazine best articulates the idea of the necessity of class divisions:

> God sets one creature higher, and another lower: one to rule, the other to be ruled. And he advanceth one above the other, yet with no injustice or wrong to any, but for the mutual help of one another the beauty and the harmony of the universe. (104)

In addition to putting forth the naturalness of class division, the minister later reminds his audience that 'it is but a little while, and master and servant must be equal; death knows no difference, the worms and rottenness will seize one as soon as the other' (151). He points out the very egalitarian nature of mortality and reminds the servant reader (a portion of the article is directed to masters and the other to servants) to 'be a cheerful worker, [and] a cheerful sufferer', thus safeguarding the traditions of class oppression, since working and suffering are unproblematically linked (154). Using precisely the kind of reasoning that E. P. Thompson rightly criticizes in *The Making of the English Working Class*, Annesley goes on to remind servants that 'shortly you shall not be called servants, but friends; not friends only but children; not children only but heirs, joint heirs with the Lord Jesus' (156). This logic regarding the inherent equality of master and servant *in relationship to God* is further bolstered by yet another argument, one that seems to be endorsed in *Tenant*: 'if all loved God the way they should, this would make the master reasonable, just and merciful; the servant faithful, diligent and constant in his obedience' (105). The relations between Arthur, Helen and Rachel illustrate this idea, since Arthur is both cruel and unkind to Rachel while the properly Christian Helen is not. Rachel, in turn, is 'faithful, diligent and constant' to the religious Helen.

[22] Note, however, that there is no definitive proof that Brontë read Wollstonecraft.

[23] For more information on Wesley and his relationship to Enlightenment philosophy see Brantley, Dryer, and Gill.

24 Thanks to Ellen Brinks, Janet Gray, U. C. Knoepflmacher, Karen McPherson, Deborah Nord, and Linda Shires for reading and commenting on earlier versions of this piece.

Works Cited

Annesley, Rev. Dr. 'Sermon on the Duties of Masters and Servants: Ephesians VI. 5-9'. *Methodist Magazine* 24 (March and April 1801): 104-12 and 151-58.

Anonymous. 'An Admonition to Youth: Sermon on 2 Timothy, II: 22'. *Methodist Magazine* 24 (October 1801): 422-28.

-----. 'On Being Unequally Yoked'. *Methodist Magazine* 34 (October 1811): 776-79.

-----. ['Cleopas']. 'Cursory Remarks on Methodism'. *Methodist Magazine* 31 (September 1808): 402-04.

-----. 'On the Education of Children'. *Methodist Magazine* 23 (August 1800): 373-77.

-----. 'On Fanaticism'. *Methodist Magazine* 24 (January 1801): 36-39.

-----. ['Mentor']. 'Hints to Young Persons'. *Methodist Magazine* 34 (August 1811): 624-26.

-----. 'The Pernicious Effects of Intoxication'. *Methodist Magazine* 28 (October 1805): 468-70.

-----. 'Practical Reflections on the Shortness of Human Life'. *Methodist Magazine* 26 (January 1803): 33-38.

-----. 'On the Religious Employment of Time'. *Methodist Magazine* 24 (June 1801): 265-69.

-----. '*The Quarterly Review* No. 8 'On the Evangelical Sects'". *Methodist Magazine* 34 (June 1811): 416-21.

-----. [B. R. G.]. 'The Shipwreck of the Namur'. *Methodist Magazine* 33 (March 1810): 111.

Barker, Juliet. *The Brontës*. London: St. Martins Press, 1994.

Berg, Mary Margaret. 'The Tenant of Wildfell Hall: Anne Brontë's *Jane Eyre*'. *The Victorian Newsletter* 71 (Spring 1987): 10-15.

Bogie, James. 'The Neglect of Family Prayer, A Source of Infinite Evil'. *Methodist Magazine* 26 (January 1803), 27.

Brantley, Richard E. *Locke, Wesley and the Method of English Romanticism*. Gainsville: University of Florida Press, 1984.

Brontë, Anne. *Agnes Grey*. 1847. London and Melbourne: Dent, 1985.

-----. *The Tenant of Wildfell Hall*. 1848. Intro. Winifred Gérin. Harmondsworth: Penguin Books, 1987.

Brontë, Charlotte. *Shirley*. 1849. Intro. and Ed. Andrew and Judith Hook. Harmondsworth: Penguin Books, 1985.

Brontë, Emily. *Wuthering Heights*. 1847. Intro. and Ed. David Daiches. London: Penguin Books, 1985.

Bury. 'An Account of Mrs Elizabeth Bury Written by Her Husband'. *Methodist Magazine* 34 (June 1811): 450-56.

Carnell, Rachel K. 'Feminism and the Public Sphere in Anne Brontë's *The Tenant of Wildfell Hall*'. *Nineteenth Century Literature* 53.1 (June 1998): 1-24.

Cunningham, Valentine. *Everywhere Spoken Against: Dissent in the Victorian Novel.* Oxford: Clarendon Press, 1975.

Dryer, Frederick. 'Faith and Experience in the Thought of John Wesley'. *American Historical Review* 88.1 (February 1983): 12-30.

-----. 'A "Religious Society Under Heaven": John Wesley and the Identity of Methodism'. *Journal of British Studies* 25.1 (January 1986): 62-83.

Eagleton, Terry. *Myths of Power: A Marxist Study of the Brontës*. 1975. London: Macmillan, 1988.

Felman, Shoshana. 'Psychoanalysis and Education: Teaching Terminable and Interminable'. *Yale French Studies* 63 (1982): 22-44.

----- and Dori Laub. *Testimony: Crises of Witnessing in Literature, Psychoanalysis, and History*. New York and London: Routledge, 1992.

Gérin, Winifred. *Anne Brontë*. London: Allen Lane, 1976.

Gill, Frederick C. *The Romantic Movement and Methodism: A Study of English Romanticism and the Evangelical Revival.* 1937. London: The Epworth Press, 1954.

Gordon, Jan B. 'Gossip, Diary, Letter Text: Anne Brontë's Narrative Tenant and the Problematic of the Gothic Sequel'. *ELH* 51.4 (Winter 1984): 719-45.

Harrison, G. Elsie. *Methodist Good Companions*. London: The Epworth Press, 1935.

-----. *Haworth Parsonage: A Study of Wesley and the Brontës*. London: The Epworth Press, 1937.

-----. *The Clue to the Brontës*. London: Methuen & Co. Ltd., 1948.

Herman, Judith. *Trauma and Recovery: The Aftermath of Violence from Domestic Abuse to Political Terror*. New York: Basic Books, 1992.

Mitzi Myers. '"Servants as They are Now Educated": Women Writers and Georgian Pedagogy'. *Essays in Literature*, 16.1 (Spring 1988): 51-69.

Paige, Lori. 'Helen's Diary Freshly Considered', *Brontë Society Transactions* 20.4 (1991): 225-27.

Shires, Linda M. 'Of Maenads, Mothers and Feminized Males: Victorian Readings of the French Revolution'. *Rewriting the Victorians: Theory, History and the Politics of Gender*. Ed. Linda M. Shires. New York and London: Routledge, 1992: 147-65.

Stevens, John. 'An Account of Leah Masters'. *Methodist Magazine* 28 (February 1805): 82-85.

Talley, Lee A. 'Subject to the Word: Evangelical Discourse and the Brontës'

Fiction'. Dissertation. Princeton University, 1999.

Wesley, John. 'Original Letter of the Reverend John Wesley, to Miss B'. *Methodist Magazine* 28 (November 1805), 520.

Wise, T. J. and J. A. Symington. *The Brontës: Their Lives, Friendships and Correspondence, Volume 1*. Philadelphia: The Porcupine Press, 1980.

Wollstonecraft, Mary. *The Vindication of the Rights of Woman*. 1792. *Feminism: The Essential Historical Writings*. Ed. Miriam Schneir. New York: Vintage Books, 1994. 5-16.

Chapter 9

Aspects of Love in
The Tenant of Wildfell Hall

Marianne Thormählen

I dare to predict that before the close of our twentieth century
posterity will discover that it has been unjust in its assessment of
Anne Brontë and *The Tenant of Wildfell Hall*, and will belatedly
come to re-discover the novel for the masterpiece it is. (Bell 321)[1]

It is fair to say that A. Craig Bell's prophecy of 1966 is in the process of being
fulfilled, though things got off to a slow start. In 1982, Arlene M. Jackson
introduced a discussion of *The Tenant of Wildfell Hall* by maintaining that Anne
Brontë seemed 'ready for rediscovery' (Jackson 198),[2] and the 1980s bore her out:
Juliet McMaster's superb close reading of the *Tenant* was published a mere six
months after Jackson's article, to be followed by other worthwhile critical
contributions, among them two books on Anne Brontë with separate chapters on
the novel.[3] Before the 1980s, discussions of *Tenant* tended to be contained in
studies of the Brontë fiction as a whole.[4] The authors of these studies would
usually draw attention to Brontë's narrowness of vision, emphasizing her didactic
purpose and downplaying her skills.[5] More recently, by contrast, commentators
on *Tenant* have detected both complexity and conscious artistry of a high order in
Brontë's fiction. Some have examined *Tenant* in conjunction with, and as a
response to, *Wuthering Heights*.[6] The interest of feminist critics in the novel is
amply warranted; for one thing, it features the situation of a married woman
powerless to detach herself by legal means from even the most depraved
husband.[7] Narratological analyses and studies of structural images have uncovered
previously unnoticed levels of sophistication in *Tenant*. All this critical activity has
contributed to bringing about that revaluation of Anne Brontë, not least of all of
her second novel, that Bell foresaw.

A great deal remains to be done, of course. The novels with which Bell
compared *Tenant*, *Jane Eyre* and *Wuthering Heights*, have generated enormous
quantities of scholarship and criticism over the years. There is scope for extensive
research on *Tenant* as well. Historically orientated investigators will find fruitful
material in, for instance, such diverse matters as its reflections of new practices
and ideas in agriculture and changing tastes in the arts.[8] Among the facets of
human relations that still await critical scrutiny are male friendship, sibling
relationships and family responsibilities. But the passion of love between man and

woman is the core of the novel, and the ensuing discussion focuses on that fundamental theme.

While a good deal of examination has been devoted to character development in *Tenant*, I want to stress two perspectives that have not as yet received the attention they deserve: love as an actuator of and driving force in human development and spiritual pilgrimage. Love rouses and stimulates individual characteristics and propensities, causing the novel's characters to develop in different directions depending on the nature of the activated qualities and on how the individual deals with the consequences of his/her passion. Happiness in love is associated with determined resistance to forces that militate against the laws of God, whereas the flouting of divine decrees breeds misery.

No other Brontë heroine lives in such constant awareness of the hereafter as Helen Huntingdon does. From first to last, she keeps her eyes fixed on eternity. The salvation of her soul, and in due course her son's, is the most important concern in her life. All her earthly aspirations in ruins, her hope of Heaven is, as she herself says to an insidious tempter, the only thing left to her (322). Her first diary comments on the birth of her son are 'thank Heaven, I am a mother too. God has sent me a soul to educate for Heaven' (228). They are followed by sombre reflections on the dangers in her child's path – dangers she prays to be allowed to help him avoid, so that he can become 'God's servant while on earth, a blessed and honoured saint in Heaven'. Death, even his, is vastly preferable to jeopardizing the hope of future bliss: she says so explicitly, both when in raptures over his innocent baby self and later, defending her child-rearing principles in Linden-car. Even at that time, when her little boy has become still more precious to her and his welfare is virtually her sole earthly preoccupation, she goes so far as to announce:

> '. . . if I thought he would grow up to be what you call a man of the world – one that has *"seen life,"* and glories in his experience, even though he should so far profit by it, as to sober down, at length, into a useful and respected member of society – I would rather that he died to-morrow! – rather a thousand times!' (31)

This attitude matches the moral tuition dispensed by countless authors of early-nineteenth-century devotional literature, however repugnant it may seem to present-day readers. At a time when many children did not survive infancy, parents did not expect to rear every son and daughter born to them. The best consolation their spiritual advisers could give them was that death was the door to instant heavenly bliss for a small and unpolluted soul. Helen shares this belief unreservedly; it is part and parcel of that faith which is, for long periods, the only source of strength that she possesses.

If she had regarded God as a stern judge, her faith could not have inspired her with such fortitude: Helen's God is, first and foremost, the very fount of love, and to her divine and human love are inseparable. In one of the key scenes of *Tenant*, the newlywed Huntingdons discourse on religion along lines that reveal a great gulf fixed between them. Arthur Huntingdon finds his bride 'too religious' and resents the fact that she forgets him in her worship. Helen replies:

> 'I will give my whole heart and soul to my Maker if I can ... and not one atom more of it to you than He allows. What are *you*, sir, that you should set yourself up as a god, and presume to dispute possession of my heart with Him to whom I owe all I have and all I am ...'
>
> . . . .
>
> 'I should *rejoice* to see you at any time, so deeply absorbed in your devotions that you had not a single thought to spare for me. But, indeed, I should lose nothing by the change, for the more you loved your God the more deep and pure and true would be your love to me'. (193-94)

The intensity of her feelings is underlined by her husband's admonition – the exhortation of a healthy sportsman in the prime of life to his girl bride – not to 'pinch my arm so, you're squeezing your fingers into the bone'.

As a number of critics have pointed out,[9] the Huntingdon marriage is a fatal mismatch of personalities which accelerates the male partner's 'progress' towards his disastrous end. Usually, Helen's high moral standards and her severity in asserting them have been regarded as operative factors; but to me they seem far less crucial than Huntingdon's frustration at not being able to possess her soul.[10] When his descent towards 'the place prepared for the devil and his angels' (Helen's aunt's description of Huntingdon's likely destination) begins (142),[11] Helen nurses him devotedly and without reproach, leaving him in no doubt of her love for him. It is only when this forbearance proves ineffectual that she actively tries to restrain his riotous living and openly shows her displeasure. During the decisive initial phase of his downward journey, her 'harshness' is thus hardly in evidence at all: what infuriates him is that there is a part of his wife – and she has left him in no doubt that it is the most important part – which he cannot control or even reach. It is clear from the start that she resists his attempts to assert his dominance over her spirit and that the only way in which he could have gained access to it would have been as a sharer in God's love. As a creature wholly of this world, he is incapable of meeting her on this level, and his annoyance with anything and anyone who affords his wife even a moment's pleasure independently of himself gives us an idea of how potent his jealousy of her God becomes. Always a powerful marriage-wrecker, jealousy is at work in the Huntingdon ménage long before the Arthur-Annabella intrigue begins. It is only logical that Arthur Huntingdon should defy his wife's unshakeable devotion to an invincible rival by heading towards the opposite camp, actively pursuing perdition in such places as 'the Hell-fire Club'.[12]

There are many couples in *Tenant*, married and unmarried;[13] but the marriage of Helen and Arthur Huntingdon holds centre-stage position for most of the book. The girl Helen's infatuation with the semi-pathologically sniggering man whose abundant curls mask his absence of firmness of character and moral feelings[14] is the most fateful instance of love as an actuator in the novel. Her passion for him is so strong that it nullifies years of patient moral education administered by her aunt; makes her forget her own avowed principles prior to her first 'season' (principles reiterated, word for word, in scores of courtesy books) to the effect that esteem must precede love; and causes her to disregard a succession of warning signs that would have deterred a far less intelligent and observant girl with some instinct for self-preservation.

Unfortunately, the two women who are Helen's best friends and whose spontaneous recoiling from Arthur Huntingdon might have given her pause indirectly weaken their cases against him by being known to prefer other suitors, real and potential. Milicent Hargrave favors her brother, as yet unknown to Helen, and Helen's aunt the male personage in the book with the lowest degree of sensual attractiveness: the dull, fussy and self-important valetudinarian Mr Boarham. The latter creation is, incidentally, one of several indications that Anne Brontë carefully worked out the *dramatis personae* in *Tenant* as a pattern of parallels, contrasts and foils: while the idea of spending so much as a week married to Mr Boarham makes any female reader shudder, his avuncular outpourings to Helen in the course of which he tactlessly expatiates on her shortcomings are in fact perfectly justified.[15] He is a far better judge of her character than Arthur Huntingdon, who ascribes angelic qualities to this all-too-human girl in a parade of clumsy and hypocritical clichés. For all the wisdom and good sense that Mrs Maxwell exhibits, one would have thought she should have known better than to set up a physically repulsive dogmatist as a rival to a handsome and charming playboy in a teenage girl's affections. Nor does she improve her position by scolding Helen for calling the disreputable old rip Mr Wilmot (the suitor supported by Helen's uncle) wicked, though she 'allowed he was no saint' – words echoed in Helen's subsequent defence of Arthur Huntingdon to her. Helen's suspicion that her aunt never knew the true nature of love (126) seems natural under the circumstances.

Physical attraction, then, is obviously the basis of Helen's love for Huntingdon, a passion so powerful that it overcomes every obstacle, including her consciousness of Huntingdon's shocking liberties with her person, the lack of tact and real intelligence of which she is likewise aware and his heartless playing with her feelings as he flirts with Annabella. But that kind of infatuation could have been overcome by a few more months of quiet country life (and perhaps another personable wooer), and the novel does not depict sensual appetites as reprehensible in themselves. Where Helen errs, and errs grievously, is in constructing a religious rationale to accommodate an inclination that has nothing even remotely spiritual about it.

Whenever Arthur Huntingdon tries to adopt religious modes of discourse, he is so blatantly insincere and doctrinally unsound that not even Helen can ignore it. During the uncertain courtship which looks as if it could equally well end in a match between him and Annabella, he utters occasional would-be pious platitudes which his conduct subsequently disproves: 'sometimes he says that if he had me always by his side he should never do or say a wicked thing, and that a little daily talk with me would make him quite a saint' (141). Waiting for her guardians' approval of her choice, Helen is compelled to recognise that the man she loves is happy to pose as a religious hypocrite to gain his ends (163 and 167-68). Perhaps Huntingdon's most ominous utterance in this context is his plea to Helen's aunt when she surprises the young lovers in the library: 'I would sooner die than relinquish her in favour of the best man that ever went to Heaven – and as for her happiness, I would sacrifice my body and soul' – Mrs. Maxwell's horror at his last words is patent in her response, 'Body and *soul* Mr. Huntingdon – sacrifice your *soul?*' (160). Forced to retract, he amends the expendable entity to 'life'. This only shows that he has no conception of the difference between giving up one's temporary possession, earthly existence, and surrendering to the forces of evil by giving up that which properly belongs to God, the soul. It is clear that he is capable of neither act, and his selfish declaration that he would rather die than permit Helen's union with a better man is not exactly a recommendation either, least of all to an elderly woman who is deeply committed to the girl's welfare and thoroughly suspicious of him.

Helen thus has no good reason to believe that she will be encouraged or even allowed to put her 'sense' and 'principle' at Huntingdon's service (141-42). However, her failure to see this is mere stupidity and self-delusion of a kind that might be excused in a teenager in love for the first time. But her arrogation to herself of the power to save another human being's soul is an act of religious hubris, exacerbated by the way in which she harnesses her spiritual vanity to her endeavor to gratify her own non-spiritual desires. As every Anglican Christian in the early- and mid-nineteenth century knew, the only agent who can save is God, and nobody can be saved who does not voluntarily open his heart to him.

Tenant in its entirety repeatedly asserts the need for the sinner to repent, freely and wholeheartedly, and no human persuader can bring him/her to that state. Lord Lowborough reforms because he is determined not to sink under vice and disgrace and finds the requisite stamina within himself. Ralph Hattersley mends his ways because he tires of dissipation and wishes to begin a new life, in which he would behave 'with all decency and sobriety as a Christian and the father of a family should do' (361-62). He gallantly ascribes his reformation to

Helen's influence; but the latter truthfully tells Milicent Hattersley that 'her husband was predisposed to amendment before [Helen] added [her] mite of exhortation and encouragement' (365). Helen's most significant act in this respect consists in silently handing him two letters from his wife, the perusal of which becomes a turning point. For all his deficiencies, Hattersley cares about his wife and children. Reading the letters transforms his view of Milicent, whose uncomplaining devotion he always took for granted to the point where she barely existed as a sentient being for him. The awareness of what she suffers beneath her meek exterior rouses his shame and breeds a resolution to abandon his former life and habits. The Hattersley marriage thus supplies a particularly striking illustration of activated love initiating the favorable long-term development of a character in Tenant.

Helen Huntingdon has sometimes been regarded as a little too perfect to engage the reader's sympathy, but as the preceding discussion has shown, her young self is seriously flawed. Her ensuing sufferings, harrowing as they are, are not incommensurate to her fault, as she herself acknowledges. If her true rehabilitation is to be achieved, she has to be stripped of every illusion and made to taste the dregs of utter humiliation. Before her engagement, her aunt begged her not to boast but watch, greeting the girl's protestations of unshakeable prudence in matters of the heart with the sceptical response, 'You have not been tried yet . . . we can but hope' (125-26). Subsequent events prove how justified that 'cold, cautious' attitude was.

Helen's trials come thick and fast after she has committed herself for life to a man whose shallow fondness for her never deserves to be called love. Not once, before or after marriage, does he show a moment's genuine concern for the welfare of the woman for whose happiness he had declared himself willing to 'sacrifice body and soul'. His reason for deciding to marry Helen and not Annabella, also beautiful, accomplished and a probable future heiress, may be that the younger girl looked like an easier proposition. A more likely explanation, however, is that Annabella, who is always exceedingly frank with Arthur Huntingdon, makes it clear to him at an early point that she means to marry a title. Before her engagement to Lord Lowborough, Annabella admits to Helen that while she has set her sights on the morose peer, she would have preferred Arthur Huntingdon – provided the latter had owned Lowborough's 'pedigree, and title, and delightful old family seat' (172).

This does not amount to saying that Huntingdon is indifferent to Helen and marries her for mercenary reasons only. His inability to possess her body *and* soul would not have bred such resentment in him if she had not mattered at all. He is clearly gratified by the desirable young girl's obvious infatuation with him, and for a brief period he enjoys showing his beautiful bride off in company. But when he tires of Helen's constant expectations to see him act against his inclinations and finds her unable to relieve his boredom, his affection for her peters out. The combination of flattered vanity, sensual satisfaction and gratification at having made an advantageous match does not survive everyday life with the real person. Far from being purged of wickedness and stimulated to saintliness by daily life with Helen (as he had claimed during their courtship), Arthur Huntingdon develops in the opposite direction. As time goes by, her spiritual strength which began by irritating and alienating him makes him positively afraid of her – a fact noted by his friends and manifest in his occasionally behaving like a guilty child before her.[16]

Disappointed in the outcome of his marriage, Huntingdon turns first to drink and debauchery of (to him) familiar kinds and then to a person who has also found that matrimony, in her case entered into for purely material considerations, did not live up to expectations. Arthur Huntingdon and Annabella Wilmot-Lowborough were always a natural pair, matched in opinions and inclinations, and Annabella's society is stimulating and entertaining to him in a way that his uncongenial wife's is not. For one thing, Annabella possesses the sole artistic accomplishment that Huntingdon really appreciates, musical ability.

It is not the least of Helen's griefs to find that this woman, of whose moral inferiority she has always been conscious, attains the aims Helen had set for herself in respect of Arthur Huntingdon, if only temporarily. While in love with Annabella, he behaves with moderation to win her approval; he does not take pleasure in teasing or confusing her; and – for once – he is serious.[17] Her departure leaves him drained of merriment, the fiendish 'low laugh' which used to torment Helen giving way to lamentations and ill-temper. Annabella has undoubtedly come closer to him than any other woman. But not even this passion, the nearest thing to love that Arthur Huntingdon ever experiences, has any real staying power: when Annabella, like Helen before her, expects him to behave in ways he has no mind to, he tires of her – '[s]he was so deuced imperious and exacting . . . now I shall be my own man again, and feel rather more at my ease' (333). Despite his brief improvement under the Annabella régime, Huntingdon hence remains essentially impervious to the influence of love – and Annabella really loves him, as the disgusted Helen is obliged to recognise.[18]

This love is entirely worldly, though. Not only does it not contain any spiritual dimension; it is a flagrant offence against the laws of God, whose love alone is perfect. That is, fundamentally, why the relationship cannot prosper and actually hastens the downfall of both protagonists. Meanwhile, Helen is forced to acknowledge an emotion which embodies a threat to herself:

> Oh! when I think how fondly, how foolishly I have loved him, how madly I have trusted him, how constantly I have laboured, and studied, and prayed, and struggled for his advantage; and how cruelly he has trampled on my love, betrayed my trust, scorned my prayers and tears, and efforts for his preservation –

crushed my hopes, destroyed my youth's best feelings, and doomed me to a life of hopeless misery – as far as man can do it – it is not enough to say that I no longer love my husband – I HATE him! The word stares me in the face like a guilty confession, but it is true: I hate him – I hate him! – But God have mercy on his miserable soul! – and make him see and feel his guilt – I ask no other vengeance! If he could but fully know and truly feel my wrongs, I should be well avenged; and I could freely pardon all; but he is so lost, so hardened in his heartless depravity that, in this life, I believe he never will. (297)

Having sidestepped duty to achieve her union with a man she loves, Helen Huntingdon spends the first years of her marriage trying to love him as a duty. It is a hopeless, protracted rearguard action: her efforts are remorselessly ground down by a succession of ordeals and disappointments, great and small, culminating in the shock of his infidelity with Annabella. The circumstances of that revelation are unusually brutal: weeks of hoping that she possesses her husband's love after all, and that he may indeed be reformed if not redeemed as a result, are followed by Helen's discovery that the ardent embrace and the whispered 'Bless you darling!' in the dark shrubbery were intended not for her but for Annabella. '[T]he burst of kindness was for his paramour, the start of horror for his wife' (284-85 and 293): this stark sentence not only sums up her personal agony and humiliation; it also spells the end of her hope that her life of sacrifice might after all be of some benefit to Huntingdon. The double blow is too great: the pathetic resolution to 'love him when I can' (257) gives way to 'I hate him!' in less than two months.

The reason why Helen's hatred is dangerous for her is that it, too, is a violation of divine precepts. Hatred of persons, as all the Brontë novels emphasize, is impermissible: it misdirects emotional energy, impedes generous and affectionate impulses between humans and, most importantly, blocks communication with God, whose forgiveness of our sins is contingent on our ability to forgive one another (Thormählen, *The Brontës and Religion* 119-43). The impulse to seek revenge for injustice must be stifled, as both Helen and Lord Lowborough, striving to keep faith with God, are aware (331-32). The latter resists the exhortation to be avenged on Huntingdon by fighting a duel with him and is derided in consequence; it is an attractive prospect for the wretched cuckold, in that it would probably lead either to the adulterer's demise or to his own liberation in death. Helen, of course, faces no temptations of that kind; but Walter Hargrave's attempts to seduce her do offer an opportunity to retaliate. Once she actually admits to finding herself contemplating that option; but her subsequent horror at her 'sinful thoughts' causes her to hate her husband 'tenfold more than ever' for having placed her in a situation where such an idea could even cross her mind (302).

The irrevocable loss of every remnant of love for Arthur Huntingdon, and its replacement by bitter, rancorous loathing, is a decisive factor in Helen's gradually evolved project of escape from the matrimonial home and from her torturer. Another is of course her concern for her son. Far from standing the slightest chance of saving her husband, Helen Huntingdon faces the prospect of being dragged down with him, along with the soul that God had, in her own words, sent her 'to educate for Heaven'. Helen's labors to counteract that corruption of little Arthur in which Huntingdon takes such pleasure, largely because he knows what exquisite pain it inflicts on his wife, may prove vain in the end: having failed to reform her husband and being compelled to register the successive warping of her own self, how can she be sure of success in this, the most vital of her obligations? When Huntingdon places young Arthur in the care of a mistress of his, posing as a governess, Helen knows that the time has come.

Among the dangers and afflictions she leaves behind as she runs away from Grassdale Manor is Walter Hargrave's four-year campaign to induce her to flee with him, or at least to have an affair with him *in situ*. The Hargrave element is a curious feature in *Tenant* in that the neighbor is presented as a tangible menace for reasons that are not readily apparent. True, Walter Hargrave is a credible and accomplished tempter: he is far more intelligent and cultured than Arthur Huntingdon; Helen enjoys their conversations, and their tastes agree in many respects. Besides, he is her best friend's brother, and he lends her some assistance in her efforts to restrain Huntingdon's evil influence on her little boy. Even so, he *is* a member of her husband's band of revellers, and she never admits to finding him in the least attractive. On the contrary, she is suspicious of him from the outset, and her diary contains no hints that she relishes his extravagant flattery. Instead of feeling comforted that one man in her surroundings claims to appreciate her worth, Helen appears annoyed by his rapturous compliments on her 'angelic' nature. Why, then, does she come to regard him as a dangerous enemy whose presence is to be avoided by ruse and endured with resolution? A simple answer would be a failure on the author's part to ensure sufficient credibility in this respect; but the extraordinary chess game suggests a more complex one. [19] The combat is, as Helen recognises from the start, 'the type of a more serious contest', the contest for her virtue, and she feels 'an almost superstitious dread of being beaten'. At a crucial point in the game, Hargrave acknowledges his disrespect for the religious obstacles to an illicit union with Helen: 'It is those bishops that trouble me . . . but the bold knight can overleap the reverend gentleman . . . and now, those sacred persons once removed, I shall carry all before me.' Watchers of the game perceive the players' agitation; Hattersley comments on Helen's trembling hand, provoking a uniquely uncivil utterance from her, 'Hold your tongue, will you?'

If Helen had only found Hargrave a nuisance, she would not have been so excited, nor would she have regarded his pestering her as a threat to her salvation. Some of her answers to his pleas imply that she has at least entertained the idea of yielding to him so far as to think about the consequences of such an act. A telling exchange occurs in chapter 37, in which Hargrave goes on the attack:

> 'I know that there are feelings in your nature that have never yet been called forth – I know, too, that in your present neglected, lonely state you are, and *must* be miserable. You have it in in your power to raise two human beings from a state of actual suffering to such unspeakable beatitude as only generous, noble self-forgetting love can give (for you *can* love me if you will; you may tell me that you scorn and detest me, but – since you have set me the example of plain speaking – I will answer that *I do not believe you!*), but you will not do it! You choose rather to leave us miserable; and you coolly tell me it is the will of God that we should remain so. *You* may call this religion, but *I* call it wild fanaticism!'
>
> 'There is another life both for you and for me. . . . If it be the will of God that we should sow in tears, now, it is only that we may reap in joy, hereafter. It is His will that we should not injure others by the gratification of our own earthly passions; and you have a mother, and sisters, and friends, who would be seriously injured by your disgrace; and I too have friends, whose peace of mind shall never be sacrificed to my enjoyment – or yours either, with my consent – and if I were alone in the world, I have still my God and my religion, and I would sooner die than disgrace my calling and break my faith with Heaven to obtain a few brief years of false and fleeting happiness – happiness sure to end in misery, even here – for myself or any other!' (321)

Hargrave runs a calculated risk in making it clear to Helen ('since you have set me the example of plain speaking') that he does not believe her indifferent to him. It is surely significant that she does not oppose him on this score but entertains the notion that a liaison between them could have entailed 'enjoyment' and 'happiness', however deceptive and transient. Her reply also intimates that renunciation will cost 'tears', and her use of the first person plural is suggestive, too.

On such indirect evidence as this, one may well suspect that the diatribes and denigrating remarks on Walter Hargrave that Helen commits to her diary form a case of overmuch protestation, and that she does feel drawn to him at some level. Perhaps she needs to remind herself, trapped in the situation from which her aunt tried to preserve her, of that lady's admonition, 'Don't boast, but *watch*'. Recording Hargrave's machinations – always in the least favorable light she can – could offer useful assistance in her endeavor not to succumb to vain and selfish impulses a second time.

Does Hargrave really love her? His pertinacity may be taken to suggest that he does (four years is a long time); but as Joseph Le Guern points out, Walter Hargrave comes across as a hunter in pursuit of his prey rather than as a constant lover (Vol. II 668). On one occasion only, Helen allows that his passion for her could be sincere:

> He made no answer, but, bending from his horse, held out his hand towards me. I looked up at his face, and saw, therein, such a look of genuine agony of soul that, whether bitter disappointment, or wounded pride, or lingering love, or burning wrath were uppermost, I could not hesitate to put my hand in his as frankly as if I bade a friend farewell. He grasped it very hard, and immediately put spurs to his horse and galloped away. Very soon after, I learned that he was gone to Paris, where he still is, and the longer he stays there the better for me.
> I thank God for this deliverance! (323)

Not until Hargrave breaks his promise and pleads love to Helen again, in a state of excitement she claims never to have seen in any man before, does she resort to the kind of language that is guaranteed to put off the most impetuous suitor. Having repulsed him literally at (palette-) knife point, she pronounces: 'I don't like you . . . and if I were divorced from my husband – or if he were dead, I would not marry you'. This is plain speaking indeed, far from the scruples she has adduced before, and Hargrave's reaction matches it: his face is 'blanched with anger' and he accuses her of being 'ungrateful', but he does not renew his solicitations.

A noteworthy component in Hargrave's campaign, and one on which he lays increasing stress as he learns more about the nature of Helen's objections, is his attempt to persuade her that her resistance amounts to a defiance of God:

> 'You have no reason now: you are flying in the face of Heaven's decrees. God has designed me to be your comfort and protector – I feel it – I know it as certainly as if a voice from Heaven declared "Ye twain shall be one flesh" – and you spurn me from you'. (342)

Hargrave cannot know that this approach is peculiarly unlikely to succeed with a woman who was once presumptuous enough to appoint herself to the function of God's instrument and who suffered agonizingly in consequence. With her experiences, nothing is more abhorrent to her than pseudo-religious arrogance.

An incident belonging to the Arthur-Annabella intrigue may be mentioned as another example of this attitude on her part: Wondering whether she ought not to make yet another effort to 'lead [Huntingdon] back to the path of virtue', Helen is forced by the addressee to read a letter to him from his mistress. The letter contains 'impious defiance of God's mandates, and railings against His Providence for having cut their lot asunder'. Invited by her husband to 'take a lesson by it', Helen resolves to do so, in the reverse direction to the one suggested by her husband: she abandons all thought of kindness to him in future. Inured to malice and mortification, she draws the line at condoning blasphemy.

In her refuge at Wildfell Hall, Helen is exposed to another attempt to persuade her to place human wishes above God's precepts. Of all the sacrilegious discourse she is obliged to endure, this is the most painful:

> 'But Helen!' I began in a soft, low tone, not daring to raise my eyes to her face – 'that man is *not* your husband: in the sight of Heaven he has forfeited all claim to ---' She seized my arm with a grasp of startling energy.
>
> '*Gilbert, don't!*' she cried, in a tone that would have pierced a heart of adamant. 'For God's sake, don't *you* attempt these arguments! No *fiend* could torture me like this!' (384-85)

At the time when she has placed her trust in a man she loves and is trying to summon enough strength to convince herself and him that they must not meet again, Gilbert Markham adopts exactly the same treacherous line of reasoning as Walter Hargrave had done on previous occasions when she was particularly vulnerable. By means of italics and emphatic language, Anne Brontë has taken care that the reader does not miss this distressing parallel. Is Gilbert himself another Hargrave, then? Helen's faithful old nurse clearly thinks so: 'doubtless she saw in me another Mr. Hargrave, only the more dangerous in being more esteemed and trusted by her mistress' (382). [20]

Gilbert Markham has generally had a very bad press. Judgements on him range from 'trivial' (Ewbank 83) and 'unheroic' (Chitham 142) to 'a hysterical egotist who always bullyingly insists on having his own way' (Scott 96). Critics have usually agreed that Brontë deliberately attempted to create a hero with human weaknesses, but the consensus is that she failed to make his humanity appealing. His violent assault on Frederick Lawrence has always been held against him, with reason; not only the act itself but also the perpetrator's subsequent callousness are disturbing to say the least. Even those who agree that he does improve and mature find him less than satisfactory as a romantic hero.[21] It is time that the case for his defence was heard.

Ewbank justly observes that the narrative structure of the novel contributes to giving the reader a somewhat unfavorable impression of Gilbert in that he cannot, after all, 'write much about his own good sides' and is 'bound to be as objective as possible' (83-84). Nor, of course, can he convey any idea of his appearance and physical attractiveness. We must also bear in mind that his addressee is his brother-in-law and best friend, who knows all about his 'sides', good and bad, and is apparently used to communicating with Gilbert in a jocular, self-depreciatory masculine idiom. Assured of Halford's sympathy and affection, Gilbert is able to tell a story against himself and does so with some relish – a fairly disarming characteristic, one would have thought. Some of the remarks he makes about his own person and conduct are richly ironic; here is one example:

> Without knowing anything about my real disposition and principles, [Mrs. Graham] was evidently prejudiced against me, and seemed bent upon shewing me that her opinions respecting me, on every particular, fell far below those I entertained of myself. I was naturally touchy, or, it would not have vexed me so much. Perhaps, too, I was a little bit spoiled by my mother and sister, and some other ladies of my acquaintance; – and yet, I was by no means a fop – of that I am fully convinced, whether *you* are or not. (32)

Of course the husband of Gilbert's sister Rose will know how outrageously their mother used to spoil him, and not only in ways Rose could stomach either. The few words about Gilbert that remain in Helen's diary confirm that he was indeed something of a fop – '[t]he fine gentleman and beau of the parish and its vicinity (in his own estimation, at least)' (379). 'Mrs. Graham' is a sharp observer and here she appears trustworthy, both as regards Gilbert's complacency and his status as the most eligible bachelor for miles around. In fact, the latter circumstance suggests a high degree of personal attractiveness: Frederick Lawrence is the 'squire' and socially above the gentleman farmer Gilbert Markham, but the local girls seem far more interested in the latter, who must therefore possess some pretty special qualities to recommend him. The only young woman who sets her cap at Lawrence is the would-be social climber Jane Wilson, who knows that her arts would be wasted on Markham in any case ('never for a moment could she number me amongst her admirers', 18).

Gilbert can hardly be blamed for failing to regret Arthur Huntingdon's demise. The fact that the first half of Helen's diary gives him more pain to read than the second is surely not so reprehensible either: it cannot be easy to read your loved one's ecstatic effusions about her passion for another, and Gilbert admits that the satisfaction he experienced in seeing that passion extinguished was 'selfish' under the circumstances (381). His disappointment at not being allowed to read what the woman he loves thought of and felt about himself hardly merits the censure it has come in for either, especially as he acknowledges that she was quite right to withhold it.

To Halford, Gilbert admits his faults and weaknesses with a candor that engenders confidence in his sincerity when depicting his virtues, necessarily a much more roundabout proceeding. The very first thing the reader learns about Gilbert Markham is that he has involuntarily incurred the displeasure of his best friend, that he regrets this state of affairs and that he is anxious to remove the constraint between them by means of very considerable labors. These labors will, if Halford wishes to be the recipient of them, amount to an atonement.[22] The word 'atone' is noteworthy, setting the key for a story in which the expiation of transgressions is a major element. The second thing we find out about Gilbert is that, although he had cherished ambitions to shine in the world, ambitions in which his fond mother encouraged him, he decided to forgo them and instead obey his father's last wish:

> He assured me it was all rubbish, and exhorted me, with his dying breath, to continue in the good old way, to follow his steps, and those of his father before him, and let my highest ambition be, to walk honestly through the world, looking neither to the right hand nor to the left, and to transmit the paternal acres to my children in, at least, as flourishing a condition as he left them to me.
>
>   'Well! – an honest and industrious farmer is one of the most useful members of society; and if I devote my talents to the cultivation of my farm, and the improvement of agriculture in general, I shall thereby benefit, not only my own immediate connections and dependants, but in some degree, mankind at large: – hence I shall not have lived in vain.' (9)

Gilbert immediately goes on to deflate the solemnity of this declaration by humorously pointing out that these exalted sentiments had little power to cheer the tired farmer on a cold, wet evening in late autumn. Nevertheless, we now know that he resisted the lure of worldly success in order to 'benefit mankind' unspectacularly in the sphere where he belongs. Not merely an admirable choice by any standards, it amounts to a conscious adoption of the classical *beatus ille* ideal, enhanced by filial piety of the kind praised by the classics. Pope's Horatian 'Ode on Solitude', which opens with the lines 'Happy the man whose wish and care / A few paternal acres bound', is perhaps the best-known exponent of this ideal in English literature; the expression 'paternal acres' in Gilbert's account is hardly there by accident.

The contrast between Gilbert the farmer, a man of the earth, and the spiritual and devout Helen is not detrimental to the former, nor is it inherently contradictory. Few people are as keenly aware of the transience of life as the owner-steward of a farming estate which has passed from father to son for generations. Even during the days of his greatest despondency Gilbert Markham is conscious of his duty, and after brief periods of neglect owing to acute misery he always remembers his responsibilities and gets on with his work. Whatever his shortcomings as an elder brother, he is aware of his obligations as a son and at least makes the occasional effort to alleviate his mother's worries about him.[23] This manifest feeling for his surviving parent lends warmth to his promise to Helen: 'I love [your aunt] for your sake, and her happiness shall be as dear to me as that of my own mother' (470). He obviously honors that commitment ('we lived in the greatest harmony with our dear aunt until the day of her death'); Halford would have known if that had not been the case.

Critical attempts to defend Gilbert, languid at the best of times, have dwelt on his emotional and moral development, and his *éducation sentimentale* is certainly a crucial factor. But before passing on to a review of it, I want to emphasize that Gilbert is something Helen has never known before: a *vir bonus*, both physically active and mentally agile, and a faithful steward. With the exception of her brother, whose concern for her is both touching and selfless, Helen's male guardians have failed her dismally: her father gave her up when she was a baby, took no further interest in her and led a less than virtuous life, ending in a drunkard's death;[24] like Helen's father, her uncle – 'a worthless old fellow enough' according to Gilbert (436) – supplies her with a concrete basis for her contention that 'many men of Mr. Huntingdon's habits . . . [live] to a ripe though miserable old age' (386);[25] and her first husband's treatment of his 'treasure' comprises a wide range of neglect and abuse. If ever a woman needed a good steward, it is Helen Huntingdon, and she is granted one in the man whose renunciation of his youthful aspirations is couched in terms borrowed from the parable of the talents – the central Biblical text on stewardship.[26] I think Gilbert's inferiority to Helen in terms of wealth and station should be viewed in the light of this circumstance: the men among whom Helen lived before, her husband especially, knew little about the work that created the wealth of their estates,[27] and Arthur Huntingdon cared nothing for the welfare of his tenants. Gilbert's difference from them in this respect is a circumstance in his favor.

But his moral and spiritual growth is of course the most apparent justification for his being rewarded with a woman of Helen's calibre. Unlike Walter Hargrave (a dreadful steward, incidentally, who tries to force his sisters into wealthy marriages with unworthy men to secure his estate and the continuation of his expensive habits), he changes decisively as a result of his love for Helen. Initially captivated by her beauty, especially on the rare occasions when it is enlivened by laughter, he comes to admire her intelligence, her strength of character and her gifts. The fact that he is a knowledgeable judge of art (Brontë's expertise in this field comes out especially clearly in chapter five, 'The Studio'), her chief talent and her livelihood when he first knows her, reinforces their bond.

Superficially, his attempt to win her has many points in common with Hargrave's, for example the efforts to gain Helen's esteem by feigned emotional restraint, the cultivation of shared tastes, and shows of interest in little Arthur. But Gilbert's intentions are honorable: he believes Helen to be free to marry him, and with the exception of the horrific lapse when he echoes Hargrave's blasphemous arguments he shows no signs of wishing to press her into an illicit affair. Nor does the dashing of his hopes send him off in pursuit of other women with capacious purses; Gilbert's love for Helen is not only an *affaire de coeur* but also, as he explicitly and repeatedly says, a matter of the soul.[28]

In one sense, the transformation of Gilbert Markham from a complacent *beau garçon*, intrigued and annoyed by the failure of a handsome woman to conform to other eligible ladies' (and his own) opinion of him, into a strong, gentle and manly hero parallels the *Leidensweg* of Helen Huntingdon: Tempered by suffering and disappointment, their natures are stripped of the vainglory of youth. Compelled to recognize their previous errors (one of Gilbert's being his irresponsible dalliance with the pert 'little demon' Eliza Millward),[29] they develop a combination of fortitude and humility that precludes opposition to divine decrees.

As Juliet McMaster has noted, the development of Gilbert's younger brother Fergus is 'an epitome of Gilbert's' (364-65):

> I bequeathed the farm to Fergus, with better hopes of its prosperity than I should have had a year ago under similar circumstances; for he had lately fallen in love with the vicar of L---'s eldest daughter, a lady whose superiority had roused his latent virtues and stimulated him to the most surprising exertions, not only to gain her affection and esteem, and to obtain a fortune sufficient to enable him to aspire to her hand, but to render himself worthy of her, in his own eyes, as well as in those of her parents; and in the end he was successful, as you already know. (471)

This single sentence, besides reassuring the reader that another worthy steward takes over the paternal acres, sums up the function of true love in *Tenant*: under its influence, human nature attains its finest blossoming on earth. The small touch of the lady's parentage points to the spiritual dimension that always adheres to the 'infectious theme of love' (450) in the novel. Throughout *Tenant*, the recurring references to the soul's inseparability from fulfilment in love remind us that the ultimate purpose of the exertions prompted by that passion is to be 'educate[d] for Heaven'.

Notes

References to *The Tenant of Wildfell Hall* are to Herbert Rosengarten's 1993 World's Classics paperback edition for Oxford University Press, a reprint of the Clarendon edition's text, with an introduction by Margaret Smith.

[1] Bell went on to compare *The Tenant of Wildfell Hall* with *Wuthering Heights*, to which he predicted that it would come to form a close rival, and with *Jane Eyre*, which he rated below Anne Brontë's book. My reason for cutting the quotation short is that I fail to perceive the superiority of any Brontë novel, or any novel at all for that matter, to *Jane Eyre*.

[2] Jackson did not, however, challenge Anne's inferior status in relation to her sisters.

[3] The two books are P. J. M. Scott's *Anne Brontë: A New Critical Assessment* and Elizabeth Langland's *Anne Brontë: The Other One*. The 1970s saw the appearance of a magisterial two-volume study in French which has been sadly neglected by English-language scholars, Joseph Le Guern's *Anne Brontë (1820-1849): La vie et l'oeuvre*.

[4] See Ewbank, 70-85, and Craik, 228-53.

[5] Craik is, despite her sympathy for and appreciation of Anne Brontë's writing, one example of this fundamentally censorious attitude; so is Terry Eagleton in his discussion of *Tenant* in *Myths of Power: A Marxist Study of the Brontës*.

[6] A leading exponent of this line in criticism on *Tenant* is Edward Chitham; see 91-109 in Chitham's and Tom Winnifrith's *Brontë Facts and Brontë Problems* as well as 133-53 in Chitham's *A Life of Anne Brontë*.

[7] A comparatively early representative is Naomi M. Jacobs' 'Gender and Layered Narrative in *Wuthering Heights* and *The Tenant of Wildfell Hall*'. For two recent feminist studies, see Elizabeth Hollis Berry, *Anne Brontë's Radical Vision: Structures of Consciousness* and Laura C. Berry, 'Acts of Custody and Incarceration in *Wuthering Heights* and *The Tenant of Wildfell Hall*'.

[8] The latter topic was not exhausted by the chapter on Anne Brontë in Christine Alexander and Jane Sellars, *The Art of the Brontës*.

[9] For example, see Scott, 78-80, and Langland, 143.

[10] I raised this point in 'The Villain of *Wildfell Hall*: Aspects and Prospects of Arthur Huntingdon', 836-37.

[11] On the likelihood that Arthur Huntingdon is heading for eternal torment, see 'The Villain of *Wildfell Hall*: Aspects and Prospects of Arthur Huntingdon', 838-39, and Thormählen, *The Brontës and Religion*, 90-95.

[12] As Herbert Rosengarten points out in his commentary in the World's Classics edition of the novel, the setting for Huntingdon's account of his leading role in Lord Lowborough's troubles appears to have been modelled on an eighteenth-century 'devil's den' of that name (478).

[13] Laura Berry contrasts the 'single unkillable couple' in *Wuthering Heights* with 'the endlessly repeated duos in *Wildfell Hall*' (32).

[14] See Thormählen, 'The Villain' (834-35).

[15] But a delicious detail illustrates the revoltingness of the man: waiting for Helen to come down and hear his proposal, he '[nibbles] the end of his cane' (132).

[16] See, for instance, 280 and 294.

[17] Juliet McMaster's article focuses on Huntingdon's laughter versus Helen's seriousness and provides a near-exhaustive analysis of this important feature in the novel.

[18] See, for example, 300.

[19] See 288-90.

[20] We might recall that Rachel herself originally thought Hargrave 'a very nice gentleman' while Helen 'still [had her] doubts on the subject' (238).

[21] Laura Berry concedes that Gilbert's reform 'qualifies him as the one who ought to to get the girl' but only after insulting him by maintaining that 'he is not psychologically so different from Huntingdon' (52 and 45n). In my view, the most perceptive analysis of Gilbert to date is the one offered by Elizabeth Langland, who stresses the chastening process he has to go through to be divested of his culpable arrogance (Langland 133-37).

[22] See the first letter to Halford in the World's Classics edition (7).

[23] See, for instance, 381, 396, and 442.

[24] See 38 and 255-56.

[25] Mr Maxwell's gout, his advocacy of the egregious Mr Wilmot's suit and Helen's aunt's mournful allusions to the unhappiness of being married to a man who does not share one's spiritual concerns and aspirations speak for themselves, and the 'experience' referred to in the chapter heading of chapter sixteen is all too obviously hers.

[26] Matthew 25:14-30; see also Luke 19:12-26. (The relevant passage in *Tenant* is found in chapter one, 9.)

[27] As Craik observes, Helen originally belongs to a class 'who can afford not to know how to farm their own land' (233).

[28] See 89 and 97 for examples.

[29] Le Guern calls her the Rosaline to Gilbert's Romeo (Vol. II 662).

Works Cited

Alexander, Christine and Jane Sellars. *The Art of the Brontës*. Cambridge: Cambridge University Press, 1995.

Bell, A. Craig. 'Anne Brontë: A Reappraisal'. *The Quarterly Review*, 304 (1966): 315-21.

Berry, Elizabeth Hollis. *Anne Brontë's Radical Vision: Structures of Consciousness.* Victoria, British Columbia: University of Victoria, 1994.

Berry, Laura C. 'Acts of Custody and Incarceration in *Wuthering Heights* and *The Tenant of Wildfell Hall*, *Novel*, 30.1 (Fall 1996): 32-55.

Brontë, Anne. *The Tenant of Wildfell Hall.* Ed. Herbert Rosengarten. Oxford: Oxford University Press, 1993.

Chitham, Edward. *A Life of Anne Brontë*, Oxford: Blackwell, 1991.

----- and Tom Winnifrith. *Brontë Facts and Brontë Problems.* London: Macmillan, 1983.

Craik, W. A. *The Brontë Novels.* London: Methuen, 1968.

Eagleton, Terry. *Myths of Power: A Marxist Study of the Brontës.* London: Macmillan, 1975.

Ewbank, Inga-Stina. *Their Proper Sphere: A Study of the Brontë Sisters as Early-Victorian Novelists.* London: Edward Arnold, 1966.

Jackson, Arlene M. 'The Question of Credibility in Anne Brontë's *Tenant of Wildfell Hall'. English Studies* 63.3 (1982): 198-206.

Jacobs, Naomi. 'Gender and Layered Narrative in *Wuthering Heights* and *The The Tenant of Wildfell Hall* '. *The Journal of Narrative Technique* 16.3 (Autumn 1986): 204-19.

Langland, Elizabeth. *Anne Brontë: The Other One.* London: Macmillan, 1989.

Le Guern, Joseph. *Anne Brontë (1820-1849): La vie et l'oeuvre.* 2 vols. Paris: Librairie Honoré Champion, 1977.

McMaster, Juliet. '"Imbecile Laughter" and "Desperate Earnest" in *The Tenant of Wildfell Hall*. *Modern Language Quarterly* 43.3 (December 1982): 352-68.

Scott, P. J. M. *Anne Brontë: A New Critical Assessment.* London and Totowa, N.J.: Vision and Barnes & Noble, 1983.

Thormählen, Marianne. 'The Villain of *Wildfell Hall*: Aspects and Prospects of Arthur Huntingdon'. *The Modern Language Review* 88.4 (October 1993): 831-41.

-----. *The Brontës and Religion.* Cambridge: Cambridge University Press, 1999.

Chapter 10

Wildfell Hall as Satire: Brontë's Domestic *Vanity Fair*

Andrés G. López

> It is very plain, that considering the defectiveness of our laws, the
> weakness of the prerogative, or the cunning of ill-designing men,
> it is possible that many great abuses may be visibly committed
> which cannot be legally punished. . . . I am apt to think it was to
> supply such defects as these that satire was first introduced into
> the world, whereby those whom neither religion nor natural
> virtue nor fear of punishment were able to keep within the
> bounds of their duty, might be withheld by the shame of having
> their crimes exposed to open view in the strongest colours, and
> themselves rendered odious to mankind. (Swift 157)

Exemplifying Swift's definition of the function of satire, Brontë's *The Tenant of Wildfell Hall* deserves to be read alongside other satires, including *Vanity Fair* and *Bleak House*. In *Wildfell Hall*, Brontë explodes several Victorian myths and misconceptions about education, marriage and the family. And, primarily, she satirizes fundamental Victorian assumptions about the natures and roles of men and women. Throughout the novel, Brontë unequivocally demonstrates the 'equality' and not the 'difference' between men and women. She constructs dual narratives of growth to highlight the equality of her narrators, Gilbert Markham and Helen Huntingdon, and simultaneously uses them as vehicles to expose the corruption in their society.[1] As Elizabeth Langland has stressed, *Wildfell Hall* 'rewrites the story of the Fallen Woman as a story of female excellence [and i]n so doing, it takes on a radical feminist dimension' (119). Such a dimension, I will argue, is also necessarily satiric, since it undercuts the conservative views that dominated Victorian thinking.[2] Brontë's novel thus provides a different perspective which contrasts sharply with those of other acknowledged male satirists of her age, especially with Thackeray's.

Like Thackeray, Brontë was aware of the 'defectiveness of [Victorian] laws, the weakness of the prerogative, [and] the cunning of ill-designing men [and women]'–of the 'many great abuses . . . visibly committed which [could] not be legally punished'.[3] Like him, Brontë chose satire as the weapon with which she could expose these 'many great abuses' and fight evil and injustice through her fiction. But Brontë's satiric method was different from Thackeray's; she purposely chose to 'lash' and not 'laugh' at vice and vicious characters – to present evil in its ugliness and not in its most 'agreeable manner'.[4]   Whereas *Vanity Fair* employs satiric humor following the Horatian model used by Fielding in *Tom Jones*, *Wildfell Hall* contains moral or savage indignation, rather than humor, following instead the Juvenalian model used by Richardson in *Clarissa*.[5] Through her two narrators, Gilbert Markham and Helen Huntingdon, Brontë directs her indignation at thoughtless characters who exhibit selfish values and harmful attitudes.   Brontë's exposure of her two principal satiric targets, the 'scandalmongers', in the first section of *Wildfell Hall*, and 'human brutes', in the second, is done 'in the strongest colours' and with the hope of 'render[ing these individuals] odious to mankind' in the manner Swift prescribes.

     In *Agnes Grey*, Agnes, as vehicle for Brontë's satire, limits what Brontë can criticize truthfully; while through the governess Brontë is able to expose Mrs. Bloomfield's and Mrs. Murray's maliciousness towards their children and the devastating effect it has on them, she cannot attack the male circle as forcefully because, from a governess' perspective, that circle is inaccessible.   Agnes, one recalls, hardly ever sees Mr. Bloomfield, Uncle Robson, or Mr. Murray.   Since Brontë does not want to strain the credulity of her audience, Agnes only reports the little that she does see of this circle as honestly as possible.   Agnes is also limited as vehicle because she can only report what occurs within these individual families and hence, Brontë cannot expose the evil in the larger society.   In *Wildfell Hall*, however, by using Gilbert and Helen as co-vehicles for her satire, Brontë gains more flexibility.   She chooses both a male and female voice to gain more authority and diversity as well.   The criticism of the upper class male circle – of Huntingdon and his cronies, whom Helen labels 'human brutes' (356) – comes from a woman who is literally 'trapped' in it and suffers from the evil of its members.   Helen can truthfully report what goes on behind the closed doors that a governess could not penetrate.   Through Helen, Brontë can expose more easily and with greater credulity the vice and vicious characters in upper class society.   Simultaneously, Brontë shows how Helen, like Agnes, becomes a victim of the system she exposes.   Through Gilbert, on the other hand, Brontë satirizes the petty folly and attitudes of several members of a farming community, including individuals from three families, the Millwards, the Wilsons, and the Markhams.   Though the characters in Gilbert's narrative are not as vicious as those in Helen's, Brontë demonstrates how their gossip and petty opinions can be equally destructive.   Just as Helen becomes the victim of the 'human brutes' she exposes, Gilbert becomes the unknowing victim of the 'scandalmongers' he exposes, who trigger in him a jealousy and hatred that ultimately lead him to violence.

     Both Gilbert and Helen are writing honestly and passionately about their life experiences – ones that have led to their individual intellectual, emotional and spiritual growth.   They each describe the variety of emotions they experience – excitement, hope, happiness, love, anger, jealousy, frustration, rage, hatred and indignation – with equal intensity. Helen writes in a journal, supposedly to be privately perused by her at some future time (this journal in a sense becomes an intimate friend to whom she can confess her misery and growing disillusionment during her most difficult trials); Gilbert writes a series of confidential letters to his intimate friend Halford: 'a full and faithful account of certain circumstances connected with the most important event of my life' (34). This is an important parallel between their respective narratives; each writer purposely sets out to tell the truth and avoid exaggeration – neither has any reason to lie.

As Langland observes, part of Helen's and Gilbert's growth process is characterized by their learning to 'recognise what is desirable in a partner' and be 'educated into the value of possessing reason, discernment, judgement, control, and restraint both for themselves and for their partner' (129). But that process goes much further; learning to control one's passion by developing reason and restraint is not enough.[6] For Brontë, real growth is measured by how well individuals can curtail their passions and develop a faith in God. This religious dimension of *Wildfell Hall* needs to be emphasized because it is an important component of the novel artistically, one which works harmoniously with its satiric dimension; Brontë wants readers to deplore and condemn the sins committed by her characters, but to forgive them – the sinners – as she believed God would. Like *Agnes Grey*, *Wildfell Hall* proposes Christian messages: that God is love, and that God's laws must supersede all man-made ones.[7] In *Agnes Grey*, Brontë conveys these messages through Agnes and Weston; in *Wildfell Hall*, she does so through Helen and Gilbert.

Both Gilbert and Helen undergo the same process of moral development that Agnes experiences in *Agnes Grey*. At a crucial point in *Agnes Grey*, Agnes characterizes her moral dilemma as follows: 'It was wrong to be so joyless, so desponding; I should have made God my friend, and to do His will the pleasure and the business of my life; but Faith was weak, and Passion was too strong' (155). Agnes ultimately learns to control her passion and turns to God for guidance. Subsequently, she is stronger spiritually, and such fortitude allows her to brave adversity, make proper choices and find happiness. It is the development of her moral nature that helps her control a stifling passion. In *Wildfell Hall*, Helen and Gilbert wage the same moral battle between passion and faith. They must each turn to God in their time of affliction. Each undergoes several difficult trials and emerges from them a better person – more humble, tolerant and self-sacrificing.

At several crucial points in her narrative, for example, Helen seeks divine assistance and each time, by pouring forth her agony to God and asking for His guidance, she reaffirms her faith, achieves a clearer vision and is re-invigorated. One such low point occurs when Helen discovers her husband's adulterous affair with Annabella Lowborough. Although Helen has by this time already begun to sense the devastating effects of her youthful error in rushing so quickly into marriage with Huntingdon (a man she hardly knows), and is living a miserable domestic life, she has as yet not relinquished the hope of effecting a change in her husband and saving their marriage. It is only when she witnesses his infidelity that she realizes the extent of her foolishness in thinking that she could change him. Helen finds Huntingdon in the garden with Annabella and hears him tell her that he no longer loves his wife (312). In her disillusionment at this discovery and with 'blighted hopes', Helen turns to God, and through her faith finds renewed hope in this moment of need:

> while I lifted up my soul in speechless, earnest application, some heavenly influence seemed to strengthen me within: I breathed more freely; my vision cleared . . . I felt [God] would not leave me comfortless: in spite of earth and hell I should have strength for all my trials, and win a glorious rest at last!
>
> Refreshed, invigorated if not composed, I rose and returned to the house. (313)

Helen's faith in God helps sustain her through the difficult days that follow this discovery and the emotional turmoil she suffers. Admirably, she finds the strength to confront her husband and informs him that in her eyes he has dissolved their sacred union and no longer needs to feign the love he cannot give. And she resolves to deal with the situation as a Christian: 'if *they* scorn me as the victim of their guilt, I can pity their folly and despise their scorn' (317). Her disillusionment, however, turns to anger and even hatred. Helen confesses in her diary the extent to which she is almost consumed by these destructive feelings; in a very moving passage she conveys her sense of outrage and degradation:

> how shall I get through the months or years of my future life, in company with that man – my greatest enemy . . . it is not enough to say that I no longer love my husband – I HATE him! The word stares me in the face like a guilty confession, but it is true: I hate him – I hate him! – But God have mercy on his miserable soul! – and make him see and feel his guilt – I ask no other vengeance! if he could but fully know and truly feel my wrongs, I should be well avenged; and I could freely pardon all; but he is so lost, so hardened in his heartless depravity that, in this life, I believe he never will. (318)

Through Helen, Brontë exposes the 'heartless depravity' of both Huntingdon and Annabella and shows how Helen becomes their victim. Helen is brought so low by them that she even entertains making her husband jealous by encouraging Hargrave's advances and confesses that 'No true Christian could cherish such bitter feelings as I do against him and her' (323). When Annabella audaciously challenges Helen by declaring: "'You need not grudge [Huntingdon] to me . . . for I love him more than ever you could do'", Helen's hatred turns to violence: 'I took her hand and violently dashed it from me, with an expression of abhorrence and indignation that could not be suppressed. Startled, almost appalled, by this sudden outbreak, she recoiled in silence' (324). Helen has difficulty controlling her emotions and passionate spirit against the provocations of Annabella and Huntingdon, but realizes she must do so, in order to face the difficult trials that may lie ahead: 'What a good thing it is to be able to command one's temper! I must labour to cultivate this inestimable quality: God, only, knows how often I shall need it in this rough, dark road that lies before me' (326). In subsequent trials, Helen will learn to exercise greater control over her passion by maintaining her faith in God.

At another point in her narrative, Helen is besieged by the selfish advances of Hargrave who tries to pressure her into having an adulterous affair with him. Hargrave repeatedly torments Helen with his attentions and she terms him her 'enemy' – an 'indefatigable foe . . . not yet vanquished . . . [who] seem[s] . . . always on the watch' (340). Though Hargrave calls Helen's religion "'wild fanaticism'" (342), it is exactly her firm religious conviction that becomes her strongest weapon against him; Helen successfully repulses his advances by reaffirming her faith:

> It is His will that we should not injure others by the gratification
> of our own earthly passions . . . and if I were alone in the world, I
> have still my God and my religion, and I would sooner die than
> disgrace my calling and break my faith with Heaven to obtain a
> few brief years of false and fleeting happiness – happiness sure to
> end in misery, even here – for myself or any other! (342)

Helen refutes all of Hargrave's subsequent arguments knowing full well that he is only interested in his own selfish, sensual and sexual gratification, and that his 'passionate protestation of the truth and fervour of his attachment' (343) is false.

Hargrave's pursuit of Helen is merely a game – a quest to satisfy his own lust and ego, not one to make Helen happy. In one scene, when Hargrave and Helen play a game of chess, Brontë demonstrates that he views Helen as an object to be obtained through his cleverness; Hargrave sees the conquering of her spirit as the equivalent of winning at chess. Helen, however, is alerted to his craftiness and does not miss the 'double meaning to all his words' when he confidently declares: "'you are a good player, – but I am a better: we shall have a long game, and you will give me some trouble; but I can be as patient as you, and, in the end, I shall certainly win'" (309). Hargrave does manage to defeat Helen at chess after removing the 'bishops that trouble [him]' (310), but in real life he loses his pursuit exactly because he is unable to undermine her religion. Helen cleverly turns Hargrave's words against him and manages to silence him; he stops pestering her and leaves for Paris. By affirming her faith, Helen uses her moral strength a second time and jubilantly 'thank[s] God for this deliverance!' (344). Hargrave's hypocrisy and romantic posturings are exposed, and his selfishness is, through Helen, forcefully condemned by Brontë.

Hargrave, however, continues his pursuit of Helen and, in a final confrontation with her in the library, he is 'determined to hazard all for victory' (362). This time, in a sexual frenzy – Helen notes she 'never saw a man so terribly excited' (363) – he attempts to overcome Helen with physical force, and she must defend herself by 'snatch[ing] up [her] palette-knife and [holding] it against him' (363). Hargrave 'flatter[s him]self . . . that though among [Huntingdon's group, he is] not of them' (360), but, in this scene, Brontë exposes him for what he actually is – a 'false villain' (366), and 'human brute' like all the rest. In fact, as Hargrave attempts to blackmail Helen into submission and exclaims: '"Your fair fame is gone; and nothing that I or you can say can ever retrieve it"', Helen's response shows him to be the basest of all the brutes, even lower than her husband: '"No one has ever dared to insult me as you are doing now!"' (363). Hargrave's views of women are pathetic and, as in earlier scenes, satirized by Brontë.

In an effort to make himself look good at the expense of Huntingdon, Hargrave informs Helen that her husband has offered her to any man who will have her, believing that this is the final barrier he needs to remove in order to win her consent. When Helen replies that '"what [her husband] prizes so lightly will not be long in his possession"', Hargrave misinterprets her words and cries out like an outraged romantic hero: '"You cannot mean that you will break your heart and die for the detestable conduct of an infamous villain like that!"'; Helen's calm and witty rejoinder: '"By no means: my heart is too thoroughly dried to be broken in a hurry, and I mean to live as long as I can"' (361), reveals Hargrave's foolishness and his deplorable lack of insight into her character and situation. Not only does he not see Helen's suffering, but he does not realize that she does not view herself as one of Huntingdon's possessions and that she has a mind and will of her own. Though this point should become obvious to Hargrave by the way Helen answers his inquiries: '"But your child?"'/ "My child goes with me."/ "[Huntingdon] will not allow it."/ "I shall not ask him."' (361), it is only when Helen grabs her palette-knife and shows herself as 'fierce and resolute as he' (363) that she startles him into recognition; only then does she gain his serious attention and get him to acknowledge two things: first, that she is a human being and not an 'image' to be 'admired', an 'angel' to be 'worshipped', or an object to be possessed and 'protected' (363), and second, the plain message she has tried to convey to him all along: '"I don't like you . . . and if I were divorced from my husband – or if he were dead, I would not marry you"' (364). The apparent victory that Hargrave feels he has won is short-lived, as Helen forces him to confess in front of Hattersley and the others that she has not yielded to his advances. Hargrave does, his own looks betray him, and Helen wins a decisive moral victory over him.

By the time Helen arrives at Wildfell Hall (her arrival coincides with the beginning of Gilbert's narrative and the novel itself), she has waged several moral battles successfully (against Huntingdon, Annabella and Hargrave, as I have shown), and each one has made her spiritually stronger. But it is only when she meets Gilbert Markham and falls in love with him that she faces her most difficult moral challenge. Brontë purposely draws a parallel in the novel between Hargrave and Gilbert and the respective temptations that they each pose for Helen. In her confrontation with Hargrave, who knows that Helen is married, Helen is resolute in making her decision to rebuff his advances because she is aware of his lustful intentions and does not love him. With Gilbert, however, Helen's decision to repulse his amorous advances is more psychologically and emotionally complex and strenuous because she does come to know his genuine "'worth'" – his "'depth of soul and feeling'" (146) – and "'disinterested affection'" (122), but cannot tell him she is married. In order to protect her identity, for fear that Huntingdon will discover her whereabouts, seek her out, and frustrate her plans to save her son a second time, Helen must keep her secret from Gilbert. She manages to remain silent for a period of time, but while she does so, Gilbert's passion for her grows immensely. Ultimately, it becomes impossible for Helen not to divulge the truth of her situation to Gilbert, and she eventually allows him to read her diary which holds her secret anguish: the reason why she has repulsed his advances, and the specific, personal details of the nightmare she has lived through. Helen's true affection for Gilbert thus tempts her to commit adultery. Her inner struggle between her passion for Gilbert and faith in God, however, though painful, is one that she faces with clarity of vision. Helen has learned from her past experiences and, because through faith she has overcome great grief, does not doubt God in this spiritual trial. She does, however, suffer emotionally once again. The tragedy of Helen's situation, as Brontë makes clear, is that now that she has finally met a man with whom she can have a meaningful relationship, she is still debarred from seeking the love and happiness she craves for her son and herself.

Though Helen is undoubtedly a central character in Gilbert's narrative, and the unraveling of her situation one of Brontë's major concerns, Gilbert's growth process is the author's main focus in this part of the novel. The one crucial difference between Helen's narrative and Gilbert's is that hers is presented to the reader without interruption, while his is not. Gilbert's narrative can be seen as having a clearly demarcated first and second part. Helen's narrative is inserted in Gilbert's narrative and does, in effect, disrupt its continuity somewhat. But, unlike earlier critics, I do not see this insertion as a flaw or failure of any kind.[8]

Brontë purposely constructs her novel this way to force the reader to make comparisons between Gilbert's and Helen's narratives, and see the immediate parallels that emerge between their respective stories. Thematically, Gilbert's narrative essentially follows the same pattern that Helen's does. The first part of Helen's diary (chapters sixteen through 32), for example, deals with Helen's emotional immaturity (excessive passion and pride) and its consequences (her youthful mistake in marrying Huntingdon with hopes of reforming him, and her subsequent domestic misery), while the latter part (chapters 33 through 44) deals with her spiritual trials (developing faith and turn to God), which leads to her recovery and emotional maturity. Similarly, the first part of Gilbert's narrative (chapters one through fifteen) deals with his emotional immaturity (excessive passion and pride) and its consequences (his youthful mistake in violently attacking Lawrence and his loss of faith in Helen); the latter part (chapters 45 through 53) deals with his spiritual trials (developing faith and turn to God), which leads to his recovery and emotional maturity. The novel thus starts with an account of Gilbert's emotional immaturity and is immediately followed by one of Helen's; structurally then, it is easier for a reader to make comparisons and see the similarity in their respective situations. The latter part of Helen's narrative, which deals with her trials and developing faith, is immediately followed by Gilbert's own trials and developing faith; again, structurally, it becomes easier for a reader to make comparisons and see the similarity in their respective situations. Thus, though the novel's structure may seem awkward, it is logically chosen by Brontë to better highlight for the reader the crucial parallels between Gilbert's and Helen's respective narratives.

No one would dispute that Helen Huntingdon becomes a victim of her husband's abuse, of Annabella's malevolence and Hargrave's lust, or can fail to see how these characters trigger her worst emotions (jealousy, rage, hatred, even violence). But what critics have failed to point out is that Brontë also demonstrates how Gilbert, like Helen, becomes a victim in the novel as well, and how the scandalmongers, Eliza Millward, Jane Wilson and Reverend Millward trigger in him the same destructive emotions. Some critics have viewed Gilbert negatively precisely because he has been seen as a victimizer of others, especially Lawrence, not as a victim himself. These critics, I believe, have not seen Gilbert's violence in the proper light. Tom Winnifrith, in fact, voicing his dissatisfaction with Gilbert and with the novel's resolution, claims that the

> conventional happy ending with wedding bells for Helen Huntingdon and Gilbert Markham . . . is not important in itself ... [because] it appears to be largely a matter of chance that the novel does not end with Helen still tied to her husband while her lover is in gaol for the murder of her brother. (62)

P. J. M. Scott writes that Gilbert Markham 'presents a self which gradually disquiets our nerves' and 'is not sufficiently far off from the monster condition for our comfort' (94, 95). Though these critics have rightfully condemned Gilbert's violence, they have overlooked that Brontë condemns it as well, and that she clearly shows both the evil of his violence and why he becomes so violent. Langland has proposed one possible explanation for Gilbert's heinous act and Brontë's reasons for depicting it this way:

> [Gilbert's] unprovoked attack on Frederick Lawrence is both irrational and violent. . . . Thematically and structurally in the novel, this episode develops the insidious effects of an indulgence that leads to masculine arrogance and abuse of power. . . .
> Modern readers have been dissatisfied with Helen's marriage to Markham precisely because he seems different only in degree not in kind from Huntingdon. (133-34)

The 'insidious effects of . . . indulgence' may, indeed, be one of the factors that leads to Gilbert's irrational and brutal act, but it is not necessarily the only factor. One must keep in mind that such 'insidious effects' of indulgence, as Brontë shows, affect women as well as men, and can lead to similar 'arrogance and abuse of power' on their part. In the case of Annabella Lowborough, for example, the 'insidious effects' of indulgence affect her as detrimentally as they do any of the other male characters in the novel, and lead to her arrogant and abusive behavior (mental not physical) towards Helen and Lord Lowborough. As Langland suggests, Gilbert may, in fact, appear 'different only in degree not in kind from Huntingdon', but, by the same token, so too does Annabella Lowborough. Gilbert's violence is thus not simply a matter of male indulgence that turns to abusive behavior. His situation is much more complex.

In the first part of Gilbert's narrative, Brontë illustrates structurally the 'insidious effects' not just of 'indulgence', but of gossip and rumor, and how such 'mindless' talk can be destructive. Gilbert's passionate nature and 'naturally touchy' temperament (58) are affected detrimentally by the mindless gossip of the scandalmongers. In a carefully arranged sequence of events, Brontë shows how Gilbert is the one who drinks the 'poison of detracting tongues' (102). Such poison unsettles him emotionally, inciting his suspicion, jealousy, anger and hate. Once aroused, these negative feelings overcome his ability to reason, lead to his misinterpretation of events, and to his verbal and physical violence against Lawrence. Each of Gilbert's confrontations with Lawrence, in fact, is preceded by Gilbert's exposure to mindless gossip. As Gilbert gradually becomes more suspicious and jealous of Lawrence, he resorts to verbal violence (coarse and insulting language) and finally to the culminating physical assault. Though Gilbert reflects at the opening of chapter ten that 'the vile slander had indeed been

circulated throughout the company, in the very presence of the victim', and that
"'the scandalmongers have greedily seized the rumour, to make it the basis of
their own infernal structure'" (108), he is, ironically, unaware that it is he and not
Helen who becomes the actual victim, and that his words shed more light on his
own situation than Helen's. The scandalmongers succeed in transferring 'their
own infernal structure' to Gilbert, causing his emotional turmoil and instability,
and this is what precipitates his heinous act of violence.

   On one of Gilbert's visits to the vicarage, Eliza arouses his temper and
suspicion. Though Eliza does not admit she is the one initiating the 'mysterious
reports', her sister Mary Millward's comment indicates that Eliza is culpable:
"'Some idle slander somebody has been inventing, I suppose. I never heard it till
Eliza told me, the other day'" (97). Before Gilbert leaves the vicarage, he looks
into Eliza's face and notices something he had not seen earlier; it is a moment of
insight for him, and an observation which alerts the reader to the way Eliza has
begun to unsettle Gilbert emotionally: 'within those eyes there lurked a something
that I did not like; and I wondered how I ever could have admired them: her
sister's honest face and small grey optics appeared far more agreeable' (97).
Gilbert confesses that he is 'out of temper with Eliza', and though he feels certain
that her 'insinuations against Mrs. Graham . . . [are] false', and leaves admitting
that he is not 'troubling [his] mind about the possible truth of these mysterious
reports', he is nevertheless left 'wondering what they were, by whom originated,
and on what foundations raised' (97).

   At the party Mrs. Graham attends (chapter nine), Gilbert overhears Miss
Eliza and Miss Wilson propagating rumors about Helen, and he is further
unsettled. Eliza insinuates that there is a resemblance between Helen's child and
Frederick Lawrence, but before she can utter his name in front of the company,
she is interrupted by Jane Wilson. Jane Wilson, who has designs on Lawrence, is
angered and tells Eliza not to repeat such 'ill-natured reports', and then
sarcastically continues: "'I presume the person you allude to is Mr. Lawrence; but
I think I can assure you that your suspicions, in that respect, are utterly
misplaced'" (100). While Eliza wants Gilbert to believe that Lawrence and Helen
are lovers to diminish his interest in Helen, Miss Wilson objects to the rumor
because her own interest is at stake. Both women, however, are eager to impute
some blame on Helen. In a scornful outburst, Gilbert tries to silence both Eliza
and Miss Wilson with words intended to deflate their outward sense of superiority
to Helen: "'We have had enough of this subject: if we can only speak to slander
our betters, let us hold our tongues'" (100). Through Gilbert, Brontë exposes
their hypocrisy; though they each consider themselves respectable persons and
"'right-minded females'" (130), the reader sees only their vanity and malice.

   Shortly after this indignant proclamation, however, Gilbert reveals how
suspicious Eliza and Miss Wilson have made him: 'the first thing I did was to
stare at Arthur Graham, who sat beside his mother on the opposite side of the

table, and second to stare at Mr. Lawrence, who sat below; and, first, it struck me that there was a likeness' (101). They also make Gilbert question his own knowledge of Helen's character: 'Did I not know Mrs. Graham? . . . Was I not certain that she, in intellect, in purity and elevation of soul, was immeasurably superior to any of her detractors; that she was, in fact, the noblest, the most adorable, of her sex I had ever beheld, or even imagined to exist?' (101). Though at this point Gilbert maintains his faith in Helen and claims that 'if all the parish... or all the world should din these horrible lies in my ears, I would not believe them', he is also emotionally distraught: 'Meantime, my brain was on fire with indignation, and my heart seemed ready to burst from its prison with conflicting passions. I regarded my two fair neighbours with a feeling of abhorrence and loathing I scarcely endeavoured to conceal' (101). Later in the same chapter, precisely because Eliza and Jane Wilson have filled Gilbert with such negative feelings, he misinterprets Lawrence's behavior: 'I noticed that he coloured up to the temples, gave us one furtive glance in passing, and walked on, looking grave, but seemingly offering no reply to her remarks. It was true, then, that he had some designs upon Mrs. Graham' (105). Gilbert is full of hatred for Jane Wilson ('the more I thought upon her conduct, the more I hated her') and 'indignation against [his] former friend' Lawrence (106). On that same evening, in such an unsettled state of mind, Gilbert has his first of two verbal confrontations with Lawrence (106-07). The second occurs about a week after the party and is related in the following chapter (ten). In their heated verbal exchange Lawrence asks Gilbert a question that Brontë wants readers to ask as well: '"What makes you so coarse and brutal, Markham?"' (111). Structurally, Brontë provides the answer; she clearly demonstrates how these two hostile encounters with Lawrence are triggered by the scandalmongers, Eliza and Miss Wilson, and how Gilbert, unknowingly, becomes the victim of their gossip.

Helen Graham knows how detrimental such gossip can be before she arrives at Wildfell Hall and does not allow herself to be affected by it. She has been the victim of it earlier at the hands of the 'human brutes', and is, therefore, more ready to defend herself against the scandalmongers. After the kind of abuse she has been subjected to at Grass-dale Manor, the gossip of the scandalmongers is mild by comparison. While the gossip about her is being circulated at the party (chapter nine), Helen removes herself from its presence and refuses to listen to the company's 'small talk'. She seeks refuge in the garden. Gilbert finds Helen with her son and asks why everyone has left her. Helen's reply, '"It is I who have left them . . . I was wearied to death with small talk – nothing wears me out like that"' (103), and confession shortly thereafter, '"I hate talking where there is no exchange of ideas or sentiments, and no good given or received"' (104), show the reader that she is guarding herself successfully from the pernicious effects of the 'poison of detracting tongues'. But Helen also bravely confronts her traducers and demonstrates her resolve to hold on to her opinions despite the views of the world. When, for example, the Reverend Millward calls on Helen to give her advice: "'to tell you both everything that I myself see reprehensible in your conduct, and all I have reason to suspect, and what others tell me concerning you'" (116), he is shocked that she is unmoved by his words. And she courageously tells him so:

> she offered no extenuation or defence; and with a kind of
> shameless calmness – shocking indeed to witness, in one so
> young – as good as told me that my remonstrance was unavailing,
> and my pastoral advice quite thrown away upon her – nay, that
> my very *presence* was displeasing while I spoke such things. (117)

In contrast, when Gilbert hears Reverend Millward explain the details of this conference with Helen, he becomes so enraged at Mr. Millward's audacity that he rushes from the house and violently slams the door behind him. Helen's 'shameless calmness' is thus sharply contrasted with Gilbert's 'excited feelings'. As his 'mind [becomes] little better than a chaos of conflicting passions', he, and not Helen, is shown to be the victim (117). Simultaneously, however, Brontë exposes Mr. Millward as a hypocrite. Though his duty as a preacher is to help others and combat falsehoods of all kinds, in this encounter with Helen he reveals a sinister excitement in spreading "'these . . . terrible reports'" (116) and directly accusing her. Though he has no knowledge of Helen's background and, hence, no proof that her character is questionable, he jumps to premature conclusions and resolutions: "'I am fully determined, Mrs. Markham, that *my* daughters – shall – not - consort with her. Do you adopt the same resolution with regard to yours?'" (117). Earlier in the novel (chapter ten), when he sees Gilbert quarreling with Lawrence, Reverend Millward confidently assumes that the dispute is about the "'young widow'" and again, without proof, advises Gilbert that "'she's not worth it!'"; he 'confirm[s] the assertion by a solemn nod', not with solid evidence (112). In this instance, Reverend Millward, once more, excites Gilbert's feelings; Gilbert calls out Mr. Millward's name in a 'tone of wrathful menace' and confesses that he is 'too indignant to apologize' (112).

The third and final confrontation between Gilbert and Lawrence (the physical assault) is triggered by the gossip of all three scandalmongers. Gilbert's growing suspicion of Lawrence leads him to misinterpret the import of a meeting between the brother and sister. On the night Gilbert and Helen profess their love for one another, and Helen promises to explain to Gilbert why they cannot be more than friends – warning him that what she has to confess is "'more than [he] will like to hear, or, perhaps, can readily excuse'" (122) – Gilbert leaves Helen in distress. He decides to return to comfort her but, as he does, he sees Lawrence and Helen walking and talking intimately in the garden, 'his arm round her waist, while she lovingly rested her hand on his shoulder' (125), and is led to believe that the two are actually lovers and that what the scandalmongers have insinuated is true. Gilbert's pain and disillusionment in this scene closely parallels that Helen experiences when she discovers her husband and Annabella in the garden (313) and is further evidence that Brontë is constructing dual narratives. After his discovery, Gilbert falls into a 'paroxysm of anger and despair' and 'like a passionate child . . . dashe[s him]self on the ground' (125). On the following day, Gilbert 'wak[es] to find life a blank, . . . [and] teeming with torment and misery'; he is pained to 'find [him]self deceived, duped, hopeless, [his] affections trampled upon, [his] angel not an angel, and [his] friend a fiend incarnate' (126-27). He decides to go out to 'cool [his] brain' (127) and conduct some business with Robert Wilson, but when he arrives at Ryecote Farm he finds 'Miss Wilson chattering with Eliza Millward' and 'between them manag[ing] to keep up a pretty continuous fire of small talk' (130). Both Eliza and Miss Wilson, whom Gilbert sees as his 'fair tormentors' (131), maliciously taunt him about Mrs. Graham, and again arouse his 'wrathful indignation': '"Ah! then you are convinced at last, of your mistake – you have at length discovered that your divinity is not quite the immaculate"' (130). The following morning Gilbert assaults Lawrence. It is significant that the encounter with Eliza and Miss Wilson (chapter thirteen) is followed immediately (chapter fourteen) by Gilbert's heinous act. Again, structurally Brontë wants readers to see how the events in each chapter are related, especially the way in which Gilbert's violence is precipitated by the 'fire of small talk' of Eliza and Miss Wilson. They, along with Reverend Millward, have been the ones who have triggered the succession of negative emotions in Gilbert that culminate in physical violence. Brontë clearly illustrates how 'mindless gossip' (language that is seemingly harmless) is actually 'poisonous' and destructive. Though Brontë obviously condemns Gilbert's brutality, she shows how he becomes so violent, so that a reader can more readily forgive him.

Like Helen, Gilbert learns to control his passion and develops a faith in God. The latter part of his narrative, like the latter part of Helen's, is devoted to his several spiritual trials and growth as a Christian. Essentially, Gilbert must battle his own selfishness by learning not only from his own experience, but from '"the experience of others, and the precepts of a higher authority"' (57).[9] Though I agree with Langland that Gilbert does learn from Helen's diary and 'must submit to [its] lessons before he can win Helen' (134), this does not happen immediately. Gilbert's initial response after reading the diary is a selfish one. He thinks it 'cruel' that the rest of it is torn away 'just when [Helen is] going to mention [him]' (400). He admits that 'the former half of the narrative was, to [him], more painful than the latter' (not what a reader would expect, since, in the latter half, Helen reveals her suffering and spiritual trials), that he 'felt a kind of selfish gratification in watching her husband's gradual decline in her good graces', and that '[t]he effect of the whole . . . was to relieve [his] mind of an intolerable burden and fill [his] heart with joy' (402). As Scott observes: 'It is appalling that in a sense he cares for her so little intrinsically, that he can turn from the first revelation of the length and breadth of her recent and current miseries to such trampling egotism' (95).

In this egotistical frame of mind, Gilbert joyfully goes to return Helen's diary, apparently under the illusion that there are now no barriers to prevent their union. After they share apologies, however, Gilbert is shocked when Helen calmly informs him that they must separate forever. He observes that 'her whole manner [is] provokingly composed, considering the dreadful sentence she pronounce[s]' (405). Unlike Helen, Gilbert's agitation is readily noticeable, and he reaches a state of 'silent, sullen despondency' (405) very much like Helen's similar 'despondent apathy' in one of her earlier trials (375). Gilbert's faith has as yet not been tested, and his passion overwhelms him. In this encounter with Helen, Gilbert faces his first important moral trial.

Gilbert misinterprets Helen's calm demeanor as a sign that she does not feel as strongly about their separation as he does: "'I cannot discuss the matter of eternal separation, calmly and dispassionately as you can do. It is no question of mere expedience with me; it is a question of life and death!'" (405). Helen's silence at this response allows Gilbert to see his mistake, and he realizes he has 'said an unjust and cruel thing', which he immediately follows with 'something worse', and Helen responds sharply: "'*Gilbert, don't*," she cried, in a tone that would have pierced a heart of adamant. "For God's sake, don't *you* attempt these arguments! No *fiend* could torture me like this!'" (405). Gilbert's argument reminds Helen of Hargrave's, and her quick response alerts him to this. Earlier in the same chapter, Gilbert, who has just finished reading Helen's diary, recognizes the similarity between his situation and Hargrave's, and notes why his own is even more trying for Helen. As he is greeted by Helen's maid Rachel, Gilbert notices 'the look of cold distrust she cast[s] upon [him]' and remarks: 'doubtless she saw in me another Mr. Hargrave, only more dangerous in being more esteemed and trusted by her mistress' (403). This encounter between Gilbert and Helen, in fact, closely parallels that between Hargrave and Helen in her narrative. The subject of Gilbert's conversation with Helen is the same as that between Hargrave and Helen earlier and deals with the difference between selfish and disinterested love. In each case, Helen tries to convince her suitor to choose the latter. But the similarities end there. After their discussion, Hargrave continues to pester Helen, attempts to physically assault her, and even to blackmail her into submission in front of his cronies. Gilbert, on the other hand, proves his 'disinterested affection' for Helen by adhering to her request that they part forever. He does not return to pester her as Hargrave does. While Hargrave does not try to see things from Helen's perspective and is unsympathetic when she implores him to help her retain the 'solace of a good conscience' (343), Gilbert is sympathetic and does try to put himself in her place. When Helen asks that Gilbert not use certain arguments with her, he is immediately penitent, realizes his mistake, and responds with conviction: "'I won't, I won't!'" said I, gently laying my hand on hers; almost as much alarmed at her vehemence, as ashamed of my own misconduct' (405-06). Gilbert also asks Helen to forgive him and agrees to do 'whatever [she] desire[s]' (406). Helen challenges Gilbert to test his faith and "'try the truth and constancy of [his] soul's love for [hers]'" (409). She tries to assuage Gilbert's fears and increase his confidence in God's goodness (410-11). Before he parts from her, Gilbert's response to Helen's question expresses his willingness to exercise his faith and place his life and future happiness in God's hands: "'Helen, I can! if faith would never fail'" (411).

Helen forces Gilbert to stop thinking of his own gratification and understand her situation and needs. In his encounter with Lawrence, Gilbert must repeat the process. He overcomes his selfishness and pride by acknowledging his error in attacking Lawrence and asking his forgiveness. This becomes his second trial. The encounter itself is awkward and tense. Lawrence, 'with equal degrees of nervous horror, anger, and amazement' is shocked to see Gilbert enter his room uninvited, and informs Gilbert he is "'in no state to bear [his] brutalities . . . or [his] presence'" (413). Gilbert recognizes the 'difficulties of [his] unenviable task', but 'plunges' into a general apology, which is soon followed by a more sincere and heartfelt acknowledgement of his brutal action: "'Yes, yes, I remember it all: nobody can blame me more than I blame myself in my own heart – at any rate, nobody can regret more sincerely than I do the result of my *brutality* as you rightly term it'" (414). This encounter with Lawrence becomes a lesson in humility for Gilbert; when he leaves, one notices he has a genuine willingness to help Lawrence and sacrifice for him: "'[I] took leave after asking if there was anything in the world I could do for him, little or great, in the way of alleviating his sufferings, and repairing the injury I had done'" (416). Gilbert's success in this trial can be measured by the close friendship that eventually develops between the two men; the mistrust and animosity that exist between them is replaced by a new intimacy, trust and respect. Gilbert begins to think of Lawrence's future happiness and helps save him from the mistake of marrying Jane Wilson. Though angered at first at Gilbert's intrusion into his affairs, Lawrence eventually sees that Gilbert is right about Miss Wilson and accepts his 'well-meant warning'. Gilbert thus plays an instrumental part in Lawrence's 'deliverance' (423).

Gilbert's greatest test of faith comes when he learns that Helen has returned to help nurse her husband through a serious illness. At first, Gilbert is distraught and, like the reader, questions Helen's action. In an exchange of dialogue with Lawrence, he reveals his 'silent anguish' and in a burst of passion calls Helen a 'fool'; he finds it 'intolerable' to think that she has taken 'this infatuated step' (427). Gilbert believes that Helen has provided Huntingdon with the perfect opportunity to "'make all manner of lying speeches and false, fair promises for the future, . . . [that] she will believe him'", and make her situation worse (427). But as Lawrence shares with Gilbert the letters that Helen sends him, Gilbert gradually realizes that her action has been prompted by her sense of duty and faith in God. In returning to comfort an individual who has been her enemy and put her through terrible agony, Helen makes a great sacrifice and behaves like a Christian. This action is similar to Agnes' in *Agnes Grey* when she returns to comfort Rosalie at Ashby Hall (193). Helen's behavior, like Agnes', is not a sign of weakness but of inner strength, and serves as an example for Gilbert of Christian humility, forgiveness and tolerance from which he learns. At the close of her first letter, Helen reveals that she is aware of the difficulty of her situation, but will not be dissuaded from accomplishing her task:

> I find myself in a rather singular position: I am exerting my utmost endeavours to promote the recovery and reformation of my husband, and if I succeed what shall I do? My duty, of course, – but how? No matter; I can perform the task that is before me now, and God will give me strength to do whatever he requires hereafter. (435)

Helen's spiritual fortitude is praiseworthy and inspires Gilbert to maintain his faith in her and put his own trust in God: "'I shall say no more against her: I see that she was actuated by the best and noblest motives in what she has done; and if the act is not a wise one, may Heaven protect her from its consequences!'" (435).

The death of Huntingdon has a profound impact on Gilbert; it becomes a lesson that sobers him into the realization that while earthly life and passions are transient, God's goodness is infinite, and the understanding and appreciation of that goodness and growth of one's soul constitute true fulfillment. By witnessing Helen doing everything possible to try and get Huntingdon to save his soul from destruction – because "'No man can deliver his brother, nor make agreement unto God for him'" (451) – Gilbert realizes that he too must work hard to save his own. He also sees how all along Helen has been trying to do the same for him, and can more fully appreciate why their separation was necessary. Gilbert learns to take more seriously the 'blessed truths' of which Helen speaks, and to 'trust' and 'comprehend' that "'God is Infinite Wisdom, and Power, and Goodness – and Love'" (451) as Huntingdon could not.

In the course of chapter 49, the most intensely religious chapter in the novel, a reader can clearly see the change that takes place in Gilbert. As the chapter opens, Gilbert confesses his secret wish for Huntingdon's death: 'I wished with all my heart that it might please Heaven to remove him to a better world, or . . . to take him out of this' (443). Though he is resigned to the thought that 'God knew best' what should be Huntingdon's fate, Gilbert is nevertheless 'anxious for the result of His decrees' (444). At the close of the chapter, however, Gilbert expresses a sense of contrition and shame that he had thought of himself at a time when Helen was enduring such suffering and another's soul was being lost:

> Poor, poor Helen! dreadful indeed her trials must have been! And
> I could do nothing to lessen them . . . it almost seemed as if I had
> brought them upon her myself, by my own secret desires; and
> whether I looked at her husband's sufferings or her own, it
> seemed almost like a judgment upon myself for having cherished
> such a wish. (451-52)

With this admission, a reader realizes that in the course of the chapter, while Brontë is documenting the loss of Huntingdon's soul, she is simultaneously showing the growth of Gilbert's. Gilbert emerges from this spiritual trial a better person and a more sincere Christian who is able to pity others, even someone he had formerly hated and wished dead: 'I experienced a painful commiseration for her unhappy husband . . . and a profound sympathy for her own afflictions . . . for I was persuaded she had not hinted half the sufferings she had had to endure' (453). He confesses that he 'had no reason to disguise [his] joy and hope from Frederick Lawrence, for [he] had none to be ashamed of '; his only joy is that Helen is 'at length released from her afflictive, overwhelming toil' (453). Gilbert is genuinely more concerned with her situation than he is with his own. He has undergone the same growth process as Helen, his faith in her and in God is manifest, and hence, the joining of their '"hearts and souls"' (487) in marriage is a testament to their equality.

Helen tries to help Gilbert because she genuinely loves him and firmly believes in God's goodness, not out of a selfish desire to prove to herself that as a woman she has special powers to bring men towards salvation, or because she sees that as her only role in life. Helen sees it as her Christian duty to help others in whatever way she can; she not only tries to help her husband and Gilbert, but also her son, Hattersley and Millicent, Esther Hargrave, and Lord Lowborough. The implication at the novel's end is that what Helen does for Gilbert he is also capable of doing for someone else.

By creating parallel narratives of growth, Brontë illustrates that men's and women's respective natures and experiences are similar and explodes the myth many Victorians believed that they occupy separate or different spheres. And herein lies the main thrust of *Wildfell Hall's* satire. Brontë's structural paradigm shows readers how men and women are equal: how they think similar thoughts, feel similar feelings, have similar passions (sexual and otherwise), have similar needs to develop, express and share their talents, and how, when young, are in equal need of parental guidance and education. As Christians, men and women also share a similar 'fallen' condition on earth, are equally capable of good and evil and, ultimately, need to turn to God.

Brontë portrays characters, such as Gilbert and Helen, Richard Wilson and Mary Millward, Frederick Lawrence and Esther Hargrave, who are thoughtful, sensitive, and self-sacrificing, as model individuals who have learned and matured from painful life experiences and whose behaviors are worthy of imitation by others. But with similar power, Brontë vividly depicts the thoughtlessness, insensitivity, and cruelty of an Arthur Huntingdon, Annabella Lowborough, Walter Hargrave, Reverend Millward, Eliza Millward, Jane Wilson and Mrs. Hargrave. By presenting several evil women and their heinous acts alongside several evil men, Brontë explodes still another widely held Victorian myth – that women were by nature 'angelic' and delicate as 'wallflowers' and could therefore serve as moral influences to men. Throughout the novel, Brontë advocates that both men and women must be equally responsible for their own actions and lives. It is noteworthy that Brontë's fictional argument for the equality of the sexes appears twenty years before John Stuart Mill's persuasive exposition in *The Subjection of Women* (1869).

Notes

[1] Charles Kingsley is perhaps the first critic to refer to *Wildfell Hall* as a 'satire, and an exposure of evils', though he ultimately declares that the 'unnecessary coarseness' found in the novel is 'a defect which injures [its] real usefulness and real worth' (Allott 271). In his unsigned review (originally printed in *Fraser's Magazine*, April, 1849, xxxix, pp. 417-32, under the title 'Recent Novels'), Kingsley sees Acton Bell (Anne Brontë) as a satirist of the Juvenalian mold realistically exposing the 'foul and accursed undercurrents' of a 'smug, respectable, whitewashed English society', and showing it 'the image of [its] own ugly, hypocritical visage' (Allott 270).

More recently, the critic Edward Chitham has argued that *Wildfell Hall* is a satire of *Wuthering Heights*. See Chitham's essay 'Diverging Twins: Some Clues to *Wildfell Hall*' in Chitham and Winnifrith. Chitham also discusses this idea in chapter nine ('Artistic Independence') of his biography of Anne Brontë, *A Life of Anne Brontë*.

[2] In *The Victorian Frame of Mind, 1830-1870*, Walter E. Houghton outlines the three main 'conceptions of woman current in the Victorian period' (348). The first, most conservative, and 'best known' view is that of 'the submissive wife whose whole excuse for being was to love, honor, obey – and amuse – her lord and master, and to manage his household and bring up his children. In that role her character and her life were completely distinct from his' (348). Cast against this conservative, popular view, one finds the concept of the 'new woman', representing the most radical thinking of the time, and emerging 'in revolt against [women's] legal and social bondage . . . and demanding equal rights with men: the

same education, the same suffrage, the same opportunity for professional and political careers' (348). Finally, as Houghton explains, '[b]etween these two poles there was a middle position entirely characteristic of the time in its mediation between conservative and radical thinking' (349). This position stressed that 'woman is *not* man [and hence, had] her own nature and function in life, not inferior to his but entirely different'; that function was 'to guide and uplift her more worldly and intellectual mate' (349). This third alternative was also popular and endorsed by several important intellectual figures throughout the age, most notably Ruskin in 'Of Queens' Gardens' and Kingsley in *Yeast*. Others include Tennyson's 'The Princess' and 'Locksley Hall' and Patmore's 'The Angel in the House' (351).

Of these three conceptions of woman Houghton outlines, it is evident that in *Wildfell Hall* Brontë endorses the second view – the concept of the 'new woman' – which represents the most radical thinking of the time on this issue. Simultaneously, however, Brontë rejects the conservative view of the 'submissive wife', as well as the more moderate, third alternative, which stresses that women occupy a separate or different sphere than men, because it is ultimately one that places them in a subservient role also. Brontë purposefully satirizes the narrowmindedness of these two views because she saw men and women occupying 'equal' and not 'different' intellectual, emotional, and spiritual spheres.

³ Working as a governess at Blake Hall and Thorp Green, no doubt, gave Brontë insight into the 'many great abuses' tolerated in her society, especially ones which occurred within domestic circles. In her 1845 diary paper there is evidence to suggest that while at Thorp Green she observed much that was 'unpalatable' about human nature and behavior, which may have eventually given her the impetus to write so forcefully against vice and vicious characters in *Wildfell Hall*: 'I was wishing to leave [Thorp Green] then, and if I had known that I had four years longer to stay how wretched I should have been; but during my stay I have had some very unpleasant and undreamt-of experience of human nature' (qtd in Shorter 144). According to Langland, 'A full awareness of [the] inequities in British law informs Anne Brontë's novel *The Tenant of Wildfell Hall*' (24-25). See Langland's discussion on this important issue (23-28).

⁴ For a full discussion of the differences between Brontë's and Thackeray's satiric methods see chapter three of my dissertation: *Exposing Vice and Vicious Characters: Anne Brontë's Satiric Art in* Agnes Grey *and* The Tenant of Wildfell Hall (90-123).

⁵ In *Clarissa*, Richardson sets out to lash and not laugh at vice and vicious characters. His satiric method is, therefore, different from Fielding's. Richardson's portrayal of Lovelace, for example, is geared towards exposing his character's crimes 'in the strongest colours', so as to 'render [him] odious to mankind'. Several critics have commented on the similarities between Richardson's and Brontë's art. W. A. Craik, for example, observes: 'With such material and such a

society, it is probably unavoidable that Anne Brontë in *The Tenant of Wildfell Hall* should resemble Richardson, especially when she employs the journal as method, and has a situation that also might have suited him' (235). Richard Stenberg observes that 'Anne's novels bear affinities to *Pamela* which are suggestive' (104). Specifically, Stenberg discusses how Brontë and Richardson grapple with narrative problems that emerge as the direct result of the protagonists' sexual innocence in the heroine-centered novel (104-117).

[6] In *A Life of Anne Brontë*, Brontë's most recent biographer Edward Chitham observes that 'throughout Anne's work there have been reminders that the belief in reason alone is insufficient. . . . Anne is warning herself and her readers against too rigid an application of the rationalist calculus' (154).

[7] Brontë's Christian philosophy which is embodied in *Agnes Grey* and *Wildfell Hall*, like that espoused by other eighteenth-century writers and characters in their creative fiction, is based on the principle of Augustinianism. The Augustinian ethic stresses the 'imperfection' of all humanity because of original sin. Derivatives of this ethic are the principles of tolerance, understanding and forgiveness. By acknowledging how all individuals share a similar imperfect or 'fallen' earthly existence, one should become more tolerant of the 'flaws' or 'faults' of others and eager to sympathize, understand and forgive them. As Donald Greene explains in *The Age of Exuberance: Backgrounds to Eighteenth-Century English Literature*: 'Augustinianism . . . centers . . . on the affirmation of man's inherent moral weakness, which he is unable to rectify merely through his own unaided efforts. . . . It can be averted only by the full emotional acceptance of the fact of one's own imperfection and of God's merciful and forgiving love, freely offered to the sinner' (95).

In *Wildfell Hall*, Brontë carries her religious thinking further than in *Agnes Grey* by introducing the unorthodox doctrine of Universal Salvation that is the logical extension of the Augustinian principle. Just as Augustinianism asks that individuals forgive one another's sins, the doctrine of Universal Salvation posits Brontë's belief that God will likewise be tolerant, understanding and forgiving in the end (that after suffering for his or her sins an individual will be purged of them and allowed to enter God's kingdom). As Stenberg has noted, this doctrine 'surfaces throughout the novel in modified form in everything from a love song to discussions of happiness in marriage' (72).

In a letter to the Reverend David Thom, Brontë expresses her belief in the doctrine of Universal Salvation: '. . . I have cherished it from my very childhood . . . in my last novel *The Tenant of Wildfell Hall*, I have given as many hints in support of the doctrine as I could venture to introduce into a work of that description'. The complete letter is reprinted in Gérin (361).

[8] In *Conversations in Ebury Street*, George Moore questioned the novel's peculiar structure; specifically, he was troubled by Brontë's insertion of Helen's diary in Gilbert's narrative and saw her artistic choice to do so as the failure in

judgment of an inexperienced novelist: 'Anne broke down in the middle of her story, but her breakdown was not for lack of genius but of experience. . . . The diary broke the story in halves' (216). Following Moore's lead, several subsequent critics have questioned Brontë's structural choices in *Wildfell Hall*. Winifred Gérin, for example, writes in her 1979 introduction to *Wildfell Hall*: 'How right was Moore! By the device of the diary the drama that wrecked Helen's life is seen at one remove, not in the heat of action, in the palpitating moments of hurt and disillusion, at the height of anger and recrimination' (14). In *Anne Brontë: Her Life and Work*, Derek Stanford writes: 'Admitted that the narration of the story, through the medium of the diary, does amount to an hiatus – a set back, even – its great interest and desperate events offer rich compensation for this' (225). Finally, Inga-Stina Ewbank, in *Their Proper Sphere: A Study of the Brontë Sisters as Early-Victorian Female Novelists*, explains what she perceives as the novel's structural problem thus: 'In the central section of the novel Helen can reveal her innermost being to the diary; in the framing letters, Markham is bound to be as objective as possible. This throws the novel out of balance; the frame fails to support the powerful middle portion' (83-84).

⁹ These are Helen's words; in a debate with Gilbert (chapter three), she defends her position on the necessity of equal education for young men and women. Helen passionately argues that it is essential for children to learn from the experience of others, as well as from the laws of God set forth in the Bible, so that they may be spared the grief of learning about evil from first hand experience (57).

Works Cited

Allott, Miriam, ed. *The Brontës: The Critical Heritage*. London: Routledge, 1974.

Brontë, Anne. *Agnes Grey*. Ed. Hilda Marsden and Robert Inglesfield. Oxford: Oxford University Press, 1988.

-----. *The Tenant of Wildfell Hall*. Ed. G. D. Hargreaves. Intro. Winifred Gérin. Harmondsworth: Penguin, 1979.

Chitham, Edward. *A Life of Anne Brontë*. Oxford: Blackwell, 1991.

----- and Winnifrith, T. *Brontë Facts and Brontë Problems*. London: Macmillan, 1983.

Craik, W. A. *The Brontë Novels*. London: Methuen, 1968.

Ewbank, Inga-Stina. *Their Proper Sphere: A Study of the Brontë Sisters as Early-Victorian Female Novelists*. Cambridge: Harvard University Press, 1966.

Gérin, Winifred. *Anne Brontë*, 2nd ed. London: Allen Lane, 1976.

Greene, Donald. *The Age of Exuberance: Backgrounds to Eighteenth-Century English Literature*. New York: Random, 1970.

Harrison, Ada M. and Derek Stanford. *Anne Brontë: Her Life and Work*. London:

Methuen, 1959.

Houghton, Walter E. *The Victorian Frame of Mind, 1830-1870*. New Haven: Yale University Press, 1957.

Langland, Elizabeth. *Anne Brontë: The Other One*. Totowa: Barnes, 1989.

López, Andrés G. *Exposing Vice and Vicious Characters: Anne Brontë's Satiric Art in* Agnes Grey *and* The Tenant of Wildfell Hall. Diss. Stony Brook University, 1991. Ann Arbor: UMI, 1991. 9205241.

Moore, George. *Conversations in Ebury Street*. 2nd ed. London: Heinemann, 1930.

Scott, P. J. M. *Anne Brontë: A New Critical Assessment*. Totowa: Barnes, 1983.

Shorter, Clement. K. *Charlotte Brontë and Her Circle*. London: Hodder and Stoughton, 1896.

Stenberg, Richard. A. *The Novels of Anne Brontë*. Diss. University of Minnesota, 1980.

Swift, Jonathan. *The Examiner*. No. XXXVIII. *English Satire*. Ed. James Sutherland. Cambridge: Cambridge University Press, 1958.

Winnifrith, Tom. *The Brontës and Their Background: Romance and Reality*. New York: Barnes, 1973.

Chapter 11

Helen's Diary and the Method(ism) of Character Formation in *The Tenant of Wildfell Hall*

Melody J. Kemp

Ever since George Moore criticized Anne Brontë's presenting of Helen Huntingdon's story in diary form (253-57), critics have tried to justify *The Tenant of Wildfell Hall*'s embedding of Helen Huntingdon's diary within the frame of Gilbert Markham's letters to his brother-in-law. Early attempts to account for the narrative frame point out that *Wildfell Hall*'s titular house suggests a response to *Wuthering Heights*, with its famous layered narratives.[1] More recent comparisons of *Wuthering Heights* and *Wildfell Hall* include the deconstructive 'Gossip, Diary, Letter, Text: Anne Brontë's Narrative *Tenant* and the Problematic of the Gothic Sequel', which argues that Brontë used multiple narratives, including spoken ones, to show that experience is irrecoverable. Other recent studies propose new reasons for the enclosure of Helen Huntingdon's narrative by Gilbert Markham's letters, among them Edith Kostka's suggestion that Helen's diary matures Gilbert.[2] I would like to propose yet another possible reason for Anne Brontë's 'oft rebuked' embedding of Helen Huntingdon's diary within Gilbert Markham's framing epistolary narrative: Brontë's exposure to Methodism, which led her to believe that character could be deliberately (re)formed, especially by means of writing and reading personal narratives – an enterprise that *Wildfell Hall* simultaneously demonstrates and hopes to effect.

I am not suggesting that Methodism is 'the clue to the Brontës' or even that Anne Brontë can accurately be termed a Methodist.[3] In 1812, when Methodism became a dissenting denomination, 'Methodist' and 'Anglican' became mutually exclusive terms, so members of the Reverend Patrick Brontë's Anglican parsonage household, established in 1812, cannot be labeled Methodists (Barker 282). However, Anne Brontë was brought up as a 'methodist' in the original sense of 'methodism' as an ordering of one's time (Gaskell 199). The name 'Methodist' had, according to George Whitefield, been bestowed upon John Wesley's followers '"from their custom of regulating their time, and planning the business of the day each morning"' (Heitzenrater, *Mirror and Memory* 16), a practice that Wesley saw as integral to his followers' attainment of Christian perfection. Emily Brontë's declaration, 'I have just made a new regularity paper! and I mean *verb sap* to do great things' (Smith, Vol. 1 263), directly connects the regulation of time with self-improvement. The regulation of her time is likely to have produced in Emily's soulmate, Anne, the assurance that one could regulate one's character as readily as one could regulate one's time. Anne Brontë's belief in self-formation may well have been further enhanced by reading Thomas á Kempis' *Imitation of Christ*, a treatise on Christian perfection that had profoundly influenced Wesley's own beliefs. The edition available to Anne Brontë, first owned by her mother and subsequently by her sister Charlotte, had been translated by Wesley himself.[4]

Although Anne Brontë cannot be labeled a 'Methodist', many of her religious beliefs were compatible with Methodist doctrine,[5] and she shared the Wesleyan antipathy for Predestination – a doctrinal stance that was undoubtedly integral to her beliefs about character. The belief that some men are unconditionally predestined to salvation and that others are predestined to damnation not only denies free will but also implies that character is predetermined. Anne Brontë's rejection of the Calvinist doctrine of Predestination – eloquently expressed in her 1843 'Word to the Calvinists' (Chitham 89-90) – would have reinforced her belief that individuals had control over the development of their own characters. Belief that the character of real humans is predestined is comparable to literary determinism. Anne Brontë's stance on Predestination led her to espouse a theory of character formation opposed to that of her sister Charlotte, whose determinism may well be traceable to her 'conviction' that 'ghastly Calvinist doctrines are true' (Smith, Vol. 1 156). Charlotte Brontë's use of phrenology further suggests that she believed character to be predetermined; Anne Brontë, on the other hand, believed that character could be self-determined.

Also important to Anne Brontë's theory of character formation must have been the issues of the *Methodist Magazine* that had survived shipment to Yorkshire from Cornwall as part of Maria Branwell's trousseau (Gaskell 146). Caroline Helstone's ability to recall the contents typical of the *Methodist Magazine (Shirley* 389) not only proves Charlotte Brontë's familiarity with the Wesleyan periodical but also suggests that Anne Brontë, on whom Caroline is primarily based (Tompkins 18-28), had been markedly influenced by them. The *Methodist Magazine* was composed largely of journals of Wesleyans, which related their subjects' conversions and their writers' attempts at character formation through the regulation of time and temper.

The composition of what are now called Emily and Anne Brontë's 'diary papers' may have been suggested by the narratives in the *Methodist Magazine* and, in Anne Brontë's case, by the diary of one of John Wesley's first followers, Benjamin Ingham, the ancestor of Anne's employees at Blake Hall.[6] Ingham's diaries are extant and show that, in addition to a strict accounting of how one had spent each hour in one's day, the Methodist diarist recorded his 'temper of devotion', recollections, resolutions broken and kept, and any special blessings he felt he had received (Heitzenrater, *Diary of an Oxford Methodist* 75). Ingham frequently conducted self-examinations, and his diary contains not just statements, but self-interrogations (Heitzenrater, *Diary of an Oxford Methodist* 19). Anne Brontë's solo diary papers, composed in 1841 and 1845, are reminiscent of Ingham's. Both recollect the time of the previous diary and, after relating what the Brontës are resolved to do in the future, speculate about the family's condition on the future date when the paper's opening is scheduled. These analyses of each family member's past, present, and future status concentrate – with typically Methodist concern for the wise use of time – on how each Brontë is employed. Unlike Ingham, Anne Brontë does not record her 'temper of devotion', but she does record her emotional state, complaining in her last diary paper, 'I for my part cannot well be flatter or older in mind than I am now' (Wise and Symington, Vol. 2 53). Like Ingham and other Methodist diarists, Anne is candid about her faults, noting in her 1841 paper, 'I have the same faults I had then [in 1837], only I have more wisdom and experience, and a little more self-possession than I then enjoyed' (Smith, Vol. 1 264).[7] If the questions Anne asks are not quite the ritual questions of Wesleyan self-examination, they are nonetheless designed to ensure that Anne makes good use of her time:

> This afternoon I began to set about making my grey figured silk
> frock that was dyed at Keighley. What sort of a hand shall I make
> of it? E. and I have a great deal of work to do. When shall we
> sensibly diminish it? I want to get a habit of early rising. Shall I
> succeed? We have not yet finished our *Gondal Chronicles* that we
> began three years and a half ago. When will they be done? (Wise
> and Symington, Vol. 2 52)

Wesley believed in human perfectibility, and the self-examining diaries he encouraged are methodical attempts by subjects to perfect themselves by retrospectively analysing their flaws and resolving to make improvements. Anne Brontë's diary papers indicate her adoption of both Wesley's belief in and method of effecting self-improvement. In their 1845 diary papers, both Emily and Anne Brontë express the hope that their brother Branwell 'will be better and do better' in the future (Smith, Vol.1 407-11) – a statement that suggests a shared belief in one's ability to will the improvement of one's own character. Anne's use of copulative verbs in the 1841 diary paper also suggests that Anne thought that one could become what one wanted to become. Anne tells us not that Emily had taught at Law Hill, but that 'Emily has been a teacher' (Smith, Vol.1 264). During the preceding four years, Branwell Brontë has 'been a tutor in Cumberland . . . and become a clerk on the railroad' (Smith, Vol. 1 264). Similarly, Emily's last diary paper announces that during their excursion to York, she and Anne 'were Ronald Macelgin, Henry Angora, Juliet Augusteena, Rosobelle? Esualdar, Ella and

Julian Egramont, Catherine Navarre, and Cordelia Fitzaphnold' (Smith, Vol. 1 408). The diary papers suggest that one can change roles or identities at will, rewriting who or what one 'is' just as authors can revise the characters of their fictions.

In short, Anne Brontë's exposure to the tenets, practices, and texts of Methodism led to a belief that 'character' could be 'methodized'.[8] As we have seen, Anne Brontë's acceptance of certain Methodist tenets made her see character not as inherent but as within human control. Brontë's exposure to Wesleyan methods of self-regulation suggested to her a means by which literary, as well as real, characters might be (re)formed. The consumption and production of self-narratives made Anne Brontë self-conscious about her own 'character' – a self-consciousness Helen Huntingdon's diary produces in her hopeful suitor in *The Tenant of Wildfell Hall*. *Wildfell Hall* is indeed, as scholars have already noted, a novel with a purpose, but that purpose is not merely to encourage readers' acceptance of the doctrine of Universal Salvation but also to demonstrate how a reader should employ his or her time in order to save, or at least improve, himself: by reading, if not by writing, narratives that will make him self-conscious about the moral status of his own 'character'.

Brontë's exposure to Methodism is apparent throughout *Wildfell Hall*. For instance, *Wildfell Hall* demonstrates a Methodist concern with employment. First, Brontë distinguishes her novel's exemplary characters from its negative characters by showing the former employed at useful tasks. Without realizing what the information reveals about his first intended's character, Gilbert describes Eliza Millward as being 'as usual, busy with some piece of soft embroidery' (48) while her sister Mary, whose worth he underestimates until much later, is 'mending a heap of stockings' (49). When he arrives for another visit at Reverend Millward's vicarage, he finds Eliza 'beautifying' a cambric handkerchief by adding a lace border (96); practical Mary is 'absorbed in the hemming of a large, coarse sheet' (97).

More importantly, Brontë demonstrates that the human need for satisfying employment is responsible for both Gilbert Markham's misguided desire to save Helen from her seeming immurement in apparently grim Wildfell Hall, which is actually her refuge, and Helen's equally foolish desire to save Arthur Huntingdon by marrying him in order to reform him. Both Gilbert and Helen want – in both senses of the word – not simply occupations but vocations. Gilbert, who is at least gainfully employed, reveals his dissatisfaction with his hereditary livelihood at the start of his narrative:

> My father . . . was a sort of gentleman farmer in ___shire; and I, his express desire, succeeded him in the same quiet occupation, not very willingly, for ambition urged me to higher aims, and self-conceit assured me that, in disregarding its voice, I was burying

my talent in the earth, and hiding my light under a bushel. (35)

Helen's need for a vocation is both more acute and, because it prompts her disastrous marriage, more dangerous. As she confesses to her diary:

> If [Huntingdon] is now exposed to the baneful influence of corrupting and wicked companions, what glory to deliver him from them! – Oh! if I could but believe that Heaven has designed me for this! (168)

Wildfell Hall's demonstration of the dangers of a lack of occupation is not confined to showing how Helen Huntingdon suffers the sad consequences of her desire for purposeful occupation. The novel also shows how a lack of occupation leads to evil consequences for others, as when the bored middle-class women of the Lindenhope neighborhood invent 'idle slander' (97) about Mrs Graham, the disguised Helen Huntingdon, to while away their time. As Gilbert's younger brother notes, "'ladies and gentlemen . . . that have nothing to do'" spend their time "'snooking about to [their] neighbours' houses, peeping into their private corners; and scenting out their secrets, and picking holes in their coats'" (80).

The chief danger of lack of occupation is the self-destructive behavior to which one's consequent boredom might lead. Like the middle-class women of Gilbert's parish, Arthur Huntingdon and his cronies are members of the leisure class. With no need for gainful employment, they resort to hunting, gambling, drinking, debauchery, and tormenting others in an attempt to fill their days. Brontë repeatedly shows that Arthur Huntingdon's lack of occupation leads, through boredom, to his dissipation. As soon as she and Huntingdon return from their honeymoon, Helen reports:

> Arthur is getting tired . . . of the idle, quiet life he leads – and no wonder, for he has so few sources of amusement; he never reads anything but newspapers and sporting magazines; and when he sees me occupied with a book, he won't let me rest till I close it. In fine weather he generally manages to get through the time pretty well; but on rainy days, of which we have had a good many of late, it is quite painful to witness his ennui. (221)

On this occasion, Arthur's boredom leads him to fill the next ten days by teasing Helen with tales of his illicit love affairs, provoking their first quarrel (221-23). The day after the quarrel, Arthur is again bored by his lack of employment:

> The reading and answering of letters, and the direction of household concerns, afforded me ample employment for the

> morning; after lunch, I got my drawing, and from dinner till
> bedtime, I read. Meanwhile poor Arthur was sadly at a loss for
> something to amuse him or to occupy his time. (224)

Unable to ruffle his determinedly imperturbable wife, Huntingdon spends his time abusing his dogs (224-25). Faced with rain again the next morning, Huntingdon resolves to make the first of what become annual visits to London (226), where he lives so dissolutely that he returns home primarily to recover his health. Huntingdon's annual house parties, with their nightly scenes of drunken excess, commence when he is again bored:

> Arthur is himself again . . . and as restless and hard to amuse as a
> spoilt child, – and almost as full of mischief too, especially when
> wet weather keeps him within doors. I wish he had something to
> do, some useful trade, or profession, or employment, anything to
> occupy his head or his hands for a few hours a day, and give him
> something besides his own pleasure to think about. (238)

At first, Helen is hopeful when Huntingdon's son proves 'an increasing source of amusement to him within doors' (277), but when her husband's amusement takes the form of teaching young Arthur to drink and swear, she begins to contemplate removing the child from his father's corrupting influence.

Ralph Hattersley, one of Arthur Huntingdon's friends, is used to show that occupation is a necessary component of successful reformation. Hattersley's resolving to change is the subject of 'A Reformation' (382-86). Gilbert's later letter to Halford reports that Hattersley has maintained his resolve for twenty years – and attributes Hattersley's success to occupations:

> As for Mr Hattersley, he had never wholly forgotten his
> resolution to "come out from among them," and behave like a
> man and a Christian. . . . Avoiding the temptations of the town,
> he continued to pass his life in the country, immersed in the usual
> pursuits of a hearty, active country gentleman; his occupations
> being those of farming, and breeding horses and cattle. (461)

Brought up according to the Methodist idea that the careful employment of one's time enables one to better oneself, Anne Brontë connects the methodical use of time with self-improvement throughout *Wildfell Hall.* Huntingdon's friend Walter Hargrave tells Helen that he would reform '"entirely and for ever"' if he had '"but *half* the inducements to virtue and domestic, orderly habits"' (261) that Huntingdon has. Even physical improvement is dependent upon regularity. When Huntingdon is seriously injured, his doctor assures him '"[he] was sure to get better, if [he] stuck to his regimen'" (434). Of course, a 'strict regimen' is 'so opposite to all his previous habits' (437) that Huntingdon fails to stick to it and dies.

Perhaps the most unusual result of Brontë's exposure to Methodism is *Wildfell Hall*'s travesty of the role of the Methodist band. Following Peter Bohler's advice, John Wesley had organized his Methodist societies into smaller groups called bands, whose members met together at least weekly to share their experiences so that each band's leader could exhort those who failed to keep their resolutions to make greater efforts (*Journal*, Vol. 1 459). Arthur Huntingdon's group of cronies, with its deleterious effect on its members, is clearly meant to be a travesty of a Methodist band. Huntingdon is, as Helen's aunt points out, "'banded with a set of loose, profligate young men'" (167). Huntingdon himself calls his group 'the society' (206). As in Methodist societies, those who fail to conform to the desired habits face expulsion (206) – except that in Huntingdon's version, resolutions to reform are discouraged, not encouraged. When Lord Lowborough determines to give up gambling (202), Grimsby encourages him to "'try once more'" (202) and insists "'I *would* have one more chance if I were you'" (203). Amazingly, Huntingdon reports that Lowborough "'kept his oath about gambling . . . though Grimsby did his utmost to tempt him to break it'" (203). When Lowborough attempts to rid himself of his new vice, drinking, his "'friends did all they could to second the promptings of his own insatiable cravings'" (203). In a parody of the Christian metaphor that a Methodist leader might have used, Huntingdon tells Helen how he "'tenderly brought [Lowborough] back to the fold'" (207).

Brontë's use of travesty highlights the importance of a personal resolve to improve by showing how Arthur Huntingdon and his cronies hinder Lowborough's desired reformation:

> 'Huntingdon, this won't do! I'm resolved to have done with it'.
> 'What, are you going to shoot yourself?' said I.
> 'No, I'm going to reform'.
> 'Oh, *that's* nothing new! You've been going to reform these twelve months and more'.
> 'Yes, but you wouldn't let me'. (208)

Resolve is necessary even to Helen Huntingdon, *Wildfell Hall*'s pure and Christian heroine, who repeatedly states her resolution not to spoil her son and, more important, to control the anger that her husband's extramarital affair provokes (326).

With its insistence on willed improvement and the dogged maintenance of virtue under adverse conditions, *Wildfell Hall* argues, with Methodist zeal, that human character is the product of human will. Not surprisingly, Brontë denigrates the contemporary 'sciences' of physiognomy and phrenology. In one instance, she uses Helen's mistaken first assessment of Arthur Huntingdon's character to demonstrate the folly of assuming that character is related to physiognomy. Helen confidently proclaims:

> 'I am an excellent physiognomist, and I always judge of people's characters by their looks. . . . For instance, I should know by your countenance that you were not of a cheerful, sanguine disposition; and I should know by Mr Wilmot's that he was a worthless old reprobate, and by Mr Boarham's that he was not an agreeable companion, and by Mr Huntingdon's that he was neither a fool nor a knave, though, possibly, neither a sage nor a saint'. (154)

When Arthur Huntingdon subsequently uses phrenology as an excuse for his lack of faith, Helen states Brontë's own sentiments when she concludes the following exchange with her husband by insisting that "'our utmost exertions are required of us all'":

> '. . . the more you loved your God the more deep and pure would be your love to me'.
> At this he only laughed, . . . calling me a sweet enthusiast.[9]
> Then taking off his hat, he added – 'But look here, Helen – what can a man do with such a head as this?'
> . . . .
> 'You see I was not made to be a saint,' said he, laughing.
> 'If God meant me to be religious, why didn't He give me a proper organ of veneration'. (218)

Huntingdon's feeling that his character is predetermined seems to stem from a belief that he is one of those irretrievably predestined to damnation, called 'reprobates' by John Calvin and 'castaways' by the Calvinist poet Cowper. Evidence certainly suggests that Brontë meant us to see Arthur Huntingdon as a Calvinist. Huntingdon's friend Hattersley once asks, "'Isn't Huntingdon as great a reprobate as ever was d – -d?'" (302). Contrasting himself with Huntingdon, Lowborough proclaims, "'Huntingdon, I am not a castaway'" (21). Significantly, Arthur Huntingdon's surname links him to the Calvinistic set of Methodists who were known as the 'Countess of Huntingdon's Connexion'. Certainly, Huntingdon's 'horror of death' (446) and the 'melancholy' (447), 'gloomy reflections' (448) and despondency with which he faces it suggests a sense of damnation. Like his friend Grimsby, he is sure that his "'end'" will be "'in hell fire'" (204).

Arthur Huntingdon is not the only character Anne Brontë uses to show the deleteriousness of pessimism about one's ability to improve one's own character. Lord Lowborough, like Huntingdon, "'lacks that sustaining power of self-esteem which leads a man, exulting in his own integrity, to defy the malice of traducing foes'" (352); sharing with Helen the stereotype of woman as redeeming angel, Lowborough does not think he can keep his resolutions not to drink or gamble unless he has a wife (209). Brontë shows that self-esteem encourages efforts at improvement, as the following exchange between Gilbert and his mother makes clear:

> 'I'm sure a finer disposition than yours, by nature, could not be, if you'd let it have fair play; so you've no excuse *that* way'.
> While she thus remonstrated, I took up my book . . . for I was equally unable to justify myself, and unwilling to acknowledge my errors . . . but my excellent parent went on lecturing, and then came to coaxing, and began to stroke my hair; and I was getting to feel quite a good boy, but my mischievous brother . . . revived my corruption by suddenly calling out: –
> 'Don't touch him, mother! he'll bite! He's a very tiger in human form . . .' (128)

When Gilbert's mother shows her appreciation of his goodness, she is able to persuade him to make the changes she desires. By hinting that Gilbert also has bad urges, conversely, his brother Fergus 'revived' his 'corruption'. The improvement that we see in Gilbert's nature during the course of the novel is connected to his need to esteem himself highly, which he can do only if he proves a worthy partner for Helen Huntingdon.

Wildfell Hall indicates that we should be optimistic that inherent tendencies can be overcome by sheer willpower. Lord Lowborough's 'constant struggles to subdue the evil promptings of his nature' (60) succeed brilliantly when he has a wife of whom he wants to be worthy (461). Although Helen Huntingdon sometimes sees in her son Arthur's 'bursts of gleeful merriment' 'his father's spirit and temperament' (334), she is determined 'to contend against' what she calls 'the father's spirit in the son' (333). The departing sketch Gilbert Markham provides of his mature stepson proves that her efforts were successful.

Anne Brontë emphasizes that an adult's willpower, and ability to effect self-improvement, is dependent upon his will being broken when he is a child. Brontë's belief that a child could learn willpower by being prevented, from infancy, from having everything he 'willed' may be derived from the childrearing advice of John Wesley's mother, Susanna, who had declared:

'self-will is the root of all sin and misery, so whatever cherishes this in children ensures their after-wretchedness and irreligion; whatever checks and mortifies it promotes their future happiness and piety. This is still more evident if we farther consider that religion is nothing else than the doing the will of God, and not our own; that, the one grand impediment to our temporal and eternal happiness being this self-will, no indulgences of it can be trivial, no denial unprofitable. Heaven or hell depends on this alone. So that the parent who studies to subdue it in his child works together with God in the renewing and saving a soul. The parent who indulges it does the devil's work, makes religion impracticable, salvation unattainable; and does all that in him lies to damn his child . . '. (*Journal*, Vol. 2 36)

Helen is determined to 'curb [her son's] will' (333) despite the opposition of his indulgent father, who tells her that she has '"broken his fine spirit with [her] rigid severity"' (387).

Thus, while *Wildfell Hall* is rather discouraging about a woman's prospects for reforming her husband, it encourages women to try to mould their sons' characters, in part by emphasizing the success of Helen's efforts on behalf of young Arthur. Faced with the likelihood of her son's genetic predisposition to alcoholism – a tendency that the child's father fosters by giving him spirits – Helen devises a plan to make her son detest alcohol:

I have succeeded in giving him an absolute disgust for all intoxicating liquors . . . . He was inordinately fond of them for so young a creature, and, remembering my unfortunate father as well as his, I dreaded the consequences of such a taste. But if I had stinted him in his usual quantity of wine or forbidden him to taste it altogether, that would only have increased his partiality for it, and made him regard it as a greater treat than ever. I therefore gave him quite as much as his father was accustomed to allow him . . . , but into every glass I surreptitiously introduced a small quantity of tartar-emetic – just enough to produce inevitable nausea and depression without positive sickness. Finding such disagreeable consequences invariably to result from this indulgence, he soon grew weary of it, but the more he shrank from the daily treat the more I pressed it upon him, till his reluctance was strengthened to perfect abhorrence. (375-76)

Helen is 'determined to enlist all the powers of association in [her] service', so 'when he was sick, [she had] obliged the poor child to swallow a little wine and water *without* the tartar emetic, by way of medicine' (376). So successful is Helen's plan that when her son is offered wine by Mrs. Markham, he 'shrank away from the ruby nectar as if in terror and disgust, and was ready to cry when urged to take it' (53).

Rather than being praised by the Markhams for the success of the method she details, Mrs Graham, as Helen now calls herself, is criticized by them. Mrs Markham warns Arthur's mother not to '"spend her life in petting him up"' (55). Of course, Mrs Markham's indulgence of her own sons makes us realize that her advice is hypocritical and prompts us to favor Helen's side of the argument. In a novel that criticizes nineteenth-century sexual stereotypes, Mrs Markham's warning that Mrs Graham will '"make a mere Miss Nancy"' of her son by '"treat[ing] him like a girl"' [55] is obviously meant to be rejected. Brontë's point in 'The Controversy' is, as Helen's argument against Gilbert (56-57) makes clear, precisely that boys should be treated like girls. As Helen tells Gilbert:

> 'You would have us encourage our sons to prove all things by their own experience, while our daughters must not even profit by the experience of others. Now *I* would have both so to benefit by the experience of others, and the precepts of a higher authority, that they should know beforehand to refuse the evil and choose the good, and require no experimental proofs to teach them the evil of transgression. I would not send a poor girl into the world unarmed against her foes, and ignorant of the snares that beset her path; nor would I watch and guard her, till, deprived of self-respect and self-reliance, she lost the power, or the will, to watch and guard herself; and as for my son – if I thought he would grow up to be what you call a man of the world – one that has 'seen life,' and glories in his experience, even though he should so far profit by it, as to sober down, at length, into a useful and respected member of society – I would rather that he died tomorrow!' (57)

The entire chapter called 'The Controversy' consists of the Markhams' and Helen's debate on the education of children. Helen is clearly the mouthpiece for Brontë's own views, while the chapter itself is a vehicle for making obvious the point of the entire novel: the reader is to benefit by the experience of others.

Wildfell Hall attempts to educate readers so that they do not go into the world ignorant of its snares. Brontë's 1848 'Preface' to the second edition defends her decision to portray vice in order to warn of its consequences:

> When we have to do with vice and vicious characters, I maintain it is better to depict them as they really are . . . To represent a bad

thing in its least offensive light is doubtless the most agreeable course for a writer of fiction to pursue; but is it the most honest, or the safest? Is it better to reveal the snares and pitfalls of life to the young and thoughtless traveler, or to cover them with branches and flowers? Oh, Reader! if there were less of this delicate concealment of facts . . . , there would be less sin and misery to the young of both sexes who are left to wring their bitter knowledge from experience. (30)

If Helen Huntingdon's diary and letters constitute 'The Warnings of Experience' (148), the narrative that frames them demonstrates the educative power of another's narrative. With the benefit of the hindsight permitted when one is recalling events that had occurred two decades before, Gilbert realizes that as a young man he 'was a little bit spoiled' (58). Filled with 'self-conceit' (35), he had become angry when he perceived that Helen's 'opinions respecting me . . . fell far below those I entertained of myself' (58). Helen's diary teaches Gilbert the dangers of spoiling and the importance of exercising self-restraint; as he tells his narratee, Halford, in 1847, he had not by 1827 'acquired half the rule over my own spirit, that I now possess' (35). Even more important, Gilbert's desire for Helen's approbation led him to mould himself into the opposite sort of husband to Arthur Huntingdon.

Wildfell Hall repeatedly demonstrates Anne Brontë's belief in the value of narrative.[10] Gilbert uses monetary metaphors to describe the introductory chapter he sends Halford in his first letter:

> This is the first instalment of my debt. If the coin suits you, tell me so, and I'll send you the rest at my leisure: if you would rather remain my creditor than stuff your purse with such ungainly heavy pieces, tell me still, and I'll . . . keep the treasure to myself. (44)

When he inserts Helen's diary into his own epistolary narrative some fifteen chapters later, he imagines that Halford will 'not, of course, peruse it with half the interest that I did' (147) – understandably so, given the 'return' that Helen gets when she 'invests' her narrative in Gilbert: an increase in his own value as a husband and an increase in the virtue with which she is credited. Helen's diary is designed to be personal; not expecting to enter into an 'exchange', she does not refer to it in economic terms. Nevertheless, her diary shows the value of narrative. Helen is often 'occupied with a book' (221), unlike her husband, who is 'sadly at a loss' (224) for something to do while she reads and who 'never reads anything but newspapers and sporting magazines' (221). Helen believes that 'if he would take up with some literary study', his life would have purpose (238). When

Ralph Hattersley finally urges Huntingdon to reform, he does so by telling him to "'turn over a new leaf'" (361).

By revealing that the community's narratives about Mrs Graham are not to be 'credited', *Wildfell Hall* may appear to suggest that only printed narratives possess worth. Actually, Brontë suggests that only narratives that are based on personal experience have value, for they are the only ones whose events we can 'credit', an investment of belief that is needed if narrative is to have its full value as an agent of transformation. Gilbert's declaration that 'none but fools would credit' (120) the first stories that arise about Helen is based on Mary Millward's supposition that "'somebody has been inventing'" them (97). Gilbert comes to doubt not only tales he assumes were invented but also those that are "'the tale as 'twas told to me'" (463). When Gilbert cannot credit the stories he hears, they have no value because – unlike Helen's dependable first-hand tale – they do not inspire action. The crediting of false narratives may have the negative value of producing bad actions. Gilbert's voyeurism leads to an observation that convinces him, erroneously, that he has 'too good reason, now, to credit their reports concerning Mrs Graham' (129), and his acceptance of the report that Mr Lawrence is Helen's lover ultimately provokes his vicious attack on this rival.

Anne Brontë demonstrates that the mediated experiences provided by others' narratives are to be preferred to direct experiences of one's own, which she shows may be misinterpreted. Helen's diary convinces Gilbert to "'discredit the evidence of [his] senses'" (145); further experience is often necessary if one is to interpret appearances correctly. Soon after she meets Mr Huntingdon, Helen is receiving unwelcome attentions from an elderly suitor when Huntingdon interferes. Looking up and seeing Huntingdon, she says, 'was like turning from some purgatorial fiend to an angel of light, come to announce that the season of torment was past' (162). As Helen's subsequent experiences as Mrs Huntingdon make clear, it is Huntingdon – not old Wilmot – who is a fiend and who will necessitate purgatorial cleansing, and Helen's 'season of torment' is just beginning. After several years of marriage to Arthur Huntingdon, Helen is delighted when he responds enthusiastically to one of her embraces; she assumes that the expression of surprise she sees when the moon shines on his face 'shows, at least, that the affection is genuine' (305-06). Only later, after the experience of seeing and hearing her husband and Lady Lowborough rendezvousing in the same shrubbery (312), does she correctly interpret her husband's shocked expression as surprise at finding that he was embracing his wife and not his mistress (314). Corrective interpretation like this is permitted by written narrative's inevitably retrospective nature, and thus makes the mediated experience provided by written narrative a more reliable guide to one's conduct than one's own experience.

If Helen's diary and letters provide interpreted experience that proves corrective to Gilbert, *Wildfell Hall* itself is patently designed to produce improvement in Brontë's readers. Brontë cannot, of course, offer us only Helen's diary and be confident that we will realize its purpose. Helen could tell her story belatedly and self-consciously, with direct addresses to the reader, but we would lose the diary's vivid immediacy. Framing Helen's narrative with Gilbert's allows Brontë to preserve the diary's authenticity while making the point that the vicarious experience provided by narratives, these two among them, can and should transform the reader. Gilbert's letters reenact Helen's naïve responses to experience and enact the transformative power of narrative on character, all the while self-consciously reminding us that the enclosed and originary narrative is a 'story' and that Helen's 'character' – in both senses of the word – encouraged Gilbert's own reformation, his reading of Helen's diary having been immediately productive of two allied emotions: 'joy' that 'her character shone bright, and clear, and stainless as that sun I could not bear to look on; and shame and deep remorse for [his] own conduct' (403). Ostensibly offered to Gilbert Markham's narratee, his brother-in-law, Gilbert's 'old-world story', 'a tale of many chapters' (34), is offered to us in the hope that it will produce in us a transformation comparable to the one Helen's diary has produced in Gilbert by making him conscious of his own 'character'.

Anne Brontë's presentation of Helen's story in diary form and her indication that Gilbert's letters to Halford are drawn from 'a certain faded old journal' (34) suggest that the writing of personal narratives further heightens one's self-consciousness about one's character and hence promotes one's attempts at character improvement, as it did for Methodist journal keepers. *Wildfell Hall* does not insist that our salvation depends on our writing Wesleyan narratives – indeed, the only part of Helen's diary that really resembles a Wesleyan journal is her description of the moment when she feels assurance of salvation (313). *Wildfell Hall* does, however, urge us to view ourselves as 'characters', with character that we should deliberately perfect in a necessary attempt to ensure our own salvation. Most important, *Wildfell Hall* encourages us to have faith – a Methodistical faith that our character is subject to our own control.

Notes

[1] 'That there is a strong similarity between some of the external characteristics of *Wildfell Hall* and *Wuthering Heights* is of course a commonplace', says Edward Chitham, who sees Anne's work as a corrective to Emily's ('Diverging Twins' 99-100). Chitham cites Linton Andrews as possibly the first to notice the similarities in the names of the titular houses, in the mode of narration and in incident (Andrews 30). Both novels also contain a multitude of characters whose given and family names begin with *H* (Liddell 94).

[2] Kostka says that 'what Brontë demonstrates in her narrative experiment

is that the simple act of reading has within its nature the means to change youthful indifference into responsible, aware adulthood' (41). Kostka's argument is obviously a forerunner of my own.

³ Half a century ago, G. Elsie Harrison pointed out the Brontë family's numerous Methodist connections and suggested that Methodism might be 'the clue to the Brontës'. In the decades since the publication of Harrison's works on the Brontës, scholarly reaction has ranged from Valentine Cunningham's unquestioning acceptance of the idea that the Brontës' response to Methodism was essentially positive to, at the other extreme, Phyllis Bentley's declaration that the Brontës displayed a '"keen animus against Methodism"' (Bentley 270).

Harrison's claims of Methodism's centrality to the Brontës is unquestionably inflated. For instance, her claim that Heathcliff's name is derived from the name 'Sutcliffe' is based on the erroneous notion that it is spelled 'Heathcliffe' (*Clue* 165). On the other hand, Harrison's suggestions that the name 'Jabes Brandenham' was derived from that of Jabez Bunting (*Methodist Good Companions* 110-11) is borne out by the similarity between an incident in Lockwood's dream and a similar occurrence during one of Bunting's sermons. Harrison may well be correct when she says the names 'Shirley', 'Hastings', 'Surena' and 'Huntingdon' (*Clue* 13-14) were suggested by figures in Methodist history, but – with the exception of Huntingdon – a Methodist source for the names adds little to our interpretation of the Brontës' prose.

⁴ The Brontë household's copy of *The Imitation of Christ* is inscribed 'M. Branwell, July 1807'.

⁵ Three of the hymns Anne Brontë wrote were adopted for the *Methodist Hymn Book*, and Charles Wesley's 'O for a Heart to Praise My God' was the first piece Brontë copied into her music manuscript book (Chitham, *Poems* 34).

⁶ Emily and Anne's earliest diary papers, written in 1834 and 1837, were joint productions. Although far from bland, they are merely familial status reports, their content reminiscent of Charlotte's 1829 'History of the Year' (Alexander, Vol. 1 04-05). Anne was away at her second post on 30 July 1841, the date she and Emily had chosen for composition of their next diary paper; each therefore composed her own 1841 diary paper, Anne's differing from the earlier compositions perhaps because those express primarily Emily's feelings – or perhaps because she incorporated features she had seen in Benjamin Ingham's diary into this and her 1845 diary paper.

⁷ Maria Frawley has already noted, 'Brontë's self-assessment draws on a rhetoric of self-chastisement and correction that one would associate with the Wesleyan heritage of her Aunt Branwell' (Frawley 36).

⁸ I am indebted to Felicity Nussbaum's 'Methodized Subjects: John Wesley's Journals' for suggesting to me a connection between the Brontës' consumption and production of diaries and Anne Brontë's theory of character development.

⁹ 'Enthusiast' was a nickname commonly bestowed upon Methodists, many of whom showed great religious fervour. Helen's aunt Maxwell, who raised her, is evidently a Methodist, for Huntingdon says that if he goes to church and behaves like a Godly man the aunt will regard him with "'sisterly love, as a brand plucked from the burning'" (188), words John Wesley used to describe himself after narrowly escaping from a fire that destroyed his childhood home.

¹⁰ Jan Gordon has already noted *Wildfell Hall*'s abundance of economic terms – though her point is different from mine.

Works Cited

Alexander, Christine, ed. *An Edition of the Early Writings of Charlotte Brontë.*
    3 vols. Oxford: Shakespeare Head Press, 1987.

Andrews, Linton. 'A Challenge by Anne Brontë'. *Brontë Society Transactions*
    14.5 (1965): 25-30.

Augustine, Saint. *The Imitation of Christ.* Brontë Parsonage Museum Library,
    Haworth. MS HAPBP: bb202.

Barker, Juliet. *The Brontës.* New York: St Martin's Press, 1994.

Brontë, Anne. Ed. G. D. Hargreaves. 1848. *The Tenant of Wildfell Hall.* London:
    Penguin, 1979.

Brontë, Charlotte. *Shirley.* 1849. Ed. Herbert Rosengarten and Margaret Smith.
    Oxford and New York: Oxford University Press, 1979.

Chitham, Edward, ed. *The Poems of Anne Brontë: A New Text and Commentary.*
    Totowa, New Jersey: Rowman and Littlefield, 1979.

-----. 'Diverging Twins: A Clue to *Wildfell Hall*'. *Brontë Facts and Brontë Problems.*
    Ed. Edward Chitham and Tom Winnifrith. London and Basingstoke:
    Macmillan, 1983. 91-109.

Cunningham, Valentine. *Everywhere Spoken Against: Dissent in the Victorian Novel.*
    Oxford: Clarendon Press, 1975.

Curnock, Nehemiah, ed. *The Journal of the Rev. John Wesley, A. M.* Standard Ed. 8
    vols. London: R. Culley, 1909-16.

'Dr Phyllis Bentley on the Brontës and Methodism', *Brontë Society Transactions*
    11.59 (1949): 270.

Frawley, Maria. *Anne Brontë.* New York: Twayne, 1996.

Gaskell, Elizabeth. *The Life of Charlotte Brontë.* Ed. Alan Shelston. London:
    Penguin Books, 1975.

Gordon, Jan. 'Gossip, Diary, Letter, Text: Anne Brontë's Narrative *Tenant* and
    the Problem of the Gothic Sequel'. *ELH* 51.4 (1984): 719-45.

Harrison, G. Elsie. *The Clue to the Brontës.* London: Methuen, 1948.

-----. *Haworth Parsonage: A Study of Wesley and the Brontës.* London: Epworth
    Press, 1937.

-----. *Methodist Good Companions*. London: Epworth Press, 1935.

Heitzenrater, Richard , ed. *Diary of an Oxford Methodist: Benjamin Ingham, 1733-1734*. Durham: Duke University Press, 1985.

-----. *Mirror and Memory: Reflections on Early Methodism*. Nashville: Kingswood Press. 1989.

Kempis, Thomas à. *An Extract of the Christian's Pattern, or a Treatise of the Imitation of Christ*. Trans. John Wesley. London: G. Story, 1803.

Kostka, Edith. 'Narrative Experience as a Means to Maturity in Anne Brontë's Victorian Novel *The Tenant of Wildfell Hall*'. *Connecticut Review* 14.3 (1992): 41-47.

Liddell, Robert. *Twin Spirits: The Novels of Emily and Anne Brontë*. London: Owen, 1990.

Moore, George. *Conversations in Ebury Street*. New York: Boni and Liveright, 1924.

Nussbaum, Felicity. *The Autobiographical Subject*. Baltimore: Johns Hopkins University Press, 1989.

Smith, Margaret, ed. *The Letters of Charlotte Brontë*. 3 vols. Oxford: Clarendon Press, 1995.

Tompkins, J. M. S. 'Caroline Helstone's Eyes'. *Brontë Society Transactions* 14.71 (1961): 18-28.

Chapter 12

A Matter of Strong Prejudice:
Gilbert Markham's Self Portrait

Andrea Westcott

In their introduction to a collection of feminist essays by women poets, Sandra Gilbert and Susan Gubar argue that female poets did not flourish as well as novelists in the nineteenth century because 'the novel allows – even encourages – just the self-effacing withdrawal society has traditionally fostered in women' (xxii). While the novel, indeed, offers greater opportunity than the poem to disappear into the created fiction, it nevertheless provides many opportunities for the female writer's ideology to find voice in, through, and around the edges of the characters. In other words, if we accept the premise forwarded by Simone de Beauvoir in the introduction to *The Second Sex* that women's role has been socially constructed, defined by men, who are seen as 'the Absolute', while women are 'the Other'' (xvi), then perhaps one of the ways for a woman to attempt to circumvent this construct is to write from her own perspective, to reveal 'the Other'.

Anne Brontë has been recognized recently as an early advocate of feminism, as one who does not privilege the male point of view in her portrait of the heroine. Instead, in *The Tenant of Wildfell Hall*, she writes 'a story of female desire' in which a woman's trangression or 'fall' in leaving her husband becomes her triumph (Langland, 'Voicing of Feminine Desire' 112-13). It might likewise be argued that neither does Brontë privilege the male point of view in her portrait of the hero. Rather Brontë presents Gilbert Markham as a flawed hero not because she cannot conceive of an ideal (in her youth Anne was as steeped in the Byronic hero as her sisters), but because she is too faithful to her own experience, to what she sees in society around her.

Anne Brontë is finally being recognized not only for the realism of her portraits of both women and men, fulfilling her desire 'to whisper a few wholesome truths' (Preface 29), but also for her implicit critique of Victorian society, and for her 'sophisticated technique of layered narratives' (Langland, *Anne Brontë: The Other One* 118). Brontë adeptly juggles her portrait of Helen's growth through adversity, her husband's unByronic decline, and the third part of this three-part main structure: Markham's self portrait. While Helen's diary has most generally been considered as the novel's heart, such an interpretation fails, I would argue, to credit Markham's narrative with the importance it deserves.

The nuances that Brontë develops in the friendship between Helen and Markham are pivotal for determining the success or failure of the narrative structure she has chosen. By attending closely to that structure – Markham's letter – the reader can observe how the epistolary form offers insights into the narrator's character. He is not just the vehicle for ensuring a 'happy ending' to Helen's story but a complex individual who is shaping his experiences as he writes his narrative from the dominant, patriarchal point of view. Thus, I would contend, Markham's autobiography becomes an occasion for Brontë's exploration of this literary form.

What critics have not focused upon is the importance of Markham's portrait as fictional autobiography. Indeed, as Markham shapes his past to portray himself in the most advantageous light, I will argue in this paper that Brontë presents an intentionally mixed portrait of her 'hero', a critique of the ideal country gentleman.

In terms of length, Helen's diary is only allotted about twenty percent more space than Markham's account.[1] In terms of ideas, since he is given first voice, Markham's narrative reflects Anne Brontë's underlying ideology by establishing a structural link which connects to her thematic concerns. As Langland observes, 'by initially making Helen Graham an object of Gilbert's narrative and not the subject of her own, the text enacts what it also presents thematically: women's objectification and marginalization within patriarchal culture' (115). Since earlier critics had not recognized this structural link, their attention has been given to the diary section.[2] Despite W. A. Craik's assertion in *The Brontë Novels* that, among other things, the narrators – Gilbert Markham and Helen Huntingdon – 'are devised in the first place to ensure conviction and a first-hand accuracy' (230), closer scrutiny alerts the reader to the need for evaluating Markham's interpretation of events.

Many critics have assumed that Anne chose a clumsy device for introducing her action.[3] Similar complaints are registered against Charlotte's first novel. Nevertheless, in using the epistolary mode, both authors create a context in which the reader can judge their narrators. Having learned from Charlotte's earlier example, Anne provides a more plausible context for her narrative. Just as in *The Professor*, William Crimsworth reveals much about his own nature in his introductory letter to his acquaintance, Charles, so, in *Wildfell Hall*, Markham unconsciously invites us to consider his real motivations for disturbing 'certain musty old letters and papers' (34) in order to provide, as he says, 'a full and faithful account of certain circumstances connected with the most important event of my life' (34).

Essentially, in his letters Markham writes an autobiographical account of the events leading to his marriage. The occasion is provided neatly by Halford's request for a return of confidence, unlike Crimsworth who writes less convincingly after seeing Charles' name in the paper. However, Markham did not comply with an earlier request. What, but an intense desire to understand the pattern of his life, which dovetails with Anne Brontë's desire to critique the pattern of her society, would induce Gilbert Markham to embark upon such a lengthy and intimate disclosure?

Gilbert's autobiography becomes an occasion for Brontë's exploration of the possibilities of this literary form. A French twist on de Beauvoir's theory here might be for the 'Other' to write as the 'Self', the male subject. Brontë's narrator, Gilbert, assumes the role of autobiographer by virtue of his desire to amuse Halford 'with an old-world story' (34), spoken by someone who, only by virtue of his marriage, has donned the patriarchal mantle of the ideal country gentleman and found it to be a most suitable fit. That each of the sisters had already experimented with the form does not necessarily speak to the Victorians' absorbing interest in autobiography, but nevertheless, the Brontës' use of the forms of autobiography does coincide with its increasing popularity. Later, Charlotte developed what she refers to as 'the autobiographical form' (qtd. in Wise 322) most fully in *Villette*. The first record of the word, by Robert Southey in 1809, suggests that the need for a term did not actually arise until the nineteenth century.[4] Earlier autobiographies – with the exception of religious confessions such as St. Augustine's *Confessions* or Bunyan's *Grace Abounding* – generally adopted an external rather than an internal focus. By the end of the eighteenth century the emphasis had changed. As Wayne Shumaker explains, 'the development of a subjective emphasis in autobiography has . . . the same kind of literary significance as the rise of the novel; and the two phenomena are clearly related' (74). Consistent with the temper of the times, the Brontës were moved like other 'men of letters' to explore the limits of this mode.

It is a mode in which the autobiographer seeks to impress his viewpoint upon the reader by presenting a believable portrait of his particular world. '[A]utobiography', as Roy Pascal explains, 'is a shaping of the past' because 'it establishes certain stages in an individual life, makes links between them, and defines, implicitly or explicitly, a certain consistency of relationship beween the self and the outside world' (9). He adds that in taking a standpoint it is the individual's 'present position which enables him to see his life as something of a unity, something that may be reduced to order' (9). Naturally, the difficulty lies in reducing a chaotic world to some semblance of order. Because it is a selective process, in the writing of autobiography, the self can be as much exposed by what is not as by what is said.

Since 'all autobiographies hold *what was* up to view in light reflected from *what is*' (Schumaker 114), the present context, then, is an essential signifier in the self portrait Markham presents. He conveys an impression of a contented man who has long since become accustomed to the generous comforts and abundant leisure that wealth provides. Yet, at the same time, Anne Brontë never presents him as a paragon. As Edward Chitham postulates, she takes *Jane Eyre*'s Rochester, 'a hugely warm-hearted, larger-than-life Byronic hero' and 'splits him in two' (142). Huntingdon would get his 'thoughtlessness, arrogance and riches' while Markham 'would walk through the book with a host of male faults' (142). Despite his material prosperity, then, Markham has not entirely buried some of his less appealing characteristics. His impulsiveness, acting quickly – even violently – and only later thinking of the consequences, surfaces in his attitude towards Halford. After lecturing on why he thinks Halford has been at fault, Markham catches himself abruptly and says, 'Well! – I did not take up my pen to reproach you, nor to defend myself, nor to apologize for past offences, but, if possible, to atone for them' (33). Markham reveals inadvertently how unconscious muscle memory dominates over conscious effort in an individual with such strong personal prejudices.

His attitude is reminiscent of William Crimsworth's in his letter to Charles. Not unlike Markham, Crimsworth makes some disparaging comments to his friend. He feels himself to be 'superior' to Charles' habit of reacting to remarks about beauty or affection with 'sardonic coldness' (1). Crimsworth's caustic frame of mind, his sharp tone, the very pretext for the letter, should strike the reader as odd. In *The Cover of The Mask*, Annette Tromly questions Charlotte's use of an epistolary mode: 'Why is he clearly more interested in telling his story than in communicating with Charles? Surely, Charlotte is asking her reader, from the book's first moments, to be aware of the centrality of the narrative voice' (22). Surely, Anne is demanding a similar involvement from her reader. Rather than dismissing either structure as ineffective, it should be remembered, as Linda Hutcheon explains in *Narcissistic Narrative: The Metafictional Paradox*, that 'the epistolary novel form, in general explicitly places the reader as letter reader within the structure of the novel' (27). The reader of this form becomes a participant and, therefore, has a responsibility to ask questions about the author's purposes.

When we pass from the letter to the beginning of the first chapter, Anne Brontë segues from the focus on communicating to revealing through autobiography. We move from Staningley in 1847 to Linden-Car in 1827, where Markham is vainly endeavoring to reconcile himself to the life of a 'gentleman farmer' (35). Here, Markham acknowledges his unruly spirit but deludes himself into believing he is capable of more than a rudimentary degree of self-control. His personal evaluations serve to expose more fully the difference between his perception of himself and the reality perceived by the reader. Brontë asks us to be aware of his dual role as a character caught in the crossfire of the action and as a narrator shaping his tale to suit his present purposes. Markham shapes his past by providing evidence of 'the progress of [his] character',[5] unaware, of course, of what else he unwittingly discloses about himself.

Since the patriarchal point of view is given voice first, Brontë sets Markham up for some irony at his own expense. In finding Mrs Graham too proud, he silently says he would 'rather admire you from this distance, fair lady, than be the partner of your home' (41). It is fitting that Markham's impressions of the widow reflect peculiarities in his own nature. He denotes her as 'a woman liable to take strong prejudices, I should fancy, and stick to them through thick and thin, twisting everything into conformity with her own preconceived opinions – too hard, too sharp, too bitter for my taste' (65). Brontë will soon offer sufficient provocation for Helen's hard exterior. In contrast, Markham has only his indulgent upbringing by his mother to account for his own propensity to twist things 'into conformity with [his] own preconceived opinions'. Of course, he will learn his error through the medium of the diary. Brontë means for the female, who feels all the effects of adversity, to instruct the male, who profits from the lesson without experiencing the pain: an ironic reversal of the education for boys and girls that Helen describes and deplores (57). However, in acting as a form of instruction, as Russell Poole argues, 'we should not exaggerate [the diary's] effect' (863). It cannot transform character traits; it simply offers Helen's testimony as a guide to action. Predictably, as we will see, Markham's autobiography reveals his inability fully to transcend his nature, which serves his author's purpose, if not his own.

Further instances of Markham's willful blindness, especially before reading the diary, are reminiscent of those of Mr Lockwood, the tenant of Thrushcross Grange. The resemblances between the two are striking, a commonplace now that *Wildfell Hall* is considered Anne's '"answer" to *Wuthering Heights*' (Chitham 142). Just as Lockwood's lack of insight into his own and Heathcliff's nature sets the tone for Emily's ironic treatment of him—he believes Heathcliff's reserve 'springs from an aversion to showy displays of feeling' (7) – so too, Markham's shortcomings offer Brontë the opportunity for besting his pride. In contrast to Emily, however, the effects reverberate more profoundly throughout *Wildfell Hall*. Whereas Lockwood distances the action, Markham partakes of it. Thus, at the end of *Wuthering Heights*, Lockwood's desire for Cathy remains unfulfilled, since she has found her mate in Hareton. Markham, on the other hand, has had his wish fulfilled. No one is affected by Lockwood's sentimental longings; conversely, Markham's fantasies have grave repercussions on the object of those fantasies.

A comparison more clearly lay between the two sets of lovers: Markham and Helen and Heathcliff and Catherine. Reaction to Markham is best termed ambivalent, as he is perceived as perfectly innocuous, on the one hand, and as inexplicably violent on the other. Such a curious combination of characteristics is central to the relationship that the author develops between the lovers. Much of the effect is created through repressed sexual tension, what George Moore calls Brontë's ability to 'write with heat, one of the rarest qualities' (253). Brontë reveals the passionate aspects of Markham's character which she combines with his pride and petulence to exploit the paradoxical qualities of human nature and, thus, to create a believable portrait. For example, Markham's jealousy is easily aroused when he suspects his acquaintance Frederick Lawrence of a romantic interest in Helen. Soon after Eliza Millward insinuates that little Arthur might be Lawrence's son, Markham's 'brain was on fire with indignation, and [his] heart seemed ready to burst from its prison with conflicting passions' (101). With no justification, he then unceremoniously accuses Lawrence of being a 'hypocrite' (107) for offering any advice on what to do about Mrs Graham.

Just as Emily does with Lockwood, Anne maintains a very deliberate distance between herself and her first narrator. She condones neither his attitude nor his actions. However, Markham is also supposed to be the romantic hero, which once again highlights the different approaches between the sisters in their attitude towards gender. Emily sympathizes with Heathcliff because she fuses the masculine and the feminine into the single soul of Heathcliff/Catherine.[6] As two halves of the same tormented spirit, Heathcliff/Catherine embody Emily's vision of the Self. All the rest in their world are the Other. For Emily, gender is not an issue; for Anne, it is. Emily assumes an equality between souls for which Anne sees no evidence. Anne, therefore, strives to present the male Self as she sees it. Thus, however reprehensible Markham's petty jealousies appear, they are realistic psychological insights into her hero's character, a character striving to give vent to his desire in a socially acceptable manner.

The most heinous example of Markham's conflicting desires occurs when, 'impelled by some fiend at [his] elbow' (134), Markham strikes Lawrence with his whip. Whether one views it as the toy symbol of power that Catherine Earnshaw never received from her father or as a simple tool for domination, it produces a 'feeling of savage satisfaction' (134) in Markham when he uses it over Lawrence's head. Furthermore, he feels no shame for his act of violence until, after reading Helen's diary, he learns the extent to which he has misconstrued events. Markham's contrition results only from recognition of this error, not from any revulsion at the deed itself, a fact that calls his moral consciousness into question.

The reader's attitude to Markham is being tested continually as the conflicting qualities within his nature are gradually revealed through his autobiography. Yet, it is necessary for the eventual outcome of the novel that Markham is regarded, at least in certain respects, as an eligible companion for Helen. Whether he is truly suitable as a mate should be evident by the time we reach the 'happy ending'. That it is the hero who must meet the standard set by the heroine is a point well illustrated by Elizabeth Langland. In exchange for telling her tale, Helen wishes 'to marry a man who consents to be the object of her beneficence and affection' ('Voicing' 114). It is a neat twist of Brontë's abilities that she makes this reversal in standards both possible and proper, despite the apparent fact that '[l]egislators, priests, philosophers, writers and scientists have striven to show that the subordinate position of woman is willed in heaven and advantageous on earth' (de Beauvoir xxii). Coming from an environment which endorses this view, as Mrs Markham says, that it is a man's business to please himself, and a woman's to please him too (79), Markham has to be taught that there are alternatives to a view that still predominated into the middle of the twentieth century.

While readers are given an opportunity – using all the available evidence – to judge Markham's conduct, Helen is only permitted to assess his 'best face'. When Lawrence conceals the real cause of his illness, Gilbert's courage fails him, and he does not confess his misdeed to Helen. She does not learn the extent of his violent strain. Events in this last chapter before the break comprise another example of Brontë '[writing] with heat', as Gilbert and Helen meet in anger but finally exchange confidences. Markham first thinks he can 'crush that bold spirit' and, exulting in his power, adds that he feels 'disposed to dally with [his] victim like a cat' (143). Helen rejects his catechism intended to insult her, but not before she witnesses an exhibition of his least appealing traits. Unaware of his display of petty malice, Gilbert's behavior is reinforced as Helen indulges him with her diary. Since 'his narrative is bankrupt' (Langland, 'Voicing' 116) at this point, progress in their relationship must cease until Gilbert reads Helen's history, 'The Warnings of Experience'.

Just before Helen's voice begins to dominate, Brontë refocuses attention on the letter to Halford, allowing Gilbert a timely reminder about present circumstances, and reiterating the comfortable image of him sitting in his study at Staningley. When we leave the young Gilbert, he is in readiness to spend the entire night consuming the precious manuscript and, as we return to him, it is morning: he is tired but elated that his beloved Helen is all that he had believed her to be. The reader never senses, as a result of the lengthy interlude, any uncertainties or unexpected shifts in the direction the author is developing her narrative. Brontë executes her plan well. Markham confesses his prejudices to Halford by saying, 'I felt a kind of selfish gratification in watching her husband's gradual decline in her good graces, and seeing how completely he extinguished all her affection at last' (402). Here the epistolary mode serves to demonstrate how little Markham is capable of change. Even with Helen as an example, Markham cannot act from altruistic motives. To his credit, he is not a hypocrite, feigning hope for Arthur's recovery and the couple's reconciliation or masking his true sentiments with comments calculated, once again, to simulate Christian piety or to match Helen's faith.

In the final section Markham's romantic, often sentimental, notions find a specific focus after his reconciliation with Helen. We observe the form they assume as he vividly reconstructs the scene following their separation, which itself is only accomplished 'by some *heroic* effort', as 'we tore ourselves apart, and I rushed from the house' (411, emphasis mine).

> I have a confused remembrance . . . of long hours spent in bitter tears and lamentations, and melancholy musings in the lonely valley, with the eternal music in my ears of the west wind rushing through the overshadowing trees, and the brook babbling and gurgling along its stony bed . . . (411)

Gilbert's 'melancholy musings' afford Brontë an opportunity to parody his clichéd romantic sentiments. His words echo Wordsworthian images of lonely valleys and babbling brooks, and his reference to 'the eternal music in my ears of the west wind' reminds the reader of Shelley's famous ode. However, unlike such poets, whose thoughts and feelings were formed in the crucible of an intense imaginative response to reality, Markham's musings offer us nothing more than a debased coinage, a counterfeit romantic effusion.[7]

One of the few critics who has appreciated the fact that Brontë's portrait of her narrator is 'foolishly sentimental' is Terry Eagleton. He points out some of Markham's idiosyncrasies:

> [S]ince it is he and not the novel who maintains that, though 'a little bit spoiled by [his] mother and sister, and some other ladies of [his] acquaintance', he is 'by no means a fop', we can take it that the book, in allowing him to protest too much, has serious reservations about his character. He is touchy and over-bred, full of rhetorical gestures and gallant clichés, alternating between tender idealisations and bursts of histrionic wrath. (130)

Brontë uses a deliberate technique of alternating between the opposing aspects of his personality, a subtle irony at Gilbert's expense. The reader is never left at the mercy of Gilbert's 'rhetorical gestures and gallant cliches' without also getting at least a hint of the author's ambivalent attitude, which makes W. A. Craik's assessment that Markham fails as a personality 'even more obviously than Charlotte Brontë's Crimsworth, because Anne Brontë has nothing to do with idiosyncrasy' (242) a difficult one with which to agree. Rather than representing a failure in Brontë's characterization, Markham's deficiencies, so shrewdly revealed by Brontë's judicious use of irony, are intrinsic to her development of his character, of his position in society, and of how he reflects his cultural heritage. The reader should be wondering by this time whether he would make 'a proper husband for Helen'.

From Markham's point of view – that is, in retrospect – there is no question about the propriety of his becoming Helen's husband. But, in writing his letter to Halford, Markham has the advantage of being the autobiographer, and 'the chief danger' in that 'is to make the line linking past and present far too exactly continuous and logical' (Pascal 15). In his interpretation of events, then, Markham is at liberty to shape the past so that it will conform to his own perspective. P. J. M. Scott expresses similar doubts about the success of their marriage: 'how can life be easy with a hysterical egotist who always bullyingly insists on having his own way?' (96). Another obstacle, making it difficult for the reader to judge whether Markham would be a fitting husband for Helen, comes in the deliberate omission of Helen's point of view. Her very silence suggests that her views might not coincide with those of her husband.

An analogous situation is to be found in the closing scenes of *The Professor* where the Crimsworths share what William suggests is an idyllic existence. Yet, subtle references question the truth of Crimsworth's autobiographical portrait. Various manifestations of his myopia make it clear that his wife is neither so happy in his company nor as inclined to his interests as he assumes. 'Although critics have tended to see only Crimsworth's romanticized portrait of Frances', as Tromly notes, 'there is ample evidence in *The Professor* that Brontë's portrait, which lurks behind Crimsworth's, is meant to be considerably more subtle, complicated, and ambiguous' (33). Their relationship is further complicated by their friendship with Yorke Hunsden, who delights in 'forc[ing] from Mrs Crimsworth revelations of the dragon within her' (C. Brontë 229). Crimsworth's passing reference to 'the dragon' – passion – reveals the inadequacy of his perceptions, just as it reveals the perspicacity of Hunsden's. Hunsden perceives an aspect of Frances' character that Crimsworth is either unwilling or unable to acknowledge. If Frances had occasion to speak her mind, there is little doubt that the dimensions of 'the dragon' would be more fully revealed.

Helen's thoughts are similarly concealed during the final scene of her reconciliation with Markham, although we do learn of her desires through her actions. Once she has worn her widow's weeds for a respectable period of time, it is she who makes the passionate overtures. This role reversal imparts a singular atmosphere to the scene at Staningley as Helen 'transgress[es] the boundaries of the masculine and feminine' (Langland, 'Voicing' 121). Markham had been intent upon seeing Helen until he discovered the extent of her sprawling domain, the news of which visibly dampened his spirits and his prospects. Consequently, when they meet, Markham's air of subdued resignation contrasts with Helen's suppressed energy. Helen acts despite her disappointment with his lame excuse about coming simply 'to see the place' (478). When she offers herself to Markham, poignantly using the medium of the Christmas rose, her passion contrasts dramatically with his self-conscious posturing. As Elizabeth Hollis Berry observes,

> [w]hen Helen reaches out through the window, reaching figuratively beyond her past and present into the future, she dramatizes an unequivocal statement of Brontë's belief in egalitarian action. This scene affirms the possibility of stepping out beyond the impress of a limiting stereotype, to break through the static icon of angelic submission and become wholly alive. (106)

While it seems we should applaud Brontë for ignoring the barriers circumscribing the angel in the house, Russell Poole, nevertheless, views this scene from another critical perspective, when he says that the 'dynamic' between Helen and Gilbert 'reminds us of the central relationship in Chaucer's "Wife of Bath's Tale"' whereby Markham's 'newfound humility' is only acceptable 'at Helen's initiative and on her terms' (864). This might imply that Helen is too domineering, but Poole's intent is to show how little Markham has matured. Through Markham's gesture, his hesitant response to Helen's overture, Brontë underscores the connection to his overall insensitivity. When he is not in a position to control events, he flounders just enough for Helen to regret making her offer, and just enough for the reader to wonder about her wisdom in finally accepting him.

The highly charged atmosphere of this scene, defined by its undercurrent of tension, might be compared to the 'happy ending' in *The Professor* where the reader should be slightly disconcerted by what is not disclosed. Both contrast with the traditional endings in many novels of the Regency and Victorian periods. One might consider the delightful love scene between Emma and Mr Knightley in Jane Austen's *Emma*, which culminates with some light-hearted irony at Emma's expense. Austen does not weave a darker texture into the relationship between the lovers. It is enough that Emma is divested of her illusions, both innocent and harmful, while still possessing the presence of mind to say '[j]ust what she ought, of course. A lady always does' (297). Austen's handling is germane here because it illustrates the contrast between a traditional ending and the more problematical ending in *Wildfell Hall*. With our knowledge of the narrator's nature, we cannot accept Markham's portrait at face value. This is unlike the situation in *Emma* where Jane Austen 'means what she says', which as Wayne Booth notes, will result in 'a happy marriage because there is simply nothing left to make it anything less than perfectly happy. It fulfils every value embodied in the world of the book' (259). An unambiguous ending could not be possible in *Wildfell Hall*, since the contours of the hero's character are more ambiguously shaded.

Helen deceives herself when she believes that the impending marriage will be characterized by a 'unity of accordant thoughts and feelings, and truly loving, sympathizing hearts and souls' (487). Helen's ideal vision is unlikely to be realized. 'Helen's final apparent self-determination is more ambiguous' (Berg 485) than numerous critics have allowed. Yet, Brontë's realistic vision is presented. One has to agree, although for different reasons, with Ewbank's comment about Markham: '[it] is impossible to believe that his mind and Helen's have much in common, and that theirs is the satisfactory true marriage, to counterbalance the central disastrous marriage' (83). Ewbank perceives the incongruity of the match, but she attributes it to a weakness in Brontë's characterization of Gilbert, rather than to a deliberate effort to delve into the psyche of a character with a startling lack of self-knowledge, whose whims have ever been indulged by his family, and whose desires have only ever been thwarted by Helen.

Markham expects the reader to accept his assertion about 'how happily my Helen and I have lived and loved together' on faith. In his parting words to Halford, he exclaims, 'I need not tell you how . . . blessed we still are in each other's society, and in the promising young scions that are growing up about us' (490). As with Crimsworth, this idyllic portrait is undermined by our knowledge of Markham's shortcomings.[8] Here is a man who, even by his own admission, is 'a little too touchy', but who, nevertheless, assures us that he has 'learned to be merry and wise' (458). Markham's *own* complacency provides the reader with the necessary clue to his unappealing traits. Indeed, if he views *himself* in this light, how must he appear to others? He is neither so merry nor so wise as he believes himself. What Helen calls his 'scruples of false delicacy and pride' (487) dominate his personality long past their reconciliation. To his credit, he is far from an innocuous individual, notwithstanding his obvious failings, as even his physical presence must make a powerful impression upon Helen. What Anne Brontë achieves here is credibility. In a society in which 'past indulgence leads. . . to moral blind-ness' (Langland, *Anne Brontë* 131), what hope could Helen have of finding a knight (such as Mr Knightley) in shining armour? Since both she and Brontë know there are none, Brontë's portrayal of Markham offers that complicated mixture of characteristics that is a human portrait.

Beyond his role in the events, Markham establishes the novel's structure in the epistolary mode. Writing the letter to Halford provides him with the opportunity to give an account of his past conduct. Then, as narrator, he attempts to dress up his account in the most flattering style he can muster, much in the same way that Crimsworth and Lockwood try to present their 'best faces'. However, Markham's fictional autobiography suffers from what Annette Tromly would call 'a pronounced constriction of outlook, a chosen containment by the autobiographer of what is irreducible in his life to the terms of a paradigm. Inevitably, these paradigms suffer from "leakage"'.[9] This leakage (Henry James' term) reveals enough about Markham's idiosyncratic character to suggest that Brontë could no more imagine a traditional happy ending for Helen's second marriage than she could for the tenant of Wildfell Hall's first soul-destroying experience. Anne Brontë has served up too many illustrations of her first narrator's strong prejudices and manipulative actions for us to think Markham's nature capable of the necessary metamorphosis.

Notes

[1] Helen is given approximately 270 pages (including eight pages – 444-52 – in which Markham's comments partially paraphrase her own) and Markham has 214 pages to himself or about 79 percent of Helen's total.

[2] Many critics have touched on the perceived failure of the narrative structure and then focused on the diary section. In *Conversations in Ebury Street*, George Moore says, 'the diary broke the story in halves' (254). In her biography of Brontë, Winifred Gérin sees the novel as 'the representation of a debauched society' (243). Richard A. Stenberg states that it is about 'a woman's loss of innocence and the dangers of marriage' (68). I. S. Ewbank, in *Their Proper Sphere*, says that 'the frame fails to support the powerful middle portion' (84). In *Myths of Power*, Terry Eagleton refers to 'the novel's curious structure, which throws into formal predominance the courtship: the stereotyped Romantic saga of the cold mistress and the baffled lover' (135). Even Eagleton who recognizes that Brontë purposely varied the focus of her novel does not grant that she was attempting

anything other than a 'stereotyped Romantic saga'.

[3] For example, Ewbank remarks that 'the machinery creaks sadly at times: there is no intrinsic reason why the framework should be in the form of letters (to a person who has no function in the novel)' (71).

[4] Richard D. Altick explains that '[b]efore 1800, only nine English poets wrote autobiographies that survive; between 1800 and 1900 at least forty-two wrote such accounts. In fact, the total of autobiographies written by British literary men of all sorts before 1800 is only about twenty-three, whereas during the next hundred years at least 175 were produced' (104).

[5] The phrase is part of John Foster's definition of autobiography in his autobiographical work 'On a Man's Writing Memoirs of Himself' (1805). It appears in Keith Rinehart's article entitled 'The Victorian Approach to Autobiography' (179).

[6] See Camille Paglia's interpretation of this relationship as incestuous in Sexual Personae (444-59).

[7] For an alternative reading of this passage, see P. J. M. Scott's Anne Brontë: A New Critical Assessment where he takes a much less ironic view of Anne's treatment of Markham (123-24).

[8] Recent corroboration that notes the 'qualified and conditional [nature of the] marriage' is offered by Laura C. Berry in 'Acts of Custody and Incarceration in Wuthering Heights and The Tenant of Wildfell Hall' (45).

[9] Tromley refers specifically to William Crimsworth, Jane Eyre, and Lucy Snowe (16).

Works Cited

Altick, Richard D. Lives and Letters: A History of Literary Biography in England and America. New York: Alfred A. Knopf, 1965.

Austen, Jane. Emma. Ed. Stephen M. Parrish. New York: Norton, 1972.

Bell, Arnold Craig. The Novels of Anne Brontë. Braunton: Merlin Books, 1992.

Berg, Maggie. Review of Anne Brontë's Radical Vision: Structures of Consciousness. English Studies in Canada 22.4 (1996): 483-85.

Berry, Elizabeth Hollis. Anne Brontë's Radical Vision: Structures of Consciousness. Victoria: University of Victoria Press, 1994.

Berry, Laura C. 'Acts of Custody and Incarceration in Wuthering Heights and The Tenant of Wildfell Hall'. Novel 30 (1996): 32-55.

Booth, Wayne C. The Rhetoric of Fiction. Chicago: University of Chicago Press, 1961.

Brontë, Anne. The Tenant of Wildfell Hall. Ed. G. D. Hargreaves. Harmondsworth, Penguin, 1979.

Brontë, Charlotte, The Professor and Emma. London: J. M. Dent, 1969.

Brontë, Emily Jane. Wuthering Heights. Eds. Hilda Marsden and Ian Jack. Oxford:

Clarendon, 1976.

Chitham, Edward. *A Life of Anne Brontë*. Oxford: Blackwell, 1991.

Craik, W. A. *The Brontë Novels*. London: Methuen, 1968.

de Beauvoir, Simone. *The Second Sex*. Trans. H. M. Parshley. New York: Random House, 1968.

Eagleton, Terry. *Myths of Power: A Marxist Study of The Brontës*. London: MacMillan, 1975.

Ewbank, I. S. *Their Proper Sphere: A Study of The Brontë Sisters as Early-Victorian Female Novelists*. London: Edward Arnold, 1966.

Gérin, Winifred. *Anne Brontë: A Biography*. 2nd ed. London: Allen Lane, 1976.

Gilbert, Sandra, and Susan Gubar, eds. *Shakespeare's Sisters: Feminist Essays on Women Poets*. Bloomington: Indiana University Press, 1979.

Hutcheon, Linda. *Narcissistic Narrative: The Metafictional Paradox*. Waterloo, ON: Wilfred Laurier University Press, 1980.

Langland, Elizabeth. *Anne Brontë: The Other One*. Totowa, NJ: Barnes and Noble, 1989.

-----. 'The Voicing of Feminine Desire in Anne Brontë's *The Tenant of Wildfell Hall*. *Gender and Discourse in Victorian Literature and Art*. Eds. Anthony H. Harrison and Beverly Taylor. DeKalb, IL: Northern Illinois University Press, 1992: 111-23.

Moore, George, *Conversations in Ebury Street*. New York: Boni and Liveright, 1924.

Paglia, Camille. *Sexual Personae: Art and Decadence from Nefertiti to Emily Dickinson*. New York: Vintage, 1991.

Pascal, Roy. *Design and Truth in Autobiography*. London: Routledge and Kegan Paul, 1960.

Poole, Russell. 'Cultural Reformation and Cultural Reproduction in Anne Brontë's *The Tenant of Wildfell Hall*. *Studies in English Literature 1500-1900* (Fall 1993): 859-73.

Rinehart, Keith. 'The Victorian Approach to Autobiography'. *Modern Philology* 51 (1954): 179.

Scott, P. J. M. *Anne Brontë: A New Critical Assessment*. London: Vision, 1983.

Shumaker, Wayne. *English Autobiography: Its Emergence, Materials, and Form*. Berkeley: University of California Press, 1954.

Stenberg, Richard A. 'The Novels of Anne Brontë'. Diss. University of Minnesota, 1980.

Tromly, Annette. *The Cover of The Mask: The Autobiographers in Charlotte Brontë's Fiction*. Victoria: University of Victoria Press, 1982.

Wise, T. J. and J. A. Symington, eds. *The Brontës: Their Lives, Friendships and Correspondence*. 4 Vols. Oxford: Shakespeare Head, 1932.

Contributors

Maria Frawley is an Associate Professor of English at the University of Delaware. The author of *A Wider Range: Travel Writing by Women in Victorian England* (1994) and of *Anne Brontë* (1996), she is currently at work on a book on the culture of invalidism in nineteenth-century England and is preparing an edition of Harriet Martineau's *Life in the Sickroom* for publication by Broadview Press.

Marilyn Sheridan Gardner lives in southeastern Louisiana with her family and teaches in the English Department at the University of Southern Mississippi in Hattiesburg. Her primary interests concern the Brontës. She is presently working on a study of *The Tenant of Wildfell Hall*.

Melody J. Kemp, doctoral candidate at Lehigh University, has taught English in Pennsylvania public schools for two decades. She participated in a National Endowment for the Humanities summer seminar on the Brontës and won a Council for Basic Education fellowship for independent study of Emily Brontë's poetry. Kemp has published on *The Knight's Tale*.

Bettina L. Knapp, Thomas Hunter Professor of French and Comparative Literature at Hunter College and the City University of New York, is the author of over fifty books including *Emily Dickinson* (1989) and *The Brontës* (1991).

Andrés G. López, Associate Professor of English and Chair of the Humanities Department at the State University of New York at Morrisville, received his Ph.D. from Stony Brook University. He is currently revising his dissertation, *Exposing Vice and Vicious Characters: The Art of Anne Brontë's Novels*, for publication.

Deborah Denenholz Morse, the author of *Women in Trollope's Palliser Novels* (1987, 1991) and numerous articles on Victorian literature and women writers, and the co-editor (with Regina Barreca) of *The Erotics of Instruction* (1997), is an Associate Professor of English and one of the first of three Distinguished Professors of Teaching at the College of William and Mary. She is currently writing a book on Victorian animals.

Julie Nash is a Ph.D. candidate at the University of Connecticut. She is the author of several published articles and reviews, and has taught writing, British literature, and women's studies at the University of Connecticut, Eastern Connecticut State University, and Gustavus Adolphus College in St. Peter, MN. She is currently completing her dissertation on servants in the novels of Maria Edgeworth and Elizabeth Gaskell.

Larry H. Peer is Professor of Comparative Literature at Brigham Young University and Executive Director of the American Conference on Romanticism. He has published books and essays on Manzoni, Byron, Pushkin, Goethe, Stendhal, Diderot, the Brontës, the Romantic manifesto, and comparative European Romanticism, and his poetry has appeared in several outlets. He is also editor of the journal *Prism(s): Essays in Romanticism*.

James R. Simmons, Jr., Assistant Professor of English at Louisiana Tech University, is the author of a number of published articles and reviews that have appeared in *Brontë Society Transactions, Victorian Studies, English Language Notes*, and *The Dickensian*. He also has a forthcoming book, *Factory Lives: Four Nineteenth-Century Working Class Autobiographies*.

Garrett Stewart, James O. Freedman Professor of English at the University of Iowa, is the author of *Dickens and the Trials of Imagination* (1974), *Death Sentences: Styles of Dying in British Fiction* (1984), *Reading Voices: Literature and the Phonotext* (1990), *Dear Reader: The Conscripted Audience of Nineteenth-Century British Fiction* (1996) and, most recently, *Between Film and Screen: Modernism's Photo Synthesis* (2000).

Barbara A. Suess, Assistant Professor of English at William Paterson University, received her Ph.D. from the University of Connecticut. She is the author of published essays on William Butler Yeats, Elizabeth Bowen, H. D., and Charlotte Perkins Gilman and is currently working on a book based on her dissertation, *Progress and Identity in the Plays of W. B. Yeats, 1892 – 1907*.

Lee A. Talley, Assistant Professor of English at California State University, Dominguez Hills, has published essays on Jamaica Kincaid and Jeannette Winterson. She is currently preparing an edition of *The Tenant of Wildfell Hall* for Broadview Press and is working on a book-length study of the Brontës.

Marianne Thormählen, Professor of English at Lund University in Sweden, has several publications including books on T. S. Eliot – *The Waste Land: A Fragmentary Wholeness* (1978) and *Eliot's Animals* (1984) – and a comprehensive study of the Earl of Rochester's poetry, *Rochester: the Poems in Context* (1993). She has also edited a volume of essays on Eliot, *T. S. Eliot at the Turn of the Century* (1994) and has published articles on the Brontës. Her book *The Brontës and Religion* appeared in 1999.

Andrea Westcott, the author of entries on Anne and Charlotte Brontë for the Facts on File *Dictionary of British Literary Characters: 18th- and 19th-Century Novels*, is an instructor of English at Capilano College. Having earned her Ph.D. at the University of Toronto where she wrote a dissertation on Anne Brontë, she has also presented papers on the Brontës and the English Country House. She is currently working on a study of duality in several Gothic novels.

Index